The Oral Tradition Today

An Introduction to the Art of Storytelling

Liz Warren

Custom Publishing

New York   Boston   San Francisco
London   Toronto   Sydney   Tokyo   Singapore   Madrid
Mexico City   Munich   Paris   Cape Town   Hong Kong   Montreal

Front cover, clockwise from top left: Marilyn Torres, Vic McCraw and Sandy Oglesby by Mark Goldstein; Guadalupe Angulo and Mike Cocanour by Liz Warren; Meca Meyers by Tanya Held; Lorraine Calbow by Mark Goodstein. Back cover, clockwise from top left: Lynn Ann Wojciechowicz, Ricardo Provencio, and Liz Warren by Mark Goldstein; Boug Bland by Liz Warren.

Printed in the United States of America

10 9 8 7 6 5 4 3 2 1

2008420167

KA/LP

**Pearson
Custom Publishing**
is a division of

rsonhighered.com

ISBN 10: 0-536-03298-X
ISBN 13: 978-0-536-03298-0

Table of Contents

Acknowledgements:

I wrote most of this book while on sabbatical from my teaching responsibilities at South Mountain Community College, which is one of the Maricopa Community Colleges in metropolitan Phoenix, Arizona. I am very grateful to work for an institution that provides such a benefit to faculty.

The book was begun as a Learning Grant, another benefit provided by Maricopa. The stated purpose of the grant was to fund a two-semester learning community whose members would write a textbook for our Art of Storytelling class. It did not prove feasible for a group of people to write a text book, but we did, after much discussion and dialogue, establish a vision, values, and mission for the book. We also outlined the chapters and what each chapter should include while thoroughly enjoying each other. This book reflects that work. The members of the learning community were Roseanne Belk, Gigi Connolly, Kathy Eastman, Nancy Jennings, Vic McCraw, Janet Means, Sandy Oglesby, Willa Ordway, Cheryl Rutherford, Jan Sloat, and Laura Watson.

Susan Klein provided the professional editing for most of the book and I am grateful for the "Alien Eye" she brought to it, as well as for the perspective provided by her years of experience working in the world of professional storytelling. In addition, Linda Evans, Joyce Story, Sandy Oglesby, Vic McCraw, Janet Means, Laura Watson, and Liz Weir read the book and provided encouragement as well as suggestions for improvement. Harriet Cole and LynnAnn Wojciechowicz devoted days to editing the manuscript for publication. I'm very thankful for their skills and their stamina.

The storytelling faculty at both South Mountain and Glendale Community Colleges have been using the chapters in their Art of Storytelling classes for the last several semesters. I'm grateful to them and to their many students who have provided me with invaluable feedback on the chapters and how to make them better. They include Doug Bland, Angela Giron, Shelle Hawn, Carol Knarr, Janet Means, Ricardo Provencio, Joyce Story and LynnAnn Wojciechowicz.

Many people gave generously of their time and talents to make this book a reality. The following people allowed me to include their original stories in the book: Guadalupe S. Angulo, Doug Bland, Harriet Cole, Don Doyle, Shean R. Howlett, Michelle Mostaghim, Ricardo Provencio, Marilyn Torres, LynnAnn Wojciechowicz, and Emil Wolfgramm. My husband, Mark Goldstein, has been the Storytelling Institute's photographer over the years, and he has allowed us to use many of his fine photographs in the book.

My biggest debt of gratitude goes to LynnAnn Wojciechowicz. This book simply would not have been possible without the blessing of her time and expertise as a storyteller, teacher, and writer. Thanks, LynnAnn!

How to Use This Book

This book has been designed to accompany a college level class in storytelling, specifically The Art of Storytelling at South Mountain Community College in Phoenix, Arizona. In that class, students tell a folktale; a myth, legend or hero tale; a fact-based story; and a personal story. They collect, summarize, and analyze stories from five broad culture areas. They tell outside of class to audiences of six or more on at least three occasions and they attend performances by professional storytellers.

The chapters are meant to be read sequentially. Doing so establishes a foundation of skills.

Each chapter includes several stories. The **List of Stories** provides the names of all the stories and their cultures of origin.

Appendix A contains story exercises, reflection questions, study questions and questions on the stories for each chapter.

Appendix B includes the forms students need to complete the range of assignments required in the class:

- Story Summary and Analysis Worksheet for use with the stories collected from the culture areas.

- In-Class Telling Report Form for use in assessing classroom telling

- Instructions and forms for the Outside-of-Class Tellings

If you are not using this book as part of a class, you may still find the forms and exercises useful to focus your attention and to assess your progress.

A note about gender and third person pronouns: When writing about a hypothetical third person, I chose to alternate gender from chapter to chapter. When necessary, I use the pronoun "she" in chapters 1, 3, 5, and 7, and "he" in chapters 2, 4, 6, and 8.

Stories and Storytelling

 **= Story and Self**
- **Story** has always been a crucial source of beauty, wisdom, and entertainment for human beings.
- The Story you tell is a reflection of your **Self.**

 = Technique, Truth, Tradition and Types
- Storytellers utilize a range of **Techniques** that can be learned.
- Storytellers are committed to **Truth** even when the stories are not factual.
- Storytellers experience a deep connection to the **Tradition** of storytelling.
- There are many **Types** or genres of story.

 **= Observe, Occupy, Object, "Once upon a time", and Open-hearted**
- **Observe** the obvious and ordinary for story details.
- **Occupy** your story fully to bring it to life.
- Know the **Object** or point of your story.
- **"Once upon a time":** Stories need strong beginnings and endings.
- Storytelling requires **Open-hearted** tellers and listeners.

 **= Research, Respect and Relate**
- **Research** variants of your story and its history.
- **Respect** the culture and context from which it came.
- Stories **Relate** information and help us **Relate** to each other.

 = Images and Insight
- Stories are sequences of **Images** conveyed by words and gestures.
- Bring all the **Insight** you have to the preparation and telling of the story.

 = Emotion, Engagement and Energy
- The **Emotion** related by the storyteller **Engages** the audience.
- Fill your stories, even the quiet ones, with the complete **Energy** of your physical, emotional, intellectual and spiritual presence.

 = Structure and Style
- Stories have **Structures** which help convey images and emotions.
- You have a personal storytelling **Style** that is all your own.

1

What is Storytelling?

What is Storytelling?

Though no one definition can encompass all the varieties of storytelling, there is a set of elements that can be used to delimit the art form.

- Storytelling is narrative: Story, or narrative, is a defining feature of storytelling, as it is of many other art forms.

- Storytelling is based in images and emotions: The story's power is vested in the images and emotions that the listeners experience.

- Storytelling is oral and aural: A storyteller speaks and the audience listens.

- Storytelling is performance: Whether the story is being told at hearthside, on a main stage in a theater, or under a tent with a thousand people listening, the teller is performing and is the center of attention.

A storytelling event requires three basic elements: a story, a storyteller, and an audience. The story can be a folk or fairytale, a myth or legend, from personal experience or family history, adapted from literature, based in biography or on a historical event, or an original creation. But it is always something more than simply relating facts or a sequence of events. A story is structured and crafted to maximize its impact and the audience's experience of it. This is why storytelling is considered an art form.

The storyteller is the medium through which the story is expressed and given life. It is through the storyteller that the audience gains access to the story. She may be telling a story that has existed for centuries or as recent as an original creation, but in either case the teller must

> From *Story*, by Harold Scheub:
>
> - Image is the basic element of storytelling.
> - The image is plotted into a linear path.
> - The images are patterned.
> - The images evoke feelings.

be open to the story's inherent integrity, while simultaneously shaping and crafting it to best suit the audience and her style.

The teller might be regarded as a sentient projector who puts the story out there for everyone to see and experience. But unlike a movie projector that does not shape or influence the content, the story is always affected by coming through a particular teller. That is why certain stories suit one teller better than another. This dynamic juggling of elements in the moment of the telling makes storytelling distinct as an art form based in narrative.

The audience is there to receive and experience the story – and to be engaged and entertained in the process. A good listener comes with an openness and readiness to listen that matches the teller's desire and intention to give the story. The audience's willingness to give themselves over to the story cannot be overestimated. The audience supports the teller as the conduit for the story, bolstering her should she falter, so that the integrity of the story is maintained.

When all these elements come together, the whole is somehow larger than the sum of the parts. A moment is created in which consciousness of ordinary reality, while not exactly lost, is at least temporarily suspended.

This synergy is represented by the diagram below. Ideally, all three elements meet in the center to create an ephemeral, unrepeatable moment of story. The center triangle, the point of convergence, represents the experience that can occur when the story, teller, and audience are merged and balanced.

What is Story?

Story is the most fundamental and profound way in which humans preserve and share information. Stories are used to convey meaning, transmit history and tradition, entertain, instruct, and inspire awe and wonder. However, stories are not reports, essays, lectures, anecdotes, jokes, diagnoses, speeches, recipes, sermons, travelogues, monologues, or newscasts. These are forms of narrative with distinctive structures or elements of their own, which may or may not include story.

The vast majority of artistic expression is based in story. A common base in story is the reason that artists and professionals in so many fields are called "storytellers." Journalists, filmmakers, writers, directors, dancers, and visual artists have all been known as storytellers. They may take stories as their foundation or content, or we may experience a sense of a story playing itself out in their work.

Once a story comes into being, it has an independent existence apart from the teller or the listener. Stories are not static or inert. They change and grow, flourish and prosper, and in some cases vanish or die.

What is a storyteller?

One often hears filmmakers and authors described as storytellers, but for the purposes of this book we are not talking about artists who express their stories in literature or film. We are talking about those who share stories as they have been shared for most of human history – from the mouth, heart, and experience of one person to the waiting ears of others.

Modern storytellers take on many roles: performer, entertainer, educator, tradition bearer, consultant, and coach. The storyteller's role is paradoxical: while on the one hand she is working in the most time-honored way – face-to-face, she must, on the other hand, also exist in a culture that relies ever more heavily on technologies that allow and encourage communication in many other forms.

Today's storytellers are countercultural, revolutionary even, because they are swimming up stream in terms of contemporary society. Our culture values technology and prefers its stories in movies and on television, and of course, in books. As a culture we invest and spend large amounts of money to create and consume stories in those formats, all of which would not exist without technology of a very high order.

In contrast, a storyteller is low tech. Storytellers rely on the "technology" of the word and spirit, the voice and heart, the tongue and ear. It's a rare commodity indeed, and one that is rarely recognized as an art form or even perceived at all.

Our culture makes such a deep and profound association between stories and books that many are unaware that people can and do tell stories to others. Every teller I know has had to explain that storytelling doesn't involve holding a book open while reading to children.

So what *do* they do? Storytellers consciously craft oral stories and share those stories purposely, face-to-face with others, in real time. For many tellers, the story exists as a series of images, pictures in their minds that they describe in a story sequence, so that the audience can see the pictures in *their* minds. Storyteller Donald Davis says that when storytelling works, the audience is *seeing* rather than *listening*.

> ## Story as Floor Plan
>
> Think of a story as a house. The storyteller is very, very familiar with the layout of the house and its contents. She starts at the front door and proceeds all the way through and out the back. She walks through the rooms in a particular sequence. As she walks through, she describes each room to you. But she may not describe it in exactly the same way each time she gives the tour. One time she may spend longer in the living room and breeze through the dining room. Another time she may mention the candlestick on the mantle and omit the vase of flowers in the kitchen, but it is still the same house, the same story.

Typically, storytellers do not memorize the stories they tell. The stories, whether as images or text or both, are *learned* so that each telling is fresh and open to serendipity and the happy accidents that make *that* telling for *that* audience on *that* particular day unique. The story needs room to breathe so that the teller, story, and audience begin to respirate together. The more deeply integrated the story is in the teller's experience, the deeper the audience's experience of the story will be.

Storytellers are not actors, although many of them come from a theatre background. The storyteller does not play the role of a particular character as an actor would. She brings all the characters, including the narrator, to life while remaining essentially herself. Deeper self knowledge is directly connected to deeper, more effective storytelling. Ideally, the storyteller is able to bring herself as a whole person to the telling of the story.

Where do storytellers get their stories?

The vast majority of storytellers rely on books and other forms of print media to find the folktales, myths, and legends they tell. There are, of course, storytellers who learned their stories in the time-honored way – from another person in a traditional or cultural context – but that is becoming increasingly rare. Once the storyteller finds a story she wants to tell, she takes the written text and recasts it in an oral form.

And of course storytellers create new stories of all kinds. They create original stories in folk tale form. They create stories from their own experiences. They create stories about their relatives and friends and about fascinating people and moments in history.

Many professional storytellers make audio and video recordings of their work, but it's rare to find a teller who believes that these recordings in any way approximate the experience of a live telling. In a live telling, the teller creates a container large enough and secure enough to hold herself, the story, and the audience. For the duration of the story, these three components create a bubble of magical reality that you can almost feel pop when the story is over. The participants – teller and listeners – are part of something that can never happen in exactly the same way again.

Where do storytellers do their work?

Storytellers perform in a wide range of venues including festivals, theatres, schools, community centers, libraries, board rooms, colleges, churches, museums, hospitals, and private homes. They teach storytelling in workshops and classes. They incorporate storytelling in consulting, counseling, training, preaching, and public speaking. Throughout the book we will meet several modern storytellers who demonstrate the range of tellers and their work.

Why do they do it?

Storytellers are motivated by the deep human need to participate in the magic that an orally delivered story can create. They care about the stories, the cultural tradition the stories come from, the impact the stories have on the listeners, and the experience of personally giving a story to others. The giving of the story and the interaction that the gift creates becomes an irresistible imperative.

Many people become storytellers to deliver a message in the most effective way. Whether the cause is peace, social justice, human values, or the environment, stories convey information more effectively and enjoyably than a lecture or a power-point presentation. That is why so many teachers are drawn to storytelling: when content is delivered through or linked to story, students are more likely to remember.

What distinguishes story telling from story writing?

In response to the question, "What is narrative?" Bill Ristow, features editor for the *Seattle Times,* responds, "The art of telling a story as if the reader is right there in the room with you, listening as you tell it out loud" (http://poynter.org/column. asp?id=52&aid=49550).

This quote captures the modern paradox of storytelling: Is it writing or speaking? For most of human history, it has been speaking. But given the dominance of writing in our culture, the word "tell" doesn't necessarily denote speaking in common usage. If Mr. Ristow had said "the art of *writing* a story," it might have made sense to a storyteller's ear. However for him, as for the culture at large, writing and telling are the same. But, in fact, they are not!

Very few of us (and perhaps no one whose consciousness has been shaped by literacy) will ever know what it is to live in an oral culture with its distinct patterns of thought, behavior, and relation to language. Nonetheless, orality is the primary mode of human communication. Oral language came first, defining human culture and expression; written language came second and much, much later in the span of history. The mind-set of orality is present all about us, especially in our personal, face-to-face interactions with others. When we tell another person about an interesting or alarming experience, review the plot of a movie we've just seen, or retell our favorite stories from childhood, our primary orality is revealed. Naturally enough, storytellers play a critical role in preserving and highlighting that capacity in our culture.

Imagine a great tree.

The trunk is story; its roots are in human experience. Its branches represent the myriad ways story manifests itself, with the largest and most central branch being the oral tradition. Since the invention of the printing press, written expression has become an ever more dominant branch of the tree. And in the last century, stories expressed in film and other media have created enormous branches.

How are story telling and story writing different?

- Writing is visual and tactile. Telling is oral and aural.

- Writing is associated with "modern" life. Orality is associated with "traditional" cultures, the "old" days.

- Many people believe that writing allows a higher level of consciousness than is possible in an oral culture. Although anthropologists, psychologists, and historians of literature have shown that this is not the case, the prejudice endures.

- Writers produce commodities that can be sold. Storytellers create products, too, but what they really create is an experience. It is almost impossible to turn the actual experience of telling and hearing an oral story into a commodity much beyond the ticket price. If you buy a book, you can read it anytime and repeatedly. But a story performance is a one-time event, and doesn't lend itself to mass marketing or to making money for other people. In earlier times, few people had the money or the need to buy entertainment products. Then, as now, the *experience* of the story was what mattered.

- Writing and reading are, by and large, solitary experiences. Telling occurs in social contexts. Writers have an audience in their readers, whose anticipated participation in what they write no doubt influences them. But the audience in a storytelling event actually participates in the creation of the event.

- A writer must write every word of the picture or experience that she wishes her reader to experience. A storyteller can arch an eyebrow and in a fraction of a second convey a skepticism that might take a writer several sentences to describe.

Overall, writing and telling are parallel, although not identical:

- Both are based in language – narrative, in particular – and both benefit from the power of narrative to give us access to other realities, deeper meanings and the archetypal realms of experience.
- Both depend on sending and receiving, although in different modalities. In writing, the author commits words to paper that are ultimately received by the eyes of the reader. In storytelling, the teller speaks and the words are received by the ears of the listeners.

The relationship between oral and written language is complicated. One Irish story scholar describes a story that was told orally, transcribed by another person, and edited by yet another. The same story was then translated from Irish to English and edited again. Where does the original oral story stop and the written version begin? What is the relationship between the two? These are questions with which storytellers must constantly grapple.

What is the difference between storytelling and theatre?

Although many modern storytellers have a background in theatre, there are some fundamental differences between being a storyteller and an actor, and between a storytelling event and a play.

- First, most storytellers do not memorize a script as actors do. They prefer to learn (but not memorize) a story – thoroughly and deeply– so that when they are telling it, they can respond freely to the particular audience in attendance. This provides dynamism, unpredictability, and freshness to storytelling that is very satisfying for both the teller and the listener.
- A storyteller does not maintain the persona of a single character. The teller portrays all the characters in the story while remaining herself.
- Actors generally relate to other actors on the stage rather than directly to the audience. In the theatre, there is the concept of the fourth wall, an invisible wall through which the audience witnesses the events on stage. In storytelling there is no fourth wall, or if there is, it is *behind* the audience. Storytellers seek to establish a relationship with the audience, at least for the duration of the story, and believe that the stronger the connection between them and the audience, the stronger the impact of the story. In some storytelling events, a high degree of participation from the audience is expected and encouraged.
- Storytellers do not use directors. In theatre, the director is responsible for interpreting the text and directing the actors in fulfilling the vision. In a storytelling event, the teller is responsible for the interpretation of the story, its development and delivery. Storytellers do, however, often use coaches who help them interpret and actualize their vision of the story.
- Storytellers do not use sets, props, or costumes. A storyteller seeks to create a world inside the listener's mind. It is her job to communicate this with words and her body rather than with objects. In this sense, the story is co-created by the teller and the listener in the moment of the telling. Many storytellers believe that props, sets, and costumes can interfere with this process.

Of course, there are exceptions to every single one of the above points. Some storytellers use directors, some use props and costumes, some portray a character while telling, and some memorize. Nonetheless, the distinctions above would apply to most tellers.

Foundations of Excellence: By What Standards are Storytellers Assessed?

Standards of effectiveness and excellence are controversial within the storytelling community. Many argue that the inherent appeal and importance of storytelling is rooted in the diverse cultural heritages, performance styles, and repertoires that storytellers exhibit, and that to set standards would be counterintuitive and counterproductive. Others argue that standards are necessary for the profession to be recognized by the larger society.

The National Storytelling Network confers the Circle of Excellence Award upon the profession's greatest practitioners. Here is how the NSN describes this award:

> **The Circle of Excellence Award** is presented to artists who are recognized by their peers to be master storytellers who set the standards for excellence and have demonstrated, over a significant period of time, a commitment and dedication to the art of storytelling.

NSN does not say what constitutes the "standards of excellence." The forty-plus storytellers who have received this award have all had significant careers that include performing in the largest and most important festivals around the country, so we know that at least one aspect of excellence is the ability to command the attention of hundreds or thousands of people. Implicit in this is the storyteller's ability to create and sustain a repertoire of size, quality and range.

To tell at a major festival (the National Storytelling Festival, for example), a storyteller must have a minimum of twelve hours of stories. Storytellers who perform at this level do not repeat a story during an event, unless requested by the producers. The storyteller must have a sizeable repertoire and must have the flexibility to adapt to the needs of the audience and to the choices made by the other tellers with whom she is performing. For example, the last teller in a concert that features several other tellers, and in which a particular mood has been established, must tell a story that complements or extends the mood. Conversely, the teller may need to change the mood by the story she chooses to tell. So, for example, if she is following a teller who has told something that left the audience somber or withdrawn, she may want to bring the mood back up to end the set. This ability to effectively co-create a storytelling experience with other tellers and the audience is a clear indicator of storytelling excellence.

It is not the only indicator, however. The repertoire of the storyteller corresponds to the "story" circle in the diagram earlier in the chapter. The other two circles are storyteller and audience. The "excellent" storyteller has:

- Mastered a body of stories which she can use with a high degree of flexibility and proficiency.
- Mastered her own performance style as an artist.
- Mastered the ability to relate to any audience with sensitivity and confidence.
- Achieved a balance of the above three components that transcends them to create a unique whole.
- Always presents work that advances and serves the art form.

This often takes years, even decades to achieve. Mastery of any art form requires a high level of commitment and dedication. Storytelling is no exception.

What does this mean for the beginning storyteller? The talents that ultimately distinguish master storytellers are often inborn. Talents such as a flair for humor, a face whose expressions render words superfluous, or a tantalizing sense of timing are nurtured and honed on the road to mastery. Excellence can take years to achieve; nonetheless, the techniques of effective storytelling can be taught.

Excellence and Ethics: A commitment to ethical and responsible practices is a standard of excellence that can be achieved at any level of storytelling expertise. Standards of ethical behavior revolve around how the teller respects the sources of the stories she tells, how she interacts with her hosts and sponsors, how she relates to her audience, how she conducts her business, and her commitment to her own continued growth as an artist. Specific practices will be described in the following chapters.

Spam

I once witnessed a moment of storytelling excellence that hinged on the tellers' abilities to complement one another. At the White Mountain Storytelling Festival in Show Low, Arizona, Michael Lacapa was first on stage. He told a hilarious story about spam, and the reverence and awe the opening of a large can could evoke in his relatives. One by one, the tellers who followed him integrated spam into their stories. One teller actually had his own story about spam. Another told a story involving the theft of food, and of course, the stolen food became spam in this telling. As each of the subsequent tellers managed to include spam in their stories, the audience began to anticipate it, and when it arrived they were delighted to witness the tellers' skill. It was a wonderful session, and in fact the only one I remember from that festival. The moment was so exceptional that the tellers and audience members spoke of it with fondness for years. The tellers hadn't planned what happened; no one expected a session on the theme of spam. And yet, through their ability to tell the right story or to adapt one when needed, the tellers created a unique moment of storytelling excellence.

Bridging Tradition and Modernity: Two Storytellers

The rapid proliferation of information technologies over the last century has severely taxed time-honored storytelling practices. As traditional tellers world wide pass on, they often take their knowledge and their stories with them. There are, however, modern storytellers, such as Eddie Lenihan and Marilyn Torres profiled below, working to preserve and promote the old stories and the folk wisdom they contain. These are just two of many storytellers who are actively engaged in the process of insuring that stories from ancient traditions, and the beliefs they carry, are recorded, honored, and told.

 **Eddie Lenihan** is a storyteller, story collector, and writer from Crusheen, County Clare, in Ireland. He has dedicated his life to recording and preserving the stories, beliefs and fairy lore of Ireland to insure that they are not forgotten and that their wisdom is available to future generations. Eddie addresses the loss of tradition in *Meeting the Other Crowd: The Fairy Stories of Hidden Ireland.*

(T)hat intimate Ireland has all but passed away. Within a single lifetime Ireland has changed from a predominantly rural to a mainly urban society. This fact underlies all. Old people, the tradition-bearers, have become virtual exiles in their own land, disregarded, unvalued. Old lore is no longer passed on, and this is for a complex of reasons. Partly it is a belief among older people themselves that they are ignorant in comparison to the new "schooled" generation. And yet those same old people have a fierce pride in their specialized knowledge from times past (3-4).

In the quote below, Eddie describes where he gets his stories:

You might ask me, and you'd be right to ask me, where do I get my stories. Well, I can tell you. The stories I get, the stories I'm telling you, are not stories from a book. These are stories that come down, down, down through the generations. I go out with my tape recorder and I collect these stories from old people, from the oldest of the old people. These are people who were not brought up with television. Most of them would not have owned a radio. They would be poor people, but they were only poor in money. They were not poor when it came to knowledge and they were not poor when it came to how to tell a story. Put yourself into one of those kitchens at night, and remember now, an Irish kitchen at that time was not the kind of kitchen you look at today. This would have been the main room of the house, usually a big room, an open fireplace and a big chimney. And you could look up that chimney and you could see the stars out. And people would gather around that fireplace at night, and if there was somebody in the locality who was good to tell a story, that person would always be welcome. . . And if somebody was able to tell a story well, that person was respected in the whole parish. Transcribed from *The Good People: Authentic Irish Fairy Tales*, told by Eddie Lenihan. Sounds True, 2001.

To bridge old and new Ireland, Eddie, who is a passionate and vivid storyteller, writes books, records audio tapes and cds, teaches, and travels all over the world to tell the stories he has collected. He thrives on opening his listeners' ears to the worldview contained in the stories:

I enjoy very much seeing such people beginning to question what they have always taken for granted; i.e., that these things were only for children, that they were old-fashioned, "stupid," out-of-date, and all the other epithets that apply to the scarcely known (*Meeting the Other Crowd*, 9).

In addition to collecting, preserving and passing on the stories and fairy lore, Eddie is committed to honoring the people who told the stories. Through his work as a living bridge, not only the stories, but the tellers as well, will be remembered and their contributions cherished.

Marilyn Omifunke Torres grew up in New York and Puerto Rico and now lives in Phoenix, Arizona. She was ordained as a Yoruba priestess when she was 22 years old. Among the Yoruba people of West Africa, storytellers such as Marilyn serve as the vehicles for transmitting the wisdom of the ancestors. She received her stories through oral transmission rather than by reading them in a book. For many years, Marilyn told these stories privately as a source of spiritual guidance. More recently, she has been telling them in public storytelling venues. About her tradition, Marilyn says:

Among the Yoruba People of West Africa (also known as the Ivory Coast), storytellers are often referred to as the "Keepers of the Records." This oral history dates as far back as 3,000 B.C. and was committed to memory by the Keepers up until the 19th century. The storyteller remains a powerful mediator for communicating the people's cultural, social, and spiritual traditions and holds the place of teacher, advisor, and healer (Interview).

Marilyn's goal as a storyteller is to become the bridge between traditional African and modern American storytelling. She does this by telling stories to her middle school students, by providing workshops on Yoruba cosmology and belief that incorporate the stories, and by telling the Yoruba myths and folktales at concerts and festivals.

One of the great challenges of bringing the stories of the Yoruba tradition to modern audiences is to insure that the stories are honored in the process.

I want my listeners to understand that these are sacred stories that carry great power. The stories reflect the totality of human and divine nature. They incorporate the origins of life, humor and sensuality, death and betrayal, and love and loss. There are many names and terms that are unfamiliar to modern audiences, so I always take time to introduce the characters and other new terms to the audience, so that they are prepared to receive the wisdom and delight the stories have to offer. And, I always seek the blessing and approval of the deities and ancestors being told about before I tell their stories (Interview).

Along with the challenges come rewards. For Marilyn, it is very gratifying to be able to create a broader awareness and appreciation of the richness of African belief and story, an awareness that has been long in coming. Her work insures that the powerful stories of the Yoruba tradition are more widely available and accessible.

Tradition and Modernity

Some scholars believe that traditional oral narrative and modern literature have completely different natures and creative origins. And in truth, in some traditions the creative freedom that modern authors have to write (tell) whatever they want would have been inconceivable. The point was to pass on a particular body of knowledge and wisdom – the tradition.

Perhaps this is at the core of what it is like to be a modern storyteller with roots in traditional telling. We often do not have the same level of freedom that writers have because we must respect the oral traditions and their modern practitioners. We are somewhere between writers and traditional storytellers, with some of the constraints and some of the benefits of each. We want to use oral narrative to create meaning and enjoyment for others. We have a wide range of stories and telling styles available to us, and we can choose what we want to use based on our preference, our particular talent, and the demands and requirements of the particular story we are creating. We don't have to be the store houses of cultural history and values that our predecessors were and this frees us to be what modern audiences need in the role of storyteller.

Part of the magic and mystery of storytelling is that we can experience the power of oral language the way our ancestors did. Many storytellers have the ability to bring a story to life. They help us transcend our literate culture and recapture something primal. We feel the presence of the oral tradition in the telling of a story layered with repetition and with a structure designed for ease in learning. Most modern storytellers rely heavily on literacy to develop their stories. At the same time, they must return a living presence to the story – the immediacy and lived-in character of the oral culture.

Memorable Quotes about Storytelling

"Although setbacks of all kinds may discourage us, the grand, old process of storytelling puts us in touch with strengths we may have forgotten, with wisdom that has faded or disappeared and with hopes that have fallen into darkness. It also connects us to joys and pleasures that have been relegated to professional entertainers. Above all, storytelling gives us love and courage for life: in the process of making up a wonderful story, new spirit is born for facing the great adventures of our lives and for giving wise encouragement to others, of any age, along their own pathways." (*The Art of Storytelling*, Nancy Mellon)

"I have an old belief – true or not as it may be – and that is that the first definite challenge to the art of the storyteller came when stories began to be written down, when for the first time, tales were no longer handed on as living substance, from mouth to mouth, no longer expelled on the breath of one storyteller to be drawn in on the breath of another. . . There is a kind of death to every story when it leaves the speaker and becomes impaled for all time on clay tablets or the written and printed page. To take it from the page, to create it again into living substance, this is the challenge – not only for the storyteller from 4000 B.C. through the Middle Ages, but for the storyteller of today." (*The Way of the Storyteller*, Ruth Sawyer)

"In western cultures, where storytelling declined drastically before the recent revival, the word 'storytelling' immediately makes 95% of adults dismissively think of children. But if they can be persuaded along to a show for adults they are astounded at the quality and magic of what they have been missing – those Grimms' fairytales weren't originally meant for kids at all." (Tim Sheppard's Storytelling FAQ: www.timsheppard.co.uk/story/faq.html#Introduction)

"Storytelling is one of the few truly universal human bonds; people in all times and places have sat down at night and told stories. Putting together words to reproduce events that engage the emotions of the listener is surely a form of art that ranks among the great human experiences." (*Other Peoples' Myths*, Wendy Doniger)

"It is the function of the storyteller to weave these two kinds of imagery – the ancient images that encapsulate the deepest dreams, hopes, fears and nightmares of a society, and the contemporary images that record the evanescent world of experience – into a single strand. . . Story is at the heart of the way humans see themselves, experience themselves within the context of their worlds. And emotions are the soul of storytelling."(*Story*, Harold Scheub)

"The stories we are willing to share with one another give our culture its values, beliefs, goals, and traditions, binding us together into a cohesive society, allowing us to work together with a common purpose. Storytelling lives at the heart of human experience—a compelling form of personal communication as ancient as language itself. Since the beginnings of humankind, we have shared through stories the events, beliefs, and values held dear by our families, communities, and cultures." (*The Call of Story:* www.callofstory.org/en/storytelling)

The Stories:

Truth & Story, a Yiddish folktale from Europe, retold by LynnAnn Wojciechowicz

Long ago, Truth walked from village to village as naked as the day he was born. He kept looking for people who would listen to him, but everywhere he went, he was shunned. Mothers grabbed their children and covered their eyes. Teen-age girls might sneak a peek, but then they'd hurry off. Teenage boys liked to taunt him and throw garbage at him. Old men turned away in embarrassment while old women gave him a fleeting smile as they followed their husbands inside. Village after village, it was always the same.

One day, while resting in the woods outside of a village, trying to decide where to go next, he heard laughter, singing, and applause. He looked through the trees and saw the villagers applauding Story as she entered the town. They even brought out fresh meats and soups and pies, offering them to Story, who agreed to have some as long as the whole village shared in the feast. It was obvious that everyone loved Story.

That evening, Story came into the woods and found Truth. "Brother Truth, why are you so sad? Why do you hide in the woods?"

Truth told Story how everyone fled from him except the teenage boys who teased him and threw rotten vegetables. He told her how horrible he felt. He wanted to share his wisdom, but no one would listen. He asked, "Is it because I am so old that everyone rejects me?"

"No, brother, your age has nothing to do with it. I, too, am very old, but the older I get, the better people like me. Let me tell you a secret: No one wants to look at the naked truth."

So, Story found some black-velvet trousers, and a fine white silk shirt for Truth to wear. She wrapped a bright blue tie around his neck and set a jaunty yellow cap on his head.

Arm in arm, they walked into the village together, Truth with Story. The villagers greeted them with warmth and love and appreciation, for Truth, wrapped in Story's clothing is beautiful. Everyone listened intently to Truth and nodded at his wise insights.

Ever since that day, Truth always travels with Story, and they are welcomed wherever they go.

© LynnAnn Wojciechowicz. LynnAnn is a storyteller and a teacher. She is humanities and storytelling faculty at South Mountain Community College. She was one of the founders of the SMCC Storytelling Institute, and is currently its director. She adapted the story from the following sources:

Baltuck, Naomi. "Truth and Parable." *Apples from Heaven: Multicultural folk Tales About Stories & Storytellers.* Linnet books, 1995.

Norfolk, Bobby & Sherry. "Truth and Story." *The Moral of the Story: Folktales for Character Development.* August House, 1999.

Sheppard, Tim. "The Story of Truth and a Story about Truth." http://www.henshall.com/blog/archives/000156.html. August 13, 2007.

"The Story of Truth & Parable." *Yiddish Folktales.* Pantheon Books, 1977.

Anansi & the Sky God's Stories, a folktale from Ghana, retold by LynnAnn Wojciechowicz

One day Anansi, that shape-shifting spider-man, was thinking. "It's not fair that Nyami, the Lord of the Sky, has all the stories of the world in that box beside his throne. He should share them. I want some. I think I'll just go up and ask him."

So, he wove a spider web all the way up to the heavens, climbing as he wove. When he got to the Sky God's throne, he bowed deeply.

"Lord Nyami, master of the universe, king of the heavens," he began, but Nyami knew Anansi, so he interrupted him.

"O.K. Anansi, what do you want today?"

"Oh your most honorable majesty, I was just wondering if you might be willing to share some of your stories with me—the ones you keep in the box by your throne. I would be willing to work for them, of course, and I would ask for just a few."

Now, Nyami did not want to share *any* of his stories with Anansi, but he was the Lord of the Universe, and as such, he could not just refuse. Instead, he came up with a plan: he would ask Anansi to perform four impossible tasks. He would be granting Anansi's request, but he would still be able to keep his stories.

"Anansi, I will give you my stories if you bring me the following: Onini, the dangerous python; Osebo, the perilous leopard; Moboro, the fierce hornets, and Moatia, the creature no man can see."

"Thank you, thank you, Lord Nyami! I will certainly bring you these creatures."

Anansi scrambled down his spider web and ran home, calling for his wife: "Aso, Aso, I need to capture Onini, the dangerous python."

"Well, get a branch from a palm tree and a length of vine . . ."

"Enough, I know" and off Anansi went. He knew that an angry python could easily squeeze a spider to death. But, he would not let that stand in his way. He got a branch from a palm tree and length of vine; then, he went to where python was dozing in the sun, after finishing a good meal.

"Onini, I need your help. My wife Aso thinks this palm-tree branch is longer than you. I think you are longer than this branch. Would you allow me to tie you up so I can measure?"

Well, python was feeling so relaxed and comfortable, he agreed, and Anansi proceeded to tie him up.

"I have to tie your tail, so you don't move forward as I am measuring. I need to tie you around the middle also. Now I need to tie your mouth, if that's O.K."

Once Anansi had Onini the python completely tied up, he slung him over his shoulder and made his way up the spider web to Lord Nyami's throne.

As he threw the python down at Lord Nyami's feet, he bowed deeply.

"I see you've accomplished my first task, Anansi. Only three more to go," stated Lord Nyami.

"Yes, Sir," said Anansi as he ran back to the spider web and scrambled down again. "Aso, Aso," he cried, "I need to capture Osebo, the perilous leopard."

"Well," came his wife's voice from their hut, "if you dig a hole . . ."

"Enough, I know" and off Anansi went. He knew an angry leopard could easily claw a spider to death. But Anansi was not about to let that stop him. He carried his shovel to the path leopard took each day when he wanted to get a drink of water from the river. Right in the

13

middle of the path, Anansi dug a deep hole. Then, he climbed out and covered the top of the hole with branches and leaves, so the hole would not be noticed. After that, he went behind the nearest bush and hid himself. He waited and waited. Finally, he saw Osebo the leopard bounding down the path, and, yes, he fell right into the hole.

Anansi came out and approached the hole. "Osebo, what are you doing down there?" he asked in a concerned voice.

"I don't know what happened," called leopard. "I never noticed this hole before. It's too deep for me to climb out. Do you think you could help me?"

"Sure," said Anansi. "Just hold up your front paws, so I can tie them together. That will make it easier for me to pull you up."

Leopard held up his front paws and Anansi proceeded to tie them together with a piece of vine. Then, Anansi picked up a large rock and threw it as hard as he could, hitting Osebo right on the head and knocking him unconscious. After that, he pulled leopard out of the hole, tied his back legs together, dragged him to his spider web, hoisted leopard on his back, and started climbing back up to the Sky God. He was very tired and out of breath when he placed leopard before Nyami's throne.

"I see you've been successful again, Anansi. Well, two more to go."

"Yes, Sir," replied Anansi as he slowly retreated back down his spider web.

This time, when he got home, he went inside the hut and had a nice drink before he asked, "Aso, I need to capture Moboro, the fierce hornets."

"Well, if you get a calabash . . ."

"Enough, I know" and off Anansi went, catching a second wind. He knew that angry hornets could easily sting a spider to death. But Anansi was never one to give up. He found a nice calabash. Aso had already prepared it to carry water by cutting the top off the gourd, scraping it out, and allowing it to dry. He went to the river and filled the calabash with water; then he put the top on it to keep the water from splashing out. Down the road he went until he came to the tree where the hornets had their nest.

First, he took off the top and sprinkled water on himself; then he sprinkled water all over the hornets' nest as he called out, "Moboro, come quickly into my calabash where it is dry. The monsoon rains have come early this year."

Bzzz, Bzzz, Bzzz, Bzzz, the hornets flew into the calabash, and when they were all inside, Anansi put the top back on, and carefully carried the calabash up to the Lord Nyami's throne. He set it gently on the ground as he bowed.

"Anansi, you have now accomplished three of my tasks. Only one remains," said the Sky God as Anansi retreated back down the spider web.

"Aso, Aso, I need to capture Moatia, the creature no man can see."

"Well, make a doll of wood . . ."

"Enough, I know" and off Anansi went. Now Anansi knew that Moatia was an invisible Tree Spirit. He also knew these fairies loved to play around the odum trees, and they loved mashed yams. So, he made a little wooden doll holding a bowl, tied a vine around its neck, and sat it at the base of an odum tree. Then he found some sticky tree sap and spread it all over the front of the doll. He mashed up some yams and put them in the bowl the doll was carrying. Then, holding the vine, Anansi crept behind some bushes to hide.

Soon enough Moatia came dancing along, spotted the doll with the mashed yams and asked, "Mmmm, little one, may I have some of your yams?"

Anansi pulled on his end of the vine and the doll appeared to nod her head in reply.

"Mmmmmmmmmm. Oh, thank you, thank you," said the Tree Spirit after finishing all the yams as she licked her fingers.

The Tree Spirit waited for a reply, but the wooden doll did not move.

"I said, 'thank you.' Do you not answer me when I thank you?"

Still the doll did not move.

"Answer me when I speak to you or I will slap you!" said the angry fairy.

When the doll did not respond, Moatia slapped its cheek. The Tree Spirit's hand stuck ito the sticky sap.

"Let go of my hand or I'll slap you again," she cried. With that, she slapped the doll on the other cheek. That hand stuck fast as well. The Tree Spirit tried to push the doll away with her foot, but her foot was then stuck in the sap. She used her other foot, but that, too, was caught. "Ohhhhhhhh" she cried.

Anansi came out from behind the bush, reached his hand behind the doll, and picked up the doll with Moatia stuck to it. Very carefully, he carried it up the spider web to the Sky God's throne.

When he set the doll and Tree Spirit down, Nyami said, "Anansi, I did not believe you could do it. The richest and most powerful of men have tried and failed. But you have accomplished four impossible tasks. From this day forward, my stories shall belong to you and they shall be called "Spider Stories.""

With that Nyami gave Anansi the box. As Anansi carried it down the spider web, he called out to all the villagers to gather round. When he got to the ground, he set the box down and told the villagers what he had done to get the stories. Then he opened the lid, and stories flew everywhere. Anansi caught some, Aso caught some, each of the villagers caught some, but there were so many, they flew all over the world. Some even made it to us, and that is why to this day, we have stories to tell. And we tell them.

© 2008 LynnAnn Wojciechowicz. Adapted from the following sources:

Baltuck, Naomi. "How All Stories Came to be Known as Spider Stories" *Apples from Heaven: Multicultural Folk Tales About Stories and Storytellers.* Linnet Books, 1995.

Cole, Joanna. "How Spider Obtained the Sky-god's Stories." *Best-Loved Folktales of the World.* Doubleday & Co., Inc. 1982.

Jones, Raymond E. and Jon C. Stott, eds. *A World of Stories: Traditional Tales for Children.* Oxford University Press, 2006.

Maguire, Jack. "Spider and the Box of Stories." *Creative Storytelling.* Yellow Moon Press, 1985.

Sherman, Josepha. "Why Anansi Owns Every Story" *Trickster Tales: Forty Folk Stories from Around the World.* August House, 1996.

A Whole Brain, a folktale from Kazakhstan retold by Sally Pomme Clayton

It was the seventh day. God had finished making the world and at last he could rest—when he realized he had forgotten something. He had forgotten to give human beings brains. So he took a jug, filled it with brains, called the Angel Gabriel and said, "Go and give human beings brains!"

Gabriel flew down to Earth and saw people everywhere. There were so many people, but there was only one jug. There were not enough brains to go round. So Gabriel gave each person a teeny, tiny drop of brains. Then he flew back to heaven with the empty jug.

When God looked down on creation, he saw that people were very unhappy. They were arguing and fighting. There was hunger, poverty and tears. People did not understand how to live together at all.

"Oh dear," said God, "human beings have only got a quarter of a brain each. I'd better make someone with a whole brain who can sort them all out."

So God made one more person and filled his brain right up to the top. God filled the man's brain with stories, songs, poems, and sparkling words. And he sent the story teller down to Earth to tell stories and sing songs, to tell and sing wisdom back into foolish human beings.

(Adapted from *Tales Told in Tents* by Sally Pomme Clayton)

2

Getting Started

"I learned that even though the story was long and complicated, I still could manage it. I know I have not mastered it, but it gave me a boost in confidence. I think this whole class experience has." (Storytelling Student, Summer 2006)

What kinds of stories will I be telling?

Storytelling requires a storyteller, an audience and a story. You are the storyteller and your classmates will be your audience. The third element of the storytelling experience is the story.

During the course of this semester you will be telling four stories:

- A folktale or fairytale
- A myth, legend, or hero tale
- A fact-based story
- A personal story

Specific strategies for finding and developing each of these stories will be provided in the following chapters. For now, here is a brief overview of the range of stories you will tell and where you will find them.

Folktales are the backbone of the oral tradition and are found in all cultures. They are fictional stories that are not regarded as true in the factual sense, although they frequently reveal truths of the human condition. Fairytales are a type of folktale that usually feature fairies or magical or otherworldly elements.

Through most of history folktales have been shared from person to person, generation to generation. Few people, especially in modern industrialized cultures like ours, learn stories in the traditional way.

> **Do you feel anxious about standing in front of people to tell a story?**
>
> Remember, a little nervousness can be a good thing. It can mean that you want to do a good job, and that you aren't taking your story or your audience for granted. Too much nervousness, though, can make for a miserable experience.
>
> Preparation and practice are the keys to an effective and successful storytelling event. This chapter and those following will provide tips and strategies to help you prepare your story and yourself.
>
> In addition, be assured that your teacher is committed to maintaining a safe telling environment for you and your classmates.

Types of Stories

Although you won't be telling stories from all these genres, you will be encountering them in your reading and research.

Folktales: traditional fictional stories from around the world (Hansel and Gretel, Godmother Death, Aslaug the Deep Minded, Anansi and the Sky God's Stories).

Fairytales: folktales with fairies or magic (The Magic Orange Tree, Beauty and the Beast, Goblin's Gloves).

Fables: short folktales with animal characters and a moral (Paca and Beetle, The Tortoise and the Hare, The Ant and the Grasshopper).

Parables: short stories with a moral, spiritual, or religious message (The Prodigal Son, Truth and Story).

Pourquoi tales: stories from around the world that explain how something came to be (The Tale of the Lizards' Tails, Why the Frog Croaks in Wet Weather, The Gossiping Clams).

Myths: stories of gods, heroes, and creation (The Hungry Goddess, Who is the Greatest Warrior? The Story of Arachne).

Legends: stories about people, events, or places that may be based in fact, but are usually fictional (George Washington & the Cherry Tree, King Arthur, St. Brigid's Cloak).

Epics: long, usually mythic, stories with many characters and intertwining plot lines. Epics may require many hours or even days to tell (The Volsunga Saga, The Epic of Mwindo, The Epic of Gilgamesh, The Ramayana).

Urban Legends: stories believed by modern people that usually have elements of horror or disgust (Alligators in the Sewer, Spiders in the Hairdo).

Hero Tales: myths or folktales that tell of the remarkable deeds of a hero (Perseus and Medusa, The Devil's Three Gold Hairs).

Tall Tales: humorous folktales that rely on wildly exaggerated characters and events (Paul Bunyan, Talking Catfish, Annie Christmas).

Historical Stories: stories based in fact about historical places, or events.

Biographical Stories: stories based in fact about living or historical persons.

Family Stories: stories created by the teller about his or her own family.

Personal Stories: stories created by the teller about him or herself.

The richest source of folktales for modern people is the library, where anthologies of stories from around the world can be found. The internet is another good source for finding folk and fairy tales, and it is becoming richer and more reliable with every passing year.

Myths and legends differ from folktales in that somebody somewhere at some time believed they were true. Myths are stories of deities and of creation. They are often considered sacred. Legends are stories about people, places, or events that actually existed. While these stories may or may not have been regarded as true by their original tellers and listeners, they are often not factual. Hero tales may be stories of heroes within a particular mythological or cultural tradition, or they may be folktales with the hero's journey structure. As with folktales, the best places to find these stories are in collections of myths and legends from a particular culture or anthologies that include stories from several traditions.

Fact-based stories, which include historical, biographical, and family stories, are about actual people and events. Whether about well-known or little-known characters or happenings, these stories often rely on a unique or innovative point of view. Once you find a person or event you want to tell about, the story will require more hands-on crafting from you than the previous two types. You will be creating this story.

Personal stories, as the name states, are about you. You will find will find, develop, and craft these stories from your life and experiences.

How Do I Choose a Story?

Many storytellers say that the story chooses the teller rather than the other way around. It's as if the story is the missing piece in a puzzle or a key to a locked door; it fits, it completes, it opens the teller.

Here is an equation to guide your selection and preparation:

Delight + Desire → Delivery

- Let Delight guide the selection of your story. The types of stories you find that truly delight you and to which you are drawn naturally will be an important indication of your emerging preferences and style as a storyteller.

- Let your Desire to share the story effectively with your listeners guide and motivate the effort you invest in the story.

- Your Delivery of the story, and your ability to bring ease and energy to it, derive from the first two.

Listen to the voice of your inner storyteller and select a story that delights you. Prepare yourself and your story in a way that allows you to fulfill your desire to tell the story to others with competence and style. Do this and your delivery will honor the story, your listeners, and you as the teller.

So, how do you find a story that makes you feel like that? The most direct and accessible way for most of us is to go to the library, get a stacks of folktale anthologies and read stories, lots and lots of stories. Or go to reliable websites on the internet and read stories, lots and lots of stories. The problem is

How to choose a story

You have to like it, really like it. Choose a story that is so appealing to you that you can't wait to share it with your family and friends. Be prepared to read many stories before you find the "right" one. You'll know the story is right because it jumps into your brain and heart. The best techniques for learning and telling a story will be useless if you don't like the story. When a storyteller attempts a story he does not like, often the audience does not connect with it.

Story anthologies authored by story-tellers are filled with stories selected and written with an ear for their tell-ability. Here are some well known standards:

Fair is Fair: World Folktales of Justice by Sharon Creeden

Wisdom Tales From Around the World by Heather Forest

The People Could Fly: American Black Folktales by Virginia Hamilton

Ready-to-Tell Tales: Sure Fire Stories from America's Favorite Storytellers by David Holt & Bill Mooney

Momentos Magicos/Magic Moments by Olga Loya

Three Minute Tales: Stories from Around the World to Tell or Read When Time is Short by Margaret Read MacDonald

that a story in print, in a book or on the screen, has been stripped to its most finite element: words on a surface. It can be very difficult to discern how great a story was or can be by reading it in a book – difficult, but not impossible. The skill of the collector or writer to convey the power of the story through the printed word alone makes the difference. Your persistence and growing story sense is also a factor in finding stories that are right for you. If you read enough and pay attention to your own reactions, you will find a story that is waiting to be told by you.

To jumpstart and then accelerate this process, listen to storytellers. Listening to well-told stories sharpens your awareness. It will also awaken you to the potential of a written story to come to life in the telling. Some storytellers report the experience of rejecting a story they have read in a book only to regret that decision upon hearing someone else tell it. The latent power and value of the story is brought to life in the telling.

Find and attend professional storytelling events. Exposure to different styles of telling will provide you with clues about the type of storyteller you may become. Listening to professionals will help you begin to bridge the gap between a story in print and a told story.

How Do I Learn a Story?

For a detailed list of strategies, carefully review LynnAnn Wojciechowicz's "Learning a Story to Tell." The sections below expand and elaborate on some of those strategies and suggest others. Keep your personal learning style in mind as your read them.

Listening and Retelling: Storytelling is a traditional oral art form. A time-honored way to learn a story is to retell one that you have just heard. After you've heard your teacher, a visiting storyteller, or a fellow student tell a story that you enjoyed, ask their his permission to retell it. If the teller allows, tell the story to someone else as soon as you can. You may be surprised to discover how much you can recall after hearing a story once.

Learning a story from a print source: The first rule of learning a story from a book or the internet is: Do not memorize it word for word. Memorization is deadly for storytelling. Here's why. When you are speaking from a memorized text, you are interacting with your memory instead of your audience. Your focus is on retrieving the words just as they were written on the page. A storyteller's focus is on creating an interaction between the story, the listener and himself. For the story to live, you must tell it in your own words and bring your unique voice to the telling. This is difficult to achieve when you are trying to remember the words and their exact sequence in the original text. Instead of memorizing, your job is to learn the story well and deeply and then tell it. This will ensure that the story begins to emerge in your own voice rather than that of its author.

Learning a Story to Tell

by LynnAnn Wojciechowicz

1. **Choose a story** that insists, "Tell Me!" Choose one that touches your heart.

2. **Read the story** pausing often to notice the pictures in your mind.

3. **Make a list of plot elements:** What happens first? Next? What is the turning point? How does it end?

4. **Think about the setting:** Where does the story take place? When does it take place (past or present, day or night, winter or summer)? What colors do you see? What can you smell? What textures do you feel?

5. **Think about the characters:** What do they look like? How do they move? How do their voices sound? What are their personalities like?

6. **Take advantage of your learning style:**

   • **If you are a visual learner:** Use colored markers, pens, or crayons, and sketch out the various scenes (like cartoon segments) showing what happens in each. As you practice telling the story, see the pictures you have created in your mind.

   • **If you are an auditory learner:** Make a tape recording of yourself reading the story and listen to it over and over. After you practice telling the story in your own words, make a new recording.

   • **If you are a kinesthetic learner:** Type the story out using your words; don't copy from the printed page. It is fine to refer to the printed story if you forget certain details; just make sure you are typing it in your own words. Later, you might practice telling the story as you move around your house. Start the story in one room; tell the next scene at a different place in the room; move somewhere else for the climax of the story; choose another spot for the ending. Do this several times, telling the same part of the story in the same place each time.

7. **Practice telling the story out loud:** Tell to a stuffed animal or a pet, to a friend, to a child, to a mirror, to a tape recorder, in the car while driving, while resting in your favorite chair, in bed before you go to sleep or when you wake up. Just tell!

8. **When you get in front of your audience,** before you start your story, look at your audience, smile, and take a few deep breaths. Allow yourself to relax.

9. **Take your time when you tell the story.** Enjoy yourself! Remember, you are giving the Gift of Story!

Learning the basics of the story: When you've found a story you want to tell and have read it several times, ask yourself these questions:

• Why do I want to tell it?

• What is the story about? List the big ideas and themes of the story.

Why Frogs Croak in Wet Weather: A Korean Pourquoi Story

Once there was a young green frog who would not mind his mother. If she said, "Go east," he went west. If she said, "Go up the mountain," he jumped in the river.

After a while the mother grew old and ill. She knew that she was about to die, so she called the young frog to her and said, "When I die, bury me by the river. Do not bury me on the mountain."

She said this because she really wanted to be buried on the mountain. She was sure her son would do just the opposite of whatever she said, as he had all his life.

Finally the old mother died and the green frog was very sad. He was sorry that he had never done what his mother wanted. So this time he was determined to do what she said to do.

Thus the green frog buried his mother beside the river. Then he worried. When it rained he was afraid the waters would rise and wash her grave away and he would sit on the riverbank and cry with a sad hoarse voice.

Today green frogs still sit and croak whenever it rains.

From *How the People Sang the Mountains Up: How and Why Stories* by Maria Leach.

- What is the sequence of events? Try to list the entire story in as few briefly written steps as you can – seven to ten maximum.

Let's try this out on the story, "Why Frogs Croak in Wet Weather."

Sequence of events:

- Frog son always disobeys mother.
- Mother is getting old, and wants to be buried on the mountain, but tells her son when she dies to bury her by the river because she knows he will do the opposite of what she asks.
- She dies, he feels bad, so he does exactly as she asked and buries her by river.
- When it rains, he worries she will wash away and he croaks this sadness.
- Since then frogs croak in wet weather.

What is the story about?

- Love, death, regret, grief
- Universal human relationships
- The origin of an animal behavior

Why do you want to tell it? Here are some common reasons:

- When I was little I lived on a farm and I can remember the frogs croaking when it rained.
- I was just like the frog in this story when I was a child.
- The mother in the story reminds me of my grandmother.
- I'm a teacher and this story will fit great in my unit on amphibians.

- My child's class is studying frogs right now. This will be perfect for them. Plus, it may remind them to obey their mothers!

- This story makes me laugh. I can just imagine the poor frog croaking away.

- This is just the kind of story I like to tell. I know it will be a good fit for me. I felt an immediate connection to the wisdom expressed in the story.

Once you've gone through this sequence of questions with your own story, tell it as soon as you can without referring to the original text. This will ensure that the story begins to emerge in your voice.

Beginnings and Endings: Knowing exactly how you're going to start the story and bring it to its conclusion can provide you with some security when you stand up to tell it. Using traditional openings like "Once upon a time . . ." or "A long time ago . . ." brings listeners into the story quickly. Traditional endings such as "They all lived happily ever after" or "If he hasn't died, he's living there still" can help you conclude a story and let your listeners know you are done.

Making a deeper connection to the story: Once you have learned the basics of the story, you are ready to deepen your relationship to the tale.

Beginnings and Endings: Story as Train

A story is a sequence of images conveyed by the storyteller through voice and body. Imagine a train with many cars on a circular track sitting at the station. The listeners wait at the station for the story to begin. The storyteller is the engineer, and the engine is the storyteller's desire to deliver a well-told story to his or her listeners. This desire gives the train its energy; it begins to move. The first car is a familiar opening: *"Once upon a time . . ."* or *"Long, long ago in a place far, far away . . ."* The second car is the first image in the story and every car afterwards carries another image. The storyteller brings the story up to speed and the audience feels the power and momentum of its forward locomotion. They hear the rhythm of the story as the image-laden cars rumble over the rails. Then, the train begins to slow, and the last car comes into view, carrying a closing image as undeniably final as a red caboose: *". . . they lived happily ever after,"* or *". . . if they haven't died, they're living there still."* Just as the caboose slides by the station, the listeners see that the engine has come all the way around and in that moment they comprehend, with a sigh of satisfaction, how the beginning led inevitably and unerringly to the ending.

- List the primary characters in your story.
  Can you think of someone who is like these characters, maybe relatives or friends, celebrities or politicians? How are your characters similar to these people? What is the nature of the similarity? Physical? Personality? Life Situation?

- What is the setting for your story? Describe the landscapes of the story. What real geographic location is like the setting? Have you ever been to such a place? Draw on those memories to enhance the images in the story. If you've never encountered such a place, do some research.

- Describe the emotional landscape of your story. Is it playful, adventurous, creative, sorrowful, endearing? Think of a time in your life when you have experienced this emotion and write about how you felt.

For example, if you were to apply these questions to "Why Frogs Croak in Wet Weather", you would first think about the frog and his mother and who they resemble in your experience. Then you would think about the landscape – a familiar river and mountains. Finally, you would ponder the emotions in the story. For some, it might be the humorous set-up of the consistently contrary frog son. For others it might be the regret of having disappointed a relative, or the grief of losing a loved one.

Learning the story vs. learning to tell the story: However you have gone about learning the basics of your story, there is only one way to learn how to tell it – and that, of course, is by telling it. Each telling will bring a new opportunity to learn something about the story, about yourself as a storyteller, or about how to relate to your audience. Experienced storytellers all say that new dimensions open up to them in the process of telling. The more the story is told, the more the relationship between teller and story deepens. Storyteller Papa Joe says, "If you want to be a storyteller, tell stories. If you want to be a better storyteller, tell more stories." This may seem oversimplified, but it is the truth.

What Will the Classroom Storytelling Experience Be Like?

After you have selected, learned, and practiced your story, the time will come to tell it to your classmates. Telling, listening, and giving feedback are the core activities of the class. Your instructor will establish a storytelling space in the classroom to enhance the telling and listening experience. The teller has four responsibilities:

- **Tell the story:** Stand in the front of the room, look around at your fellow storytellers, take a deep breath, and begin.

- **Receive appreciations and other feedback from your classmates:** Appreciations are the most important thing for an emerging teller to hear. You need to know what went well in the story.

- **Listen to others tell their stories:** When you are not telling, your job is to listen with focus and concentration. This is the best kind of support you can give another storyteller.

- **Participate in the appreciations and feedback for your classmates:** If you have listened with concentration, you will be better able to tell the storyteller what went well.

Peer Coaching: In many performing arts, coaching means critique. The focus is on the weak points and what needs to be improved. Storytelling approaches coaching from a different point of view. The initial focus is on what the teller has done well.

First, tellers receive appreciations from classmates and the instructor. From that point on, the teller controls the feedback. The teller has the option to ask the listeners questions. He may want to know if the ending was clear, or if the characters were distinct. The teller may then choose to receive questions from the listeners. The listeners ask questions about parts that are unclear or incomplete. The last step the teller may choose is suggestions. Suggestions are kept to a minimum for beginners.

It is the teller's responsibility to be aware of the type of feedback he wants. The instructor has the responsibility to ensure that the feedback process remains positive and constructive. In this way the storytelling space remains safe for all concerned. This model of coaching is common amongst storytellers. It is described in more detail by Doug Lipman in *The Storytelling Coach: How to Listen, Praise, and Bring out People's Best*.

After you tell your story: Once you have told your story and received your feedback, it is essential to reflect on your experience.

- Describe the process you used to prepare to tell this story.
- Describe the experience of telling the story in class.
- What feedback did you get? What effect did the feedback have on you? How did it make you feel?

24

- What did you learn about the story or yourself from the telling?
- What do you plan to do differently the next time you tell?
- What do you plan to do just the same?

Reflecting on your experience, absorbing your success, and making plans to continue your artistic development will ensure that you get the most out of your in-class telling experience. Consistent self-assessment helps you internalize what you have learned.

Foundations of Excellence

Researching, selecting, learning, crafting, and practicing stories are the ongoing creative tasks of the storyteller. As you learn what stories mesh with your emerging style and how best to learn and practice them, you are building the foundation of your own personal excellence as a storyteller.

Another element to add to your base of skills is a focus on your commitment and readiness to tell the story to others with confidence and ease. Here are some strategies to help you accomplish this:

- Learn the story and make it your own as soon as possible. If you have two weeks before you are scheduled to tell, don't wait until the thirteenth day to begin.
- Learn the story thoroughly, but do not memorize it.
- Practice the story as often as possible with real listeners. Start off with two or three people, and then tell to increasing numbers. Practice gives you the sense and experience of relating a story to an audience.
- Your voice is your bottom-line tool. You must be heard by your listeners. A conversational tone may be appropriate for two or three listeners as you practice, but it will not be loud enough when you are telling to a room full of classmates. Practice with an audience of several people so that you can learn what level of volume and projection is necessary for the story to be heard.

Relating to your listeners: Storytelling is a face-to-face art form. The relationship that is created during the story is one of the things that makes storytelling distinct as an art form. We relate a story to our listeners, and at least for the duration of the story, we are in a relationship with them. Making eye-contact with your listeners is crucial and communicates your commitment and readiness to tell a story. Look at your audience.

Facing Performance Anxiety: Preparing to do something new can be exceedingly nerve-wracking. You may, quite naturally, feel anxious about your first telling. Most students are more confident after they have successfully told for the first time and know what the experience is like.

One of the most common fears of beginning storytellers is that they will forget their story as they are telling it. In fact, it is very, very rare for someone, even a beginner, to forget his story. Of course, the better you know your story, the less likely you are to forget it. The key is to know the story as well as you can.

But what if you do forget it? What should you do? If you do forget your story, stay calm. Just take a moment to orient yourself to where you were in the plot and pick it back up. If you need to stop and start over, feel free to do that. If you are in the middle of a story and realize you forgot to tell something important, introduce it at that point without apologizing or breaking the story. Say, for example, you forgot to mention that Jack's granny gave him a special devil-catching sack before he left home. Once Jack meets the devil, just introduce it then. "Now, before he left home, Jack's granny had given him a special devil-catching sack."

Remember that you and your classmates are all in the same boat. They will be pulling for you. If you do stumble, your listeners will be forgiving. They are counting on the same level of support from you.

Excellence and Ethics: Citing the source of the story being told is the foundational responsibility of the storyteller. Tell your audience the following, as applicable:

- The name of the story
- The author or collector of the story
- The source of the story
- The author of the source if different from the author/collector of the story
- The cultural source of the story
- The genre or type of story
- The fact that permission (if required) has been granted to the storyteller

Providing your audience with this basic information must become part of your regular habit as you tell stories. It is your absolute minimum ethical standard, upon which other standards of ethics and excellence are built.

So for example, if I had just told "Why Frogs Croak in Wet Weather," I would say, "That story is called "Why Frogs Croak in Wet Weather." It's a Korean folktale collected by Maria Leach in her book *How the People Sang the Mountains Up.*

A college classroom is a safe harbor as far as copyright is concerned. For those who intend to work in public schools or libraries, that safe harbor, known as fair use, will still apply. Be aware that if you intend to tell copyrighted material outside of these and a few other very specific contexts, you must obtain permission from the copyright holder(s).

Getting Started in Storytelling: A Trusted Voice and Two Newcomers

Susan Klein was minding her own business, happily teaching in a kindergarten/first-grade class at Oak Bluffs Elementary School in Martha's Vineyard, Massachusetts, when her call to storytelling – which she had been trying to ignore – could no longer be denied. A friend called her and said that Susan needed to hear a storyteller who was performing in the schools and would be offering stories for adults that evening. Susan said, "Oh no. I don't want anything to do with that." But her friends came to her house and dragged her off. "They told me, 'This is what you do. You talk story.' And they made me go." The storyteller was Jay O'Callahan, and when he came out to tell, he stood in front of a cement block gymnasium wall. "No props, no costumes, no creative lighting – just a tall thin man with a stunning imagination and the ability to transport his listeners. We were off."

Susan went from anticipating a dreadful evening to receiving the first inkling of the birth of a new career path within the twenty-five minutes it took Jay to tell the story of Magellan. "Jay became the mutineer captain, Cartagena, one minute, and Big Antonio gaming with the other men aboard ship, the next. I was so involved I could feel the motion of the sea hauling us southward." When the performance was over, she asked Jay if he taught storytelling. He happened to be adjunct faculty at Lesley College where she was completing her master's degree. So, she gathered up sixteen of her fellow teachers and neighbors and made the arrangements for Jay to teach a four-weekend class in story-

College where she was completing her master's degree. So, she gathered up sixteen of her fellow teachers and neighbors and made the arrangements for Jay to teach a four-weekend class in story-telling. She then spent the next four years creating and maintaining a repertoire that would work in a school system. At the end of that four years, she was ready to leave her teaching job.

> I just wanted to know if I could do it. My principal insisted I take a leave of absence instead of quitting, but I knew I had to try to make it as a storyteller. All the stories say you're supposed to go see the wise old woman before you go seek your fortune. So I went to see my mother. She said, "You've been a waitress, an actress, a seamstress, a teacher, but nothing that you've done makes your eyes shine like this storytelling business. Besides that, Susannah, you'll never own yourself until you sing your heart's true song." (Interview)

So, at age thirty Susan quit her job, loaded up her bronze Chevette and left Martha's Vineyard. "I had $300 and nine days of work scheduled for the rest of my life. But I did have a solid repertoire." When she completed her nine days in Western Massachusetts, she headed south – somewhere she wouldn't need to buy heating oil.

It was 1982. The storytelling revival and the National Association for the Preservation and Perpetuation of Storytelling were ten years old, but there were few professional tellers and even fewer role models. She went to every festival she could and slept in her car. She signed up to tell at the festival story swaps. The producers and featured tellers heard her. It wasn't long until she was being featured herself. As she traveled from festival to festival and from town to town, she presented herself to libraries and schools and was often hired. Word spread, and within just a few years, she was one of the busiest and best-known storytellers working in America. The repertoire she spent four years honing, composed mostly of folktales, served her very well.

> Story structure is inherent in the old tales. If one steeps oneself in 398.2 in the library and then does the back-up research, one can build a solid knowledge of story crafting through the time-less examples provided by traditional material.
>
> One of the things that is so alluring about folktales is you discover that all the human stories have been told. You meet yourself within the confines of the story journey. We're all there in the old tales. When something within a folktale resonates with your own story, it calls you to be its voice. And then the responsibility begins. You do whatever you need to do to get to the root of what it means to you and the truth that resides in the story. That truth then informs your derivative version – and your life. It enhances the day-to-day experience of living.
>
> What could be more fabulous than living a life mapped out in the realms of imagination? That happens when you take on a career in storytelling; you are embarking on an archetypal journey, and life as you knew it is over. The tasks and challenges come as they have for every seeker. The rewards are never gained without the magical beings along the way dispensing their gifts. (Interview)

Her substantial repertoire now includes folktale and myth, as well as autobiographical, fact-based, and literary tales. She has built a career balanced between performing and providing a wide range of services to storytellers and authors including coaching, leading workshops, producing recordings, and editing written material. Her own books and recordings have received many awards. In 2001, she received the Circle of Excellence Award presented by the National Storytelling Network.

Within the storytelling community, Susan is known for her impassioned advocacy of professional ethics. Her book *Ethics, Apprenticeship, Etiquette, Courtesy, and Copyright* is required reading for

Dustin Loehr has been performing all his life. He started taking tap dancing lessons when he was three years old, and says, "I never *wanted* to be a dancer – I always *was* a dancer." Dance led him to theater and by the time he was in high school he was an experienced performer and had no doubt that his life path was in acting and dancing.

On a whim he went on an audition for a spot as a youth teller for the 2005 Mesa Storytelling Festival. The audition was being run by Don Doyle, the festival's artistic director. Dustin told a story about a time he fell while tap dancing in a talent show. Don encouraged him to tell it again and to incorporate his tap dancing. They both loved the result. Dustin got one of the youth teller slots and Don helped him to craft a small repertoire of stories that fit his style and which were well served by his unique approach to them. Dustin remembers the day of the festival very clearly:

I was nervous. My mom and dad and grandparents were there. I stood with my tap shoes in hand and my tap board under my arm ready to take the stage. I had rehearsed my story for the umpteenth time that morning. The idea of not memorizing my story was frightening at first; however, I soon discovered the freedom that came along with telling from the heart and I learned to love it. I was one of the only Youth Tellers to tell twice that day, and my first performance was in the largest tent, full of over three hundred squirming kids. One of the featured tellers, David Novak, gave me the greatest advice that morning. He said, "If you are nervous, you should open with your tap, something you know you can do well," I listened to David, and after my tap intro, I dove into the story. (http://youthstorytelling.com/youth_spot.html)

Dustin has been a youth teller at the Mesa Storytelling Festival every year since. This year he decided that storytelling is what he wants to do with his life. He loves the independence and authority it gives him as an artist. He says that when he acts he must become a character that someone else has written. When he dances someone else's choreography, it is like being their puppet.

When I tell, I know that it is me up there. It is one hundred percent Dustin Loehr. The audience is seeing and hearing my words, my taps and my moves. When I include tap in my stories, I'm not just dancing; I'm making music with my feet and telling stories with that music. When I tell I'm free – free to express myself using both my training in theatre and in dance. (Adapted from http://youthstorytelling.com/youth_spot.html)

Dustin uses tap in a range of ways when he tells. In some stories, he uses tap as a refrain, or to bracket or frame the story. In others, each character has a unique tap signature, and changes in tempo or intensity signal changes in the character's state of mind. Dustin has some stories which include little or no dancing, since not all stories he feels compelled to tell are served by the inclusion of tap.

Dustin has devoted himself to storytelling with great passion and drive. He is building a repertoire, seeking performance opportunities, and furthering his training by taking classes at the SMCC Storytelling Institute, and working with mentors. Working with trusted mentors is one of two pieces

Dustin has devoted himself to storytelling with great passion and drive. He is building a repertoire, seeking performance opportunities, and furthering his training by taking classes at the SMCC Storytelling Institute, and working with mentors. Working with trusted mentors is one of two pieces of advice he offers to beginning tellers. The other is, "When you find a story, make it your own, put yourself into it, and recognize yourself in it. It's you. Love it."

Kassandra Rubalcava is in the eighth grade at the Tertulia Precollege Community Charter School in Phoenix, Arizona. She has been telling stories for the past two years. Her teacher, storyteller Marilyn Torres, introduced her to storytelling.

I was in 7th grade and I was learning English. I was afraid to speak English in front of others. The only language I spoke was Spanish. Ms. Torres had an idea to help me speak in front of people. She asked me if I wanted to tell a story with her. She said she would tell in English and I would tell in Spanish. From that moment, doors opened for me to become a storyteller. (Interview)

When telling in tandem, Marilyn first tells a portion of the story in English; Kassandra then tells the same chunk in Spanish. This has required Kassandra to be as familiar with the story in English as she is in Spanish. Her English comprehension has improved as has her confidence with the language.

Kassandra immediately displayed considerable talent as a storyteller. She has a natural facility for selecting and connecting to the stories she tells. She enjoys using her voice to bring the stories to life. She has a compelling stage presence and is able to quickly engage her listeners.

Kassandra and Marilyn have performed together at Tertulia and community festivals, including the Mesa Storytelling Festival where Kassandra was selected as a youth teller for 2007. There she met Peter Cook, a storyteller from Chicago. Peter is deaf and he tells in sign language. As he tells, a voice interpreter speaks for the hearing audience.

One of my best storytelling experiences was when I had the opportunity to meet an amazing storyteller, Peter Cook, who is deaf. He helped me realize that your weaknesses can become your strengths. He motivated me to not stop dreaming. Whatever I want, I can achieve. (Interview)

Kassandra has begun to perform on her own in Spanish, and plans to tell in English as well.

I see myself as a storyteller in the future. I see myself traveling around the world telling stories. I want to tell stories in other languages, not just in Spanish and English. Storytelling is important to me because I can communicate with people through stories. I am able to express myself in a way that people are not used to. Storytelling has helped me find myself and discover one of my talents. (Interview)

The Stories:

A Story and a Song, a folktale from India, retold by A. K. Ramanujan

A housewife knew a story. She also knew a song. But she kept them to herself, never told anyone the story or sang the song.

Imprisoned within her, the story and the song were feeling choked. They wanted release, wanted to run away. One day, when she was sleeping with her mouth open, the story escaped, fell out of her, took the shape of a pair of shoes and sat outside the house. The song also escaped, took the shape of something like a man's coat, and hung on a peg.

The woman's husband came home, looked at the coat and shoes, and asked her, "Who is visiting?"

"No one," she said.

"But whose coat and shoes are these?"

"I don't know," she replied.

He wasn't satisfied with her answer. He was suspicious. Their conversation was unpleasant. The unpleasantness led to a quarrel. The husband flew into a rage, picked up his blanket, and went to the Monkey God's temple to sleep.

The woman didn't understand what was happening. She lay down alone that night. She asked the same question over and over: "Whose coat and shoes are these?" Baffled and unhappy, she put out the lamp and went to sleep.

All the lamp flames of the town, once they were put out, used to come to the Monkey God's temple and spend the night there, gossiping. On this night, all the lamps of all the houses were represented there – all except one, which came late.

The others asked the latecomer, "Why are you so late tonight?"

"At our house, the couple quarreled late into the night," said the flame.

"Why did they quarrel?"

"When the husband wasn't home, a pair of shoes came onto the verandah, and a man's coat somehow got onto a peg. The husband asked her whose they were. The wife said she didn't know. So they quarreled."

"Where did the coat and shoes come from?"

"The lady of our house knows a story and a song. She never tells the story, and has never sung the song to anyone. The story and the song got suffocated inside, so they got out and have turned into a coat and a pair of shoes. They took revenge. The woman doesn't even know."

The husband, lying under his blanket in the temple, heard the lamp's explanation. His suspicions were cleared. When he went home, it was dawn. He asked his wife about her story and her song. But she had forgotten both of them. "What story, what song?" she said.

(From *A Flowering Tree and Other Oral Tales from India,* by A.K. Ramanujan)

Stone Soup, a folktale from Europe, retold by D. L. Ashliman

A tramp knocked at the farmhouse door. "I can't let you in, for my husband is not at home," said the woman of the house. "And I haven't a thing to offer you," she added. Her voice showed unmasked scorn for the man she held to be a beggar.

"Then you could make use of my soup stone," he replied, pulling from his pocket what appeared to be an ordinary stone.

"Soup stone?" said she, suddenly showing interest in the tattered stranger.

"Oh yes," he said. "If I just had a pot full of water and a fire, I'd show you how it works. This stone and boiling water make the best soup you've ever eaten. Your husband would thank you for the good supper, if you'd just let me in and put my stone to use over your fire."

The woman's suspicions yielded to her desire for an easy meal, and she opened the door. A pot of water was soon brought to a boil. The tramp dropped in his stone, then tasted the watery gruel. "It needs salt, and a bit of barley," he said. "And some butter, too, if you can spare it." The woman obliged him by adding the requested ingredients. He tasted it again. "Much better!" he said. "But a good soup needs vegetables and potatoes. Are there none in your cellar?"

"Oh yes," she said, her enthusiasm for the miracle soup growing, and she quickly found a generous portion of potatoes, turnips, carrots, and beans.

After the mixture had boiled awhile, the man tasted it again. "It's almost soup," he said. "The stone has not failed us. But some chicken broth and chunks of meat would do it well."

The woman, recognizing the truth of his claim, ran to the chicken yard, returning soon with a freshly slaughtered fowl. "Soup stone, do your thing!" she said, adding the chicken to the stew.

When their noses told them that the soup was done, the woman dished up a healthy portion for her guest and for herself. They ate their fill, and — thanks to the magic stone — there was still a modest bowlful left over for her husband's supper.

"My thanks for the use of your pot and your fire," said the tramp as evening approached, and he sensed that the husband soon would be arriving home. He fished his stone from the bottom of the pot, licked it clean, and put it back into his pocket.

"Do come again," said the thankful woman.

(Reconstructed from various European sources. © 1998 by D. L. Ashliman. http://www.pitt.edu/ ~dash/type1548.html#proverb)

The Gossiping Clams, a Suquamish (Native American) folktale, retold by Naomi Baltuck

Long, long ago, when the world was new and the animals could talk, clams were the most talkative of all. And no wonder, for their mouths stretched the full length of their bodies. The clams not only loved to talk, they told stories as well. Some of the stories were true and some were not.

"Did you know," said one clam to Eagle, who was eating a fish on the beach, "that Raven says he is a much better hunter than you?"

Eagle's feathers ruffled in annoyance. "Perhaps that is true," scoffed Eagle, "if picking at carrion can be called 'hunting'."

Once when Otter came down to the beach to splash in the water, another clam said to him, "I don't think you make yourself foolish when you come down to play in the waves."

"Who said I look foolish?" demanded Otter.

"I really shouldn't say," said the clam, "but you might go and ask Beaver. Beaver thinks that everyone should work as hard as she does."

It wasn't long before all the animals were quarreling with each other, and all because of the stories that the clams were spreading. Raven finally got so tired of all that gossiping that he called a council meeting and invited all the animals. Bear, Eagle, Mink, Otter, Wolf, and many others came. It was decided at that meeting that, in order to preserve the peace, a way must be found to put a stop to these unkind stories.

"Beaver," said Raven, "we cannot decide how to punish the clams. You are a good worker. We know that you will keep working until you discover a solution, so we have chosen you to rid us of this problem."

Beaver thought and thought, and at last she thought of a plan. She gathered up armloads of the clams—every last one of them—and carried them to the edge of the water.

"What are you doing?" they asked in alarm.

"You shall see soon enough," replied Beaver. "Never again will you spread your mean-spirited tales."

Beaver waited there until the tide went out and then, quickly, she buried each and every one of those clams in the sand. The clams were outraged! When Bear came down to walk along the beach, one of the clams opened its mouth to tattle on Beaver. But as soon as it did, sand and water ran in, and all the poor clam could do was spit out the water and close its mouth.

Even today, if you walk along the beach at low tide, you might see a little spurt of water squirting up from beneath the sand here and there. That is just a clam spitting out the water it swallowed when it opened its mouth to gossip!

(From *Apples from Heaven* by Naomi Baltuck)

3

How to Tell a Folktale

"At first I thought, nobody could believe this story. But then I thought 'who cares?'
I started really wanting to tell it. I could imagine myself telling it – even the
weird parts." (Storytelling Student Fall 2004).

Why begin by telling a folktale?

We begin with folktales because they are the foundation of the world storytelling tradition and, as such, are the most logical and obvious place to begin. Folktales give us access to the riches inherent in story without the risk of telling about our own lives. Telling folktales allows us to share a small part of ourselves while wrapped in the colorful cloak of the oral tradition. Therefore, it is the perfect place to begin.

Trust the Story

Folktales are deeply ingrained in human consciousness – a cultural DNA you might say. You've encountered folktales and stories with similar structures all your life in movies, children's books, video games, television shows, comic books, and novels – anything with narrative. Some of you may have heard them told by family or friends. You already know the structure of the folktale whether you are conscious of it or not. It corresponds to a pattern you've been exposed to over and over again. Your mind will recognize it as will your heart.

To trust the story is to trust this deep foundation of experience with narrative you have been building all your life. When you choose a story that resonates with you, you are beginning the process of tapping your wellspring of story knowledge. Working with the story – learning and practicing it – awakens your deep understanding of the folktale pattern.

Take the time to consciously learn a folktale and to find your ingrained story expertise. Doing this honors the story. Then, when the time comes to tell in front of others, the story will return the favor by making itself readily available to your tongue. You can trust the story!

The strength of the folktale resides in its structure. By telling folktales we absorb the quintessential story structure, a template by which to learn and understand all other story types.

In addition to the power that folktales can lend to beginning storytellers, they are the quickest route available to experiencing the delight mentioned in the last chapter. Here are some of the ways a folktale can serve up delight:

- **Personification:** Many folktales include personification – when human characteristics are attributed to non-human entities and objects. Lamp flames are personified, for example, when they congregate in a temple to gossip. This is a key part of the folktale "The Woman Who Knew a Story and a Song" included in the last chapter. While unexpected, such personification is accepted in a folktale. Your mind can picture talking lamp flames. Folktales feature talking animals, talking objects, talking spirits – talking everything! All reality is animated and available to move the story along.

- **Blurring the edges of reality:** In folktales the boundaries between this world and other worlds are permeable. The story, "What Happens When You Really Listen," is about a story-telling event. In this story, a main character not only listens to a story, he physically enters that story in order to assist one of its characters. Then he returns to his seat. This is more than a metaphor for the power of story. We can actually picture the man diving into the story and then resuming his role as listener. The folktale doesn't ask us to believe; it assumes we do believe. This narrative confidence, supported by the structure of the story, aids us in the suspension of disbelief that is an integral part of our enjoyment.

- **Instant transformations:** In "The Woman Who Knew a Story and a Song," the story and the song, in addition to being animated, have the ability to transform themselves. One becomes a coat and the other a pair of shoes. In the well-known folktale "The Golden Ball," the princess throws her frog suitor against the wall in disgust, and he becomes a prince. In Cinderella, the pumpkin that was transformed into a coach returns to its previous form at midnight.

- **Mystifying tasks and daring adventures:** The heroes and heroines in folktales step boldly into the fray, even when they are given impossible tasks. They climb mountains of glass, slay three-headed giants, and retrieve objects from magical realms. The tasks and adventures engage us; the ability of the character to complete them inspires us and gives us hope.

- **Satisfying conclusions:** Folktales begin with a problem but end in resolution. Good is rewarded; evil is punished. Help comes at just the right time. Lessons are learned in time to take action. Characters live happily ever after.

As we listen to a folktale, we also watch it unfold on the inner movie screen of our imagination. This awakening is one of the most important gifts of folktales. We experience the action and reality of the story within ourselves.

What is a folktale?

In the previous chapter you read that folktales are the backbone of the oral tradition and are found in all cultures. In general, they are stories that are not regarded as factual, although they frequently reveal truths of the human condition. Here are some of the basics of the folktale:

- Folktales are a universal part of human experience. Throughout history, people have told folktales, loved folktales, and shared folktales with others.

- Folktales are traditional, which means that in their living context they were handed down from generation to generation. The focus for the teller was not on originality, but on passing the story on as it was received. The folklorist Stith Thompson writes:

  > In contrast to the modern story writer's striving after originality of plot and treatment, the teller of a folktale is proud of his ability to hand on that which he has received. He usually desires to impress his readers or hearers with the fact that he is bringing them something that has the stamp of good authority, that the tale was heard from some great storyteller or from some aged person who remembered it from old days. (*The Folktale*, 4)

- Because of their grounding in tradition, folktales can survive and be recognized over the millennia. Despite their inherent conservatism, folktales do change. As a story is passed from teller to teller, each infuses it with a personal flavor. Or as a given culture changes over time, the folktale evolves in order to remain culturally relevant. The characters, their challenges, the setting, and even the outcome may change, yet the story may still be recognizable as a particular type of folktale. As a folktale moves from one culture to another, it is adapted by the tellers to fit the distinct culture, values, and environment of the new place.

> Be aware that the perspective on folktales and other genres of story you are receiving in this book reflects European and North-American folklore scholarship. The classification of stories into specific genres such as folktale, myth, or legend is based in observation and can be useful for understanding stories and their functions in various contexts. This is especially true for stories from cultures that trace their roots to an Indo-European source. But the system doesn't always work as well on stories from other cultures.

- Modern Americans are often familiar with only a handful of stories, but a stunning diversity of folktales exists worldwide. The same *type* of story appears in many cultures, bearing that culture's unique imprint upon it.

- Common features of folktales include repetition, simple unelaborated characters, and minimal description. Folktales usually have traditional openings and closings which mark the boundaries of the telling experience for the listeners.

- The terms "folktale" and "fairytale" are often interchangeable in popular usage. For scholars, the folktale is generally considered the older more basic form and is the umbrella term that may contain many other types of stories.

Why are folktales important?

"I would ask you to remember only this one thing," said Badger. "The stories people tell have a way of taking care of them. If stories come to you, care for them. And learn to give them away where they are needed. Sometimes a person needs a story more than food to stay alive. That is why we put these stories in each other's memory. This is how people care for themselves. One day, you will be good storytellers. Never forget these obligations." (From *Crow and Weasel* by Barry Lopez, 60)

Folktales carry wisdom and cultural values. They provide patterns and models for thinking and acting. They give us experiences of beauty and power. Is it possible that "sometimes a person needs a story more than food to stay alive?" Someone who has experienced chronic hunger would probably not agree, but it is a very common metaphor used to express the vital importance of story to people's lives. Folktales allow us to step back in time, to step into the story stream that has been flowing for all of history; our ancestors may have heard a story like the one we are hearing or the ones we are telling. They allow us to share an experience with people we will never meet, but who told or heard the same story. Such experiences connect us to our own ancestors and to other ancestors throughout time and all over the globe.

Folktales are important because they are the foundation of narrative expression. Throughout time, folktales and other types of stories have been a primary source of entertainment and a break from reality. The storyteller was the source of education and entertainment. The storyteller offered news, history, romance, war, and tradition. The forms in which we now receive entertainment and information are all based in narrative and image, the primal form of which is an orally transmitted folktale.

Rafe Martin, a storyteller and author, also speaks to the idea of story as food:

> Folktales are soul's nourishment; are food. Without them we are never quite ourselves, never who we might have been. And they must be recast in words. Only then can they come alive in our own interior images, only then can they live, become us, enter our bloodstream, hearts and bones and empower our lives. (From "Why Folktales?" http://rafemartin.com/ articles.htm#folk)

Where Do I Find Folktales?

The two best places to encounter the world's diversity of folktales are the library and the internet. Looking for folktales on the internet can be both rewarding and frustrating. There is a wealth of material but not all sites are reliable. Confirm the validity of online sources by consulting your instructor.

One of the richest sites for folktales is *The Folklore and Mythology Electronic Texts* (http://www.pitt.edu/~dash/folktexts.html) maintained by D.L. Ashliman, a retired folklore professor. He has collected hundreds of stories and organized them by type or basic plot. The best way to use his site is to take the time to scroll through and look for story titles or types that catch your interest.

Storyteller Heather Forest's site (http://www.storyarts.org/library/index.html) contains a library of folktale plots as well as 26 of Aesop's fables. Her concise, evocative retellings are very useful for storytellers.

Sur La Lune (http://www.surlalunefairytales.com/) offers a wide range of storytelling resources, including annotated folktales, access to full-text e-books, and a discussion forum. The annotations offer the history of the folktales as well as similar tales and modern interpretations.

While the internet is quick and efficient, there are advantages to browsing the shelves at a library. Here are the kinds of things you will find:

- Books of folktales from a single culture

- Anthologies with stories from many cultures

- Children's picture books illustrating a single folktale

The book you really need is often right next to the one you intended to find.

Story Nourishment

Early in my development as a storyteller, I was anxious to get the story just right when I told it. Sometimes I fell in love with the printed words. Other times I fell in love with the way I had rewritten the story. I told myself I wasn't memorizing, just learning it very, very precisely. Once I was preparing to tell "The Master Key," from Howard Schwartz's *Gabriel's Palace: Jewish Mystical Tales*. The story is about a man who is given the opportunity by his rabbi to blow the shofar (ram's horn) for the holiday of Rosh Hashanah. He becomes obsessed with doing it perfectly. He studies and takes meticulous notes on all the secret meanings associated with the blasts of the shofar. On the day he is to blow the ram's horn, just at the crucial moment he realizes that his notes have disappeared and in that moment his heart breaks.

> Then weeping bitter tears, he blew on the shofar with his broken heart, without concentrating on the secret meanings. And the shofar rose up in long and short blasts and carried all of their prayers into the highest heavens. And everyone who heard him blow the shofar that day knew that for one moment heaven and earth had been brought together in the same place.

It was the opening created by the man's broken heart that gave the blasts of the shofar the power to rise to heaven. His broken heart was the "master key" that opened every door in that holy place.

I loved that story then and I still do. But would you believe it? I had told it many times before I realized that it was about me! It hit me like the proverbial ton of bricks. It was speaking directly to my desire to get every word in the story perfectly. I really had to think about the fact that I might be impoverishing the story by my focus on saying the words just so. Was it possible that the story would have more power if I were able to tell it from my heart? These were questions that were at the core of my development as a storyteller.

I haven't abandoned my love of words in a story, and I know that the words are the vehicles that transmit the images to the listeners. But I also know that becoming too attached to them can blunt the story's power.

A story from a different time, place, and culture provided me with a mirror of my own behavior and with a model for a different way of living. This is how a story can nourish and sustain the soul and spirit.

How do I learn to tell a folktale?

The strategies for learning a story described in the previous chapter will serve you with any story you are trying to learn. Some specific features of the folktale will aid you in learning it.

- **Repetition of plot elements:** Repetition is found in many folktales and has been used by storytellers over the centuries to aid in recall as well as to create rhythm and to encourage participation. Plot elements may be repeated as in the story of "Goldilocks and the Three Bears". In the bear's house, Goldilocks goes through the same sequence three times. Each test has three elements. She encounters porridge, chairs, and beds, and in each case she tests Papa's, Mama's, and then Baby's.

- **Repetition of refrains:** In the story "Jack and the Beanstalk," each time Jack sneaks into the giant's house, the giant says, "Fee, Fi, Fo, Fum! I smell the blood of an Englishman. Be he alive or be he dead, I'll grind his bones to make my bread."

- **Beginnings and endings:** Most folktales begin and end with some sort of formulaic phrase – "Once upon a time..." and "They lived happily ever after" being the best known. These are a boon to both the teller and the listener. They give the teller a reliable way to open and close the story. These phrases signal the boundaries of the story for the listeners.

- **Abbreviated archetypal imagery:** Folktales are generally marked by a lack of description so the images remain accessible and powerful in an archetypal way. Folktales do not require much descriptive language, but the teller should be aware of any specific colors that are used in the story. Usually very few colors are mentioned, and when a specific color is used it often carries symbolic freight. Think of "Goldilocks," or "Little Red Riding Hood."

Some Traditional Openings:

- Once upon a time when the world was new, there was only one language. (Seminole)
- In ancient times in a distant land. . . (Jewish)
- In the beginning before anything that lives in our world was created. . . (Tsimshian)
- Once upon a time and be sure 'twas a long time ago. . . (English)
- Once upon a time, not my time, not your time, but one time. . . (Appalachia)
- A fable! A fable! Bring! Bring it! (Kanuri)
- This story, my dear young folks, seems to be false, but it really is true, for my grandfather, from whom I have it, used always to say, "It must be true, or else no one could tell it to you." (German)
- There was, there was not, in times long forgot . . . (Iraqi)

Some Traditional Closings:

- They lived happily ever after, while here we sit grinding our teeth. (Italian)
- Her luck had turned and brought her every kind of happiness from that day forward. (India)
- There were great rejoicings everywhere and the King and the Queen were married again and lived contentedly to their happy end. (German)
- From the sky fell three apples: one to me, one to the storyteller, and one to the person who has entertained you. (Armenian)
- If they have not died, they are living happily to this day. (Hungarian)
- There now is the story for you from the first word to the last, as I heard it from my grandmother. (Irish)
- Mulberry, mulberry that makes two. I've told my story. So must you! (Syrian)
- All I can say is, if they haven't left off their merrymaking yet, why, they're still at it. (Norse)

(From *Once Upon a Time They Lived Happily Ever After* by Herrick Jeffers)

- **Generalization and polarization:** Sizes and distances in folktales are usually polarized in relation to each other – big or little, tall or short, far or near. These words may seem indistinct or imprecise, but they allow listeners to see their own ideas of big or small. Language that is too detailed or exact interferes with the listeners' imagination. In a folktale the next town would be "a long way away" rather than "thirty-seven miles."

Using a storyboard to learn a story: If the teller sees the pictures of the story clearly, so will the audience. Storyboarding is a simple and effective technique to help you learn your story by concentrating on its images.

- Using a blank, unlined piece of paper create twelve open boxes.

1	2	3	4
5	6	7	8
9	10	11	12

- Starting in the upper left hand corner, draw the first scene in your story. Moving left to right, in the next box, draw the next scene, and keep filling the boxes until you've worked through the story.

- Don't worry about your drawing skills. Stick figures are perfectly fine.

- Be sure to use color - colored pencils, markers, crayons – whatever you like. Although the folktale itself will probably include few references to color, use it in your drawing as you see it in your imagination. Color has an impact on your memory and will help you learn the story.

- Practice telling the story using your storyboard rather than a print version of the story.

- Tell the story to someone else using your storyboard.

Below is a storyboard created by a former student for a story called "Refereeing a Fairy Hurling Match," taken from *Meeting the Other Crowd* by Eddie Lenihan. See if you can trace the action of the story in the drawing. Here is the story in brief:

A man was riding his bicycle home when a fairy man stopped him and asked if he would referee their hurling match. The man agreed, only because he was afraid of what they would do if declined. He was led to the pitch where he met the two teams. The play was fierce and there were many fouls. At half time the players left the field and the man was wondering how it was all going to work out. If the fairies were disappointed in the outcome of the game, would he be allowed to leave? The players returned to the pitch and when the game was almost finished there was only one point difference. Just then the team that was one down scored a goal, evening the score. Even though there was a minute left on the clock, the man blew his whistle to end the game. The fairies were delighted with the way he conducted the match and asked if he would referee again some time. He agreed and they parted company, but he never took that particular road home again.

Back to the Wild

A folktale in a collection is like an animal in a zoo. An anthology of folktales is a zoo for stories. Like the single lion in his too small cage, we find a folktale from Africa wedged between one from Japan and another from Italy. Just as the zoo keepers work to preserve the animals, so too do the folktale collectors and anthologizers hope the folktale will survive in its two-dimensional home. In neither case are we seeing the captured thing in its natural glory. It would be a mistake to think that you were knowledgeable about all lions after seeing just one pacing in his cage. Similarly, reading just one Cinderella story does not begin to hint at the range of Cinderella type stories recorded all over the world. And one Cinderella story could never hope to reveal the amazing diversity of folktales around the world, just as seeing one lion can't begin to hint at the diversity of all mammals.

As a caged lion is but a pale reflection of a lion thriving in his natural habitat, a folktale in a book has been stripped of its context. The words collected on a page were once part of a living story moment. There was the storyteller with life experience and expertise. There was the place – was it by a peat fire in Ireland or around a samovar in Turkey? And the listeners were there, sitting close, eyes wide in wonder or closed in contemplation. Was it a rainy night, a cold one? Or did a warm breeze ruffle the branches of a desert tree as the listeners and the teller sat beneath it? Even if the book can tell us a little about the moment, and many don't even provide that, it can never give us the complete experience.

Continued

Back to the Wild (continued)

Both zoos and folktale anthologies allow us to experience what they contain outside of their natural habitats. Some animals and some folktales might not survive if not preserved in a zoo or in a book. Seeing a lion in a zoo is better than not having seen a lion at all – for us at any rate if not for the lion. Sometimes, animals in artificial wildlife preserves are able to be returned to their natural habitat.

Our job as storytellers is to open the cages – open the pages – and return the stories in books to something like their natural habitat - back to the wild.

Foundations of Excellence

A storyteller's instrument is the body. The story and the teller's body and voice should become a seamless integrated whole. For some tellers this means moving only the mouth. For others it means a highly kinetic presentation of the story.

Whatever the storyteller's physical style, the body's gestures and attitude do not exist independently of the story and should serve to enhance the story. The body, facial expressions, and voice must all serve to take the listeners into the actions and images of the story. If instead they call attention to the teller, then the teller is not doing an effective job.

So what does this mean for the beginning teller? Here are some tips to help tell the story with your whole body:

- Stand while telling so your entire body is available to the story.

- Allow the story to inform your body during the telling.

- Let gestures occur naturally in the context of the story.

Once you have the "feel" of the story viscerally, some conscious choices can be made to ensure that both body and voice support the story:

- Posture and carriage can be used to indicate differences in characters. For example, standing tall with straight shoulders could indicate a young soldier; slumped shoulders might show disappointment or weariness.

- Instead of trying to use an accent or making a "special voice" for each character, use more subtle variations in volume and pacing to distinguish characters.

Excellence and Ethics: One of the storyteller's most important responsibilities is determining whether or not she has the right to tell a particular folktale. As with most aspects of public life, there is a socio-political component to this decision. Does a European-American teller have the right to tell Native American stories? European-American culture has intentionally sought to dismantle Native American life-ways. How can it be right for members of a dominant culture to tell the stories of a culture that their own has damaged? This raises thorny ethical questions.

When modern storytellers do choose to tell stories from a culture other than their own, and most do, they have a strict obligation to learn as much as they can about the culture and story as they can before they tell it. In fact, this obligation exists for *all* the stories tellers choose to use in performance, no matter what the story's cultural background. Students in a college class have latitude in choosing stories, but everyone must be sensitive to the folktale's origin.

Anyone who is paid for telling stories in any context must have permission to tell stories not in public domain. Stories published since 1923 are subject to copyright law and not in public domain. The exception to this rule is stories told in educational contexts by teachers and librarians, as was mentioned in the previous chapter. Copyright issues are not cut and dried, and can be quite intricate, but "fair use" covers the educational context.

Storytellers often adapt folktales. It's often desirable to update a story's language. Sometimes a storyteller may decide to streamline a long story by eliminating characters or episodes deemed unnecessary or superfluous to a good telling. Other times, the teller may need to flesh out a story skeleton. When implemented effectively, these techniques bring new energy and ideas to folktales. But in all cases, the inherent integrity of the story must be respected.

One way that storytellers put their unique artistic stamp on a folktale is to forge a new one from three distinct variants. The Norse folktale "Aslaug the Deep Minded" included at the end of this chapter is a variant of the "Clever Manka" folktale type. Other variants of this story include "Catherine, Sly Country Lass" from Italy and "Clever Mary Anne" from Ireland. Though they are all the same story type, each has its own distinct details. While maintaining the consistent set of motifs that define a particular tale type, a storyteller developing a derivative version chooses details from the variants to create something never heard before. The teller must be careful to work within the boundaries of the tale type and its traditional elements.

The storyteller's core work lies in finding new variants, discovering the oldest known version of the story, researching the scholarship on the story – then creating a new version – all to bring the story alive for modern listeners. For example, all the variants of "Clever Manka" have the same basic story line:

- a clever young woman is asked questions by the king which she answers.
- she marries the king.
- she is asked to leave upon interfering with one of his rulings.
- she is allowed to take the thing from the palace she loves the most, which turns out to be the king.

To change any of these elements would result in something that is not "Clever Manka" or any of her cousins.

A storyteller who can't find other versions of a story in order to create a new version or who falls in love with a particular version by an author or storyteller must secure permission to tell it. It is always best to get that permission in writing.

Passion and Innovation: Three Storytellers

Dovie Thomason says that the key to storytelling is listening, and she doesn't believe that young people should necessarily be encouraged to enter the world of storytelling with the intent to compete or become professional storytellers. "They need to be in the audience listening. I think of the teachers that I've had, and a lot of them don't know that they ever taught me because I was just sitting there listening. Nobody would have encouraged me to tell stories – or let me tell – when I was young. Just because you can talk doesn't mean you can be a storyteller."

Dovie was born in Chicago to Lakota and Kiowa Apache parents. She grew up in Texas and New Mexico. She has been telling professionally for over thirty years, and her many awards and commendations include the Wordcraft Circle of Native Writer's Traditional Storyteller of the Year award in 2002 and the Circle of Excellence award from the National Storytelling Network in 2007. Her recordings have received awards from the Parents' Choice Foundation and the American Library Association. She is a passionate advocate for storytelling and for doing the work it takes to be a responsible artist.

She is featured frequently at festivals nationally and internationally, but she says that now, unlike fifteen or twenty years ago, she is often the only teller doing traditional folk material. She speculates, as do many modern storytellers, that this may be because it is easier to tell from personal experience than it is do the work necessary to tell folk material, especially from cultures other than the teller's own.

> Every profession has professional courtesy and ethics. You would not call "Swan Lake" Goose Lake and dance it. You wouldn't dance it and say it's your version of what some old Russian did. The context that is often lacking in modern storytelling is that this requirement for ethical behavior is not unique to storytelling. If you copy a Van Gogh, it is forgery and if you quote great literature without giving a reference, it is plagiarism. Yet many of us never stop to think there are the same protocols in storytelling. We regard it as folk art rather than fine art. We are more careful with what we consider fine art. To become a ballerina or a musician, you work with a master and progress through a set of circumscribed steps. In folk arts it gets fuzzier – much of the material is in the public domain. It doesn't get the same consideration for being true intellectual property as other literature does. Even among professionals we still hear arguments like, "But I really like that story," or "I'm introducing cultural diversity." The key is to know how to do it appropriately and to take moral as well as legal responsibility for what we do with the stories of other people and cultures. (Interview)

Dovie says that the key to telling stories from other cultures is to learn as much about the culture as you possibly can.

It begins with respect. If you really respect a culture, you have to have some idea of what the culture is. Think about numbers, colors, and animals. Don't assume that they mean the same thing in another culture as they do in your own. For example, for several years I was traveling to Ireland regularly. I got to know a lot of Irish tellers, heard stories I loved, and was even encouraged by some of the tellers to tell their stories. But I knew I couldn't do it. In my mouth it would come out Native. Those threes – three maidens or three tasks – would make me nervous and pretty soon there would be four maidens and four tasks as there are in my tradition, and the story would no longer be Irish.

And even within a tradition it's dangerous to generalize. I was deep into the study of Iroquois story and I knew that for them the turtle represents the land. I sent a beautiful little turtle as a gift to a friend. She was Ponca and her husband was Nakota. A few days later my friend called and said, "I hope you think that's funny!" I thought, "Oh no, what did I do?" My friend said, "You just wished a pregnancy on me! In our house, turtle is a fertility symbol." The lesson is don't generalize. You can't say "Indians" say red means this or bear means that. If you study one culture to get your information right, you can't generalize that to the next culture.

There *are* those people who are willing to do ten times the work to transcend their birth skin. People like Diane Wolkstein, Heather Forest, Rafe Martin, Laura Simms, Gay Ducey, and others. They know they have to work harder. They know they need to collect many more versions, sit with it longer, crawl into it – crawl out of it – and even then, they present the story with humility and many provisos. They hugely acknowledge their responsibility and their debt to those who opened the story and its tradition to them. People who do it right are undaunted by the amount of work involved. (Interview)

To teach people about how their own cultural meanings can color or influence their telling she asks, "Tell me what thunder means to you. What does a rainbow mean?" Most European-Americans will say that thunder is ominous or frightening or that rainbows mean unity, or sudden good fortune.

But for some Pueblo peoples, for example, a rainbow is a pretty bad sign, since it means the rain moved off. In other tribes, thunder is cleansing, healing medicine, generally male and sometimes a bird, but never terrifying and never "angels bowling". If you don't know these things, how can you prevent your own meanings from creeping into the story?

As a native, I tell stories from my own tradition and Native nations who have adopted or included me over the years. I've worked among the Navajo a lot, but I don't tell a single Navajo story. Although I'm an insider as far as being Native, I'm an outsider as far as being a Navajo. I'm intimately familiar with that land having grown up in Texas and New Mexico, but not with the stories. I honor that by keeping my mouth shut.

Non-natives seek permission to tell a story so that they have the "right" to tell it, but focusing on "rights" and "permission" is not a Native point of view. For us, it's about the responsibility that comes with making choices. I've never been given permission to tell anything. I've listened, sought answers and realized that I have to take personal responsibility for my actions. Telling the wrong story, or even telling the right story at the wrong time might imbalance the seasons, or endanger someone I love. Am I willing to take the consequence of that?

To give or withhold permission would be me taking responsibility for another person. Culturally, that's disrespectful. People are free to make their own choices; but we need to educate them about the consequences. Just because you *can* do a thing doesn't mean you *should.* Isn't that the lesson of all those Coyote stories? Sometimes the best thing is to just control yourself and keep your mouth shut. (Interview)

Dovie says that in her experience, elders and mentors, "coupled with a lifetime of independent research" have been more important to her training and education as a storyteller than formal classroom instruction in an academic institution. She advises storytellers to:

Follow no teacher – especially me. I don't want to go down the road and hear that you were trained by me. And I don't take workshops, either. To maintain myself as a storyteller I tell and tell and tell, and I listen and listen and listen. I'm not an extrovert. I'm no fun at parties. I'm an observer. Telling stories is about taking the time to really watch and listen. (Interview)

Fran Stallings met **Hiroko Fujita** in Japan in 1993. They discovered a mutual passion for storytelling and in 1995 conducted their first American storytelling tour, which they have repeated almost every year since.

Fran, who lives in Oklahoma, had been a professional storyteller for many years when she met Fujita-san. Fujita-san had worked for forty years as a kindergarten teacher and primary grade librarian in Fukushima where she grew up and in Kashiwa City, just east of Tokyo. Together, Fran and Fujita-san invented a style of non-translation telling that allow each of them to tell stories to listeners whose languages they do not speak.

When Fujita-san is in America, the focus is on her stories. Fran introduces each story by giving a brief synopsis of the plot and by showing the audience the gestures that Fujita-san will use and explaining their reference. She and Fujita-san teach the audience a few of the Japanese words they will need to participate in the story. Fran never tells the ending. That serves two purposes. Not only does it keep the audience focused on trying to follow the story, it enhances the delight when they discover that they actually can comprehend the story even though they don't speak Japanese. When Fran is in Japan, they reverse their roles for their Japanese listeners. It is often a revelatory experience for listeners in both countries.

"I didn't understand a word she said – but I understood the story!"

We have heard this from audience members of all ages in twenty U.S. states. . . . The melody and the dance can communicate so effectively that our audiences follow the meaning of the story and enjoy it – even when they don't understand a word of the lyrics. (From "More Than Words: Storytelling Without Translation" by Fran Stallings, in *Tell the World: Storytelling Across Language Barriers* by Margaret Read MacDonald)

In every performance, Fujita-san enriches the experience by incorporating traditional Japanese children's songs and games. She believes this is crucial to the enjoyment of the story. The use of old games and songs preserves cultural roots, reinforces bonds between generations, and lays the groundwork for literacy. Beyond all that, it's just terrific fun. A member of their audience described the experience as follows:

> I saw them last Thursday at the Santa Rosa public library and when I looked around at all the little itty-bitties there, I wondered how they would ever sit still through the stories. But, oh my, was I surprised. There wasn't a peep from any of them! They sat there transfixed. And they joined in on everything, including counting in Japanese!
>
> Fujita-san is so clever and funny as she tells and manipulates her puppets and props, the kids stay with her all the way... and there's usually a surprise ending that transcends cultural and language boundaries that results in the kids howling with laughter. It's amazing how one's imagination soars with stories told this way.
>
> A boy sat in front of me, probably five or six years old, with his arms crossed and a kind of "leave me alone" attitude. But about ten minutes into the first story, he was completely into it and, sure enough, when the leaping frogs came along, he was first in line to take part. (Adapted from a post by Jackie Baldwin to the Storytell Listserv, April 16, 2008)

In Japan, Fujita-san is known as an "ohanashi obaasan" – a storytelling granny – and the Japan Folktale Society considers her a "national living treasure." She learned her stories from her neighbors.

> When I was a child, I listened to stories from the farmer who cultivated the field next door. When we saw a frog jump, he told me a story about how this frog came out of an old woman's *juubako* [special stackable boxes]. When a dog piddled, he told a story about why dogs raise their hind leg. . . . What joy that gave me! Stories start when people face each other. I wish to share that joy with children. (From *Stories to Play With: Kids' Tales Told with Puppets, Paper, Toys, and Imagination* by Hiroko Fujita, adapted and edited by Fran Stallings, 87)

Fran and Fujita-san's partnership has been very productive. Three books of Fran's world tales, edited by Fujita-san have been published in Japan. Fujita-san has two books in English: *Stories to Play With*, edited and adapted by Fran, and *Folktales from the Japanese Countryside*, which features 46 of Fujita-san's traditional stories, many in English for the first time. In addition, Fujita-san has completed 31 volumes of stories in Japanese, some of which are now being translated into English. In 2003, Fran and Fujita-san received the National Storytelling Network's International StoryBridges Award in recognition of their work spanning cultural and linguistic divides.

The Stories:

The Magic Orange Tree, a tale from Haiti, retold by Diana Wolkstein

CRIC? CRAC!
There was once a girl whose mother died when she was born. Her father waited for some time to remarry, but when he did, he married a woman who was both mean and cruel. She was so mean there were some days she would not give the girl anything at all to eat. The girl was often hungry.

One day the girl came from school and saw on the table three round ripe oranges. *Hmmmm.* They smelled good. The girl looked around her. No one was there. She took one orange, peeled it, and ate it. *Hmmm-mmm.* It was good. She took a second orange and ate it. She ate the third orange. Oh-oh, she was happy. But soon her stepmother came home.

"Who has taken the oranges I left on the table?" she said." Whoever has done so had better say their prayers now, for they will not be able to say them later."

The girl was so frightened she ran from the house. She ran through the woods until she came to her own mother's grave. All night she cried and prayed to her mother to help her. Finally she fell asleep.

In the morning the sun woke her, and as she rose to her feet something dropped from her skirt onto the ground. What was it? It was an orange pit. And the moment it entered the earth a green leaf sprouted from it. The girl watched, amazed. She knelt down and sang:

"Orange tree,
Grow and grow and grow.
Orange tree, orange tree.
Grow and grow and grow,
Orange tree.
Stepmother is not real mother,
Orange tree."

The orange tree grew. It grew to the size of the girl. The girl sang:

"Orange tree,
Branch and branch and branch.
Orange tree, orange tree,
Branch and branch and branch,
Orange tree.
Stepmother is not real mother,
Orange tree."

And many twisting, turning, curving branches appeared on the tree. Then the girl sang:

"Orange tree,
Flower and flower and flower.
Orange tree, orange tree,
Flower and flower and flower,
Orange tree.
Stepmother is not real mother,
Orange tree."

Beautiful white blossoms covered the tree. After a time they began to fade, and small green buds appeared where the flowers had been. The girl sang:

"Orange tree,
Ripen and ripen and ripen.
Orange tree, orange tree,
Ripen and ripen and ripen,
Orange tree.
Stepmother is not real mother,
Orange tree."

The oranges ripened, and the whole tree was filled with golden oranges. The girl was so delighted she danced around and around the tree, singing:

"Orange tree,
Grow and grow and grow.
Orange tree, orange tree,
Grow and grow and grow,
Orange tree.
Stepmother is not real mother,
Orange tree."

But then when she looked, she saw the orange tree had grown up to the sky, far beyond her reach. What was she to do? Oh she was a clever girl. She sang:

"Orange tree,
Lower and lower and lower.
Orange tree, orange tree,
Lower and lower and lower,
Orange tree.
Stepmother is not real mother,
Orange tree."

When the orange tree came down to her height, she filled her arms with oranges and returned home.

The moment the stepmother saw the gold oranges in the girl's arms, she seized them and began to eat them. Soon she had finished them all,

"Tell me, my sweet," she said to the girl, "where have you found such delicious oranges?"

The girl hesitated. She did not want to tell. The stepmother seized the girl's wrist and began to twist it.

"Tell me!" she ordered.

The girl led her stepmother through the woods to the orange tree. You remember the girl was very clever? Well, as soon as the girl came to the tree, she sang:

"Orange tree,
Grow and grow and grow.
Orange tree, orange tree,
Grow and grow and grow,
Orange tree.
Stepmother is not real mother,
Orange tree."

And the orange tree grew up to the sky. What was the stepmother to do then? She began to plead and beg.

"Please" she said. "You shall be my own dear child. You may always have as much as you want to eat. Tell the tree to come down and you shall pick the oranges for me." So the girl quietly sang:

"Orange tree,
Lower and lower and lower.

Orange tree, orange tree,
Lower and lower and lower,
Orange tree.
Stepmother is not real mother,
Orange tree."

The tree began to lower. When it came to the height of the stepmother, she leapt on it and began to climb so quickly you might have thought she was the daughter of an ape. And as she climbed from branch to branch, she ate every orange. The girl saw that there would soon be no oranges left. What would happen to her then? The girl sang:

"Orange tree,
Grow and grow and grow.
Orange tree, orange tree,
Grow and grow and grow,
Orange tree.
Stepmother is not real mother,
Orange tree."

The orange tree grew and grew and grew and grew. "Help!" cried the stepmother as she rose into the sky. "H-E-E-lp. . . ."
The girl cried: "*Break!* Orange tree, *Break!*"
The orange tree broke into a thousand pieces . . . and the step mother as well.
Then the girl searched among the branches until she found . . . a tiny orange pit. She carefully planted it in the earth. Softly she sang:

"Orange tree,
Grow and grow and grow.
Orange tree, orange tree,
Grow and grow and grow,
Orange tree.
Stepmother is not real mother,
Orange tree."

The orange tree grew to the height of the girl. She picked some oranges and took them to market to sell. They were so sweet the people bought all her oranges.
Every Saturday she is at the marketplace selling her oranges. Last Saturday, I went to see her and asked her if she would give me a free orange. "What?" she cried. After all I've been through!" And she gave me such a kick in the pants that that's how I got here today, to tell you the story – "The Magic Orange Tree."

(From *The Magic Orange Tree and Other Haitian Folktales* by Diane Wolkstein.)

About this tale, storyteller Susan Klein says:

Stories hit us where we live. When I was telling to my K-1 students 25-30 years ago, I came across Diane Wolkstein's *The Magic Orange Tree*, a collection of Haitian folktales. I fell in love with the title story as did my students. I have great respect for Diane's scholarly work. In 1981, I had the opportunity to meet her at a literature conference. I requested her permission to tell the story and hopefully to record it one day. Diane granted me permissions to go forward. Then she sang the "Orange Tree" song for me into a tape recorder, so I'd have the melody correct.

"Orange Tree" holds a special place in my heart for a number of reasons. It is the story that has gleaned the most consistent joyful response in the years of telling to children in thirty-seven states and for the Department of Defense Dependents Schools in Europe. Though my former K-1 students are deep into their thirties, on any chance meeting, I'll still be greeted with, "Hey, Miss Klein, you still telling 'Orange Tree'?" I was told recently in the post office by a former student, "Miss Klein, I have one of your tapes. My little girl—she's five—we love listening to 'Orange Tree' together."

What makes that story so tenacious? Well, deep within the layers of the story lies the key to the courage and strength required for any little being to become individuated . . . to know who she is. (Interview)

Aslaug the Deep-Minded, a Norse folktale, retold by Harriet Cole

Sigurd Dragonslayer and his beloved Brynhilde had a child, a girl named Aslaug. Little Aslaug was hardly more than an infant when the wicked Queen of the Burgundians cast the spells that drew Sigurd to her daughter and Brynhilde to her son. Thus the child lost both her parents. Soon they were dead; her father a victim of her mother's anger, her mother a victim of her own grief.

Heimar, Brynhilde's foster-father, saw the danger to little Aslaug. Out of love for the child and her mother, he built himself a great harp with a hollow column and placed the little one inside. Slinging his harp over his shoulder, he traveled into the world as a *skald*, a maker of song and story. As Aslaug lay curled in the darkness, safe from prying eyes, she added her voice to that of the harp and it is said that the instrument sang with an oddly sweet tone. The child grew into a beautiful little girl during the years she rode hidden in Heimar's harp. One evening, they found themselves far from the halls of men, with nowhere to seek shelter other than a peasant's hut. With Aslaug inside the harp, Heimar knocked on the door. "Is there food for me here? And a bed for myself and the harp I carry?

"There is, if you give us gold," the peasant said.

"I pay in song and story, not gold," Heimar told him. "That is good enough for the hall of a king; it will be good enough for you."

The peasant's wife looked at Heimar and his harp and nodded. "It will do." She watched him carefully as he placed the harp near, but not too near, the fire. She watched him even more carefully when he took up the harp and sang. After the fire had been banked and Heimar lay sleeping, she whispered to her husband. "He has something hidden in that harp of his. Gold or some other treasure. Kill him and it shall be ours."

So the peasant waited until Heimar lay snoring. Then he took his knife and cut the *skald's* throat. At once the wife took up a hammer and smashed the column of the harp. "Let's see what we have here." There lay Aslaug, curled into silence, her ice pale blue eyes wide in the flicker of the firelight.

"This is not quite what I expected." The woman poked Aslaug. "What's your name, girl?" Aslaug said nothing.

The woman poked Aslaug again. "What's wrong with you? Have you no name?" Aslaug still said nothing.

"Very well," the peasant woman said. "If you can't say your name, I'll give you one. Kraka, that's who you'll be. You're mine now and you will do as I say." She smeared Aslaug's head with pitch to hide her golden hair, but still the girl said nothing. She dressed her in rags and set her to scrubbing and carrying, and tending the hogs, but Aslaug never spoke.

Aslaug, daughter of Sigurd Dragonslayer became Kraka, the peasant's thrall. She grew into young womanhood without speaking a word to her captors and they called her stupid. Her life with Heimar, his tales of her parents, faded into a dim memory.

One day King Ragnar, known as Lodbrok for his habit of wearing breeches made of the hairy hides of goats, beached his ship not far from the peasants' hut and sent his men to bake bread on their fire. The peasants fled, but Aslaug hid nearby listening to the voices of the warriors. Remembering whose daughter she was, she washed the pitch from her head and combed out her hair which fell like a golden blanket to her feet. When Ragnar's men saw her, they were so enthralled they burned the bread they were baking. The king was not best pleased when the men returned to the ship with the burned bread.

"But Ragnar," the boldest protested. "There was this girl. This beautiful girl, with ice pale blue eyes and golden hair."

"Where is she now?" Ragnar asked.

The warriors shrugged. "She ran away when she saw us. But she was beautiful, beautiful enough to be a queen. We can go back and get her — then you'll see for yourself."

Ragnar had been married once before to a woman named Tora, who had died. He had loved his wife very much and he said to his men, "I'll not marry again until I find a wife who is as clever, as deep-minded as Tora was. If you can find this beautiful girl, you must give her an egg and tell her to hatch it into a chick, grow the chick into a hen, slaughter the hen and stew it for my supper tomorrow night."

"But Ragnar — "

"Do as I say."

So the men went back to the peasant's hut, found Aslaug and gave her an egg. "Our king, Ragnar Lodbrok says to you, 'Hatch this egg into a chick, raise the chick into a hen, slaughter the chicken and stew it for tomorrow's supper'."

Aslaug took the egg, turned it over in the palm of her hand. Then she went to the meal safe in the corner of the kitchen and took out a measure of millet. "Give this to Ragnar Lodbrok. Tell him to sow it, cultivate it, harvest, dry and thresh it by morning so I have something to feed my hen."

The men returned to Ragnar with the millet not at all sure how he was going to react. When they gave him Aslaug's message he began to laugh. "This may be the girl for me."

"Oh she is," they assured him. "She is beautiful."

"But is she truly deep-minded?" he asked. "Go back and give her my thanks for the millet. Then tell her I want to see her. It must be neither day nor night. She must be neither dressed nor undressed, walking or riding, empty or full."

"How can she be all that?" they asked. But they returned to the hut and gave Aslaug Ragnar's message.

The next morning Aslaug left the peasant's hut at dawn, neither day nor night. She wrapped herself in a fishing net and rested one leg over the back of a goat and put an onion in her mouth.

When Ragnar saw her, neither dressed nor undressed, he immediately fell in love. She went with him onto his ship and gave the peasant couple no more thought. The two were married and, in due time, Aslaug gave birth to a son who was nothing like other men. She named him Ivar, and he was called "Boneless" for he was all gristle inside and had to be carried on a shield. Nevertheless, he grew up to be a terrifying warrior.

Some years after the marriage, it began to be whispered that Ragnar's wife was a peasant, a thrall, a woman without a dowry, whom he had taken on a raid. Ragnar was a proud man and it galled him to hear the whispers. One day he said to Aslaug, "I am done with you. Go away and live somewhere else. My next wife will be the daughter of the King of Sweden."

Aslaug was very angry, but she smiled at him. "I will do as you wish, Ragnar, if I may take the one thing from your hall that I love the best."

"Why not?" Ragnar asked himself. "She's been a good wife. It is not her fault she is the child of a peasant." So he agreed.

"Then let us share one last meal," Aslaug said.

Ragnar drank deeply of the ale she brewed for him and fell asleep. When he woke the next morning, he found himself in a small cabin in the woods. "What am I doing here?" he roared. "And where is here, anyway?" Then he saw Aslaug. "And what do you have to do with all this?"

She smiled at him. "You did say I could take the one thing I love best from your hall. And that one thing is you."

Ragnar took a deep breath. "I can't stay married to a woman who is a thrall, a peasant's child."

"You aren't married to a thrall or a peasant's child," Aslaug told him. She then explained how Heimar had hidden her inside his harp and taken her from the Court of Burgundy. "When I fell into your hands, it didn't seem to matter whose child I was, so I said nothing. Now that it does, you should know that my father was Sigurd Dragonslayer, the greatest of the Vølsungs and my mother was Brynhilde, the Valkyrie. I shall soon bear a child, a son, and you will see his ancestry in his eyes."

When Aslaug's second son was born, the pupils of his eyes were slitted like those of a snake. Ragnar gave up all thought of ending his marriage to Aslaug and named the child for her father. Men called him Sigurd Snakeyes and he grew up to be a warrior who was even more terrifying than his brother.

(c)2008 Harriet Cole. Harriet is an author and storyteller. She completed the Certificate in Storytelling at South Mountain Community College in 2006.

She created her adaptation of this story from the following sources: Cole, Joanna. "Clever Manka" in *Best Loved Folktales of the World*. New York: Anchor Books, 1983

Grimm, Jacob and Wilhelm, *The Peasant's Clever Daughter*. Magaret Taylor, trans.http://classiclit.about.com/library/bl-etexts/grimm/bl-grimm-pcleverd.htm

Thorpe, Benjamin. *Northern Mythology*. London: Edward Lumley, 1985 http://books.google.com/books?id=6YkAAAAAMAAJ&pg=PA113&lpg=PA113&dq=aslau g+kraka&source=web&ots=FWIf9ohcm-&sig=bJ4I6b98YkREImx9Bam_gKE_fJQ&hl =en#PPA110,M1

Paca and Beetle, a folktale from Brazil, retold by Heather Forest

A green and gold parrot watched a small brown beetle crawl along the endless riverbank. "Good Morning," squawked the parrot. "Where are you going?"

"I am on a long journey," replied the beetle.

Just then, a paca, a small rat-like creature, ran by. The swift-footed paca dashed circles around the beetle and laughed. "You are going on a journey? You crawl so slowly that it will take your entire life to reach your destination! If you could move as I do, you would be more likely to accomplish something. Look at how fast I can run!"

Paca demonstrated his speed by darting to and fro. "You will never get anywhere!" he mocked. "You are too slow!"

The brown beetle ignored the paca's insulting words and kept creeping along.

The parrot looked down at the two and said, "Paca, your words are boastful but not necessarily true. Beetle is slow, but he gets where he wants to be. Perhaps the two of you would like to have a race. Each of you go to the tree around the river bend as fast as you are able. I will give whoever gets there first a new coat as a prize."

Paca said, "Surely with my speed I will win! I would choose a fine yellow coat with black spots like the jaguar. That would be a fitting replacement for my brown and white fur."

Beetle replied, "I agree to the race, and if I win, I want a coat just like yours, my wise parrot friend."

"Very well," said the parrot. "Go as fast as you can!"

Paca dashed off along the riverbank. "Oh, I shall have a long tail too!" he shouted as he sped away. Suddenly he stopped, breathless, and said to himself, "Why rush? The beetle won't arrive for hours!" He walked the riverbank at a comfortable pace, thinking about his beautiful new fur.

When he arrived at the tree, a small voice said, "What took you so long, my friend?"

Paca's eyes grew wide at the sight of the little brown beetle.

"How did you get here so quickly?" asked the paca.

"I flew," the beetle replied.

"You flew?" screamed the paca. "I didn't know you could fly! You cheated!"

The parrot interrupted, "Beetle did not cheat! I told you both to go as swiftly as you could. Beetle won the race fairly. Just because you were unaware of Beetle's hidden talent doesn't mean that he shouldn't have flown to win. Beetle does not brag about flying. He keeps wings modestly folded and uses them only when necessary."

Paca grumbled and went away wearing his plain brown and white color. Meanwhile, the little beetle's back began to shine, for all time, a bright green like the wing feathers of the parrot. Tiny golden spots, the color of the parrot's head, twinkled all over his shell.

(From *Wisdom Tales from Around the World* by Heather Forest)

The Tale of the Lizards' Tails, a folktale from Japan, retold by Hiroko Fujita

A long time ago, when God was making the animals and human beings, he gave tails to dogs and cats for many different animals — but not to lizards.

The lizards thought it would be better for them to have tails when they walked, especially when they turned corners. So they went to God to ask if he had any extra tails.

God said, "As a matter of fact I gave tails to human beings but they think their tails are of no use. I'll go to the humans and get the tails for you."

So God went to the humans and said, "Can I have those tails back?"

The humans said, "Yes, these tails are just a bother to us." And they gave the tails back to God. God adapted the tails from human style to lizard style, and put them onto the lizards.

The lizards are so thankful to God that they handed the story down from parents to children, from children to grandchildren. "This is the tail which the human beings gave to us. If ever they act like they want it back, we must return it."

So even a lizard of the present generation will drop his tail off and run away as soon as a human acts as if she wants it back.

But humans haven't been handing this story down from generation to generation. They don't tell their children that humans gave tails to the lizards, and so children nowadays don't understand why lizards drop off their tails when humans try to grab them. They think, "Lizards just leave their tales behind; that's their nature," when in fact this behavior is due to the way lizards have handed down the story and have taught their children, "We must return our tails to humans when we see them."

Oshimai! [The End!]

(From *Folktales from the Japanese Countryside* by Hiroko Fujita)

The Monkey and the Crocodile, a folktale from Chiapas, Mexico, retold by Olga Loya

Once there was a monkey who wanted to eat bananas, but they were on the other side of the river. The river was very wide, and he didn't know how to swim. He tried making a little raft, but the moment he got it into the water it sank. How he hated being wet!

He got out of the water, and while he was drying, he sat staring across the water at those sweet delicious bananas. He wanted them so badly.

Just then, he saw a big crocodile swimming close to the edge of the shore. "Oh, Señor Cocodrilo!" Monkey called out. "I am very hungry. I want to eat those bananas that are on the other side of the river, but my mother never showed me how to swim. Will you take me on your back to the other side?"

"Fine," said Crocodile.

With one jump, Monkey climbed on Crocodile's back. Crocodile swam to the other side where the bananas were.

Upon arriving, Monkey said, "Señor Cocodrilo, would you please wait for me a minute? I will be right back. I will eat fast so you can take me back."

"Fine," said Crocodile.

Monkey ate happily. He even brought a banana to eat on the way back. He jumped on Crocodile's back. "Take me right to the other side of the river," he demanded.

Crocodile started swimming, but not in the direction Monkey had asked him to. Instead, Crocodile was taking him along the edge of the river.

"Señor Cocodrilo, where are you taking me? This isn't the way to my house."

"I am taking you to my house," Crocodile said as he continued to swim.

Monkey didn't like the sound of that! "Why, thank you for the invitation!" he said uncertainly. "But I really need to get home!"

"I'm not inviting you," Crocodile replied gruffly.

"Good, let's go to my house!" Monkey said.

"No, you're coming home with me whether you like it or not."

Monkey knew he was running out of options. He asked the only question that remained to be asked. "Why?"

"Because my wife is sick and the healer said for her to get well she has to eat the brains of a monkey."

"Oh, Señor Cocodrilo, why didn't you tell me about the brains before I got on?" Monkey replied. "I left my brains sunning on the other side of the river. Let's hurry and get them so we can take them to your wife before she dies."

"Let's return, then," said Crocodile.

When they arrived at the spot where they had started, Monkey said, "My brains are on the other side of my house, in the afternoon sun. I am going to go get them and then I will return."

He got off Crocodile's back and ran beyond Crocodile's reach. Then he called, "The day that my brains get out of my head, that is the day I die." Then Monkey ran away laughing and laughing.

That is how Monkey saved his own life.

About this story Olga Loya writes: I was visiting a mission in the village of Yajalone in Chiapas, Mexico, telling and collecting stories. One day a man named José Chávez came to see me at the mission. He knew I was working on a translation of a videotape featuring stories told by an elder in the Tzeltal tribe. He came and sat down next to me and told me this story.

(From *Momentos Magicos/Magic Moments* by Olga Loya)

4

How to Tell a Myth, a Legend, or
a Hero Tale

"Over the centuries we have transformed the ancient myths and folk tales and made them into the fabric of our lives. Consciously and unconsciously we weave the narratives of myth and folk tale into our daily existence." (Jack Zipes)

What is a Myth?

In everyday usage, the word "myth" means falsehood, an unsubstantiated or erroneous belief, a superstition. "It's a myth that the earth is flat." In the context of *story*, the word means the opposite. Myths are stories that contain important cultural and religious values and information. Greek myths, for example, are part of a mythological and religious system that no longer has a population of believers. Nonetheless, somebody somewhere at some time invested the stories with the full force of religious belief. The same holds true for any mythic story from any culture around the world. That means that the stories and the events and entities they describe are part of the sacred life of the culture to which they belong. The stories themselves may be considered sacred. This is not to say that they were always taken literally by their believers. As with most religious traditions, some people believe the stories are literal truth, some take them as metaphors, and others fall between those two points on the continuum of belief.

Myths are set before time or "in the beginning." The characters include gods and goddesses, semi-divine human heroes, and all the firsts – the first animals, first plants, first humans. Mythic stories that take place after creation still feature the divinities as characters. The stories often hinge on their actions, usually in response to human foibles, as in the story of Arachne in this chapter.

Myths take on the big issues in human life – the origins of the cosmos, the mysteries of life and death. They tell us how to interact with deities, how to function as a "good" man or woman, and how to survive major life transitions. As such, myths are often more explicitly concerned with human values, more intentionally meaningful, than are folktales.

Any single myth is always part of an interconnected set of stories known as the mythology of a culture or religion. The mythology of a culture usually functions to lay out a great cycle of existence, from creation through destruction. It first explains how everything came to be, tells the most impor-

---

Oh, the people you'll meet!

The characters in myth are dazzlingly diverse: gods and goddesses, tricksters and wizards, heroes and warriors, farmers and artists, beauties and beasts, and the foulest villains and monsters. Yet despite the range of fabulous characters we encounter in myths, somehow they are still familiar. We know these people.

We recognize the characters in myths, and for that matter in folktales, because they are built upon archetypes. Archetypes are the original or fundamental pattern upon which a character is realized. For example, the archetype of "king" includes the following elements: male, great power, extreme wealth, and high status. These elements of the "king" archetype are universally recognizable in human culture. Kings around the world bear different titles and wear splendidly unique royal garments but we recognize them whenever and however they appear because they are built upon a shared archetypal structure.

The concept of the archetype is most associated with the Swiss psychologist Carl Jung, who believed that archetypes exist in a collective unconscious shared by all humans. These archetypes are utilized by an individual's unconscious mind. It is from the collective unconscious that storytellers the world over and throughout the millennia have drawn not only the characters, but the types and structures of stories and myths.

Archetypal characters do not exist in myth alone. They exist in our lives. We may never have known a king, but we have known powerful males: perhaps a father, or an employer, or a mentor. The archetype in a story connects to the archetype in our personal experiences and the connection energizes the story's latent meaning. The people we meet in myth are often the people we already know!

---

tant stories, and may also relate the end and regeneration of existence. Most mythological systems contain the following types of stories:

- **Creation myths** tell how life began, how the universe was created, how the earth was formed and populated by humans, animals, and plant life. They also tell of the birth of the gods and goddesses. Related stories are called origin stories, or pourquoi stories, and may tell how a particular feature of the landscape, or a particular creature and its habits came to be. "The Story of Arachne," for example, tells how spiders came to be and why they weave webs. Arachne's name became the basis of the scientific name for spiders – arachnids.

- **Myths of gods and goddesses** tell about the creation or appearance of the deities and their distinctive attributes and powers. They also tell about how the deities interact with each other and with humans. These stories teach humans how to interact with the gods and goddesses, the benefits of winning their favor, and the perils of offending them. Arachne, for example, suffers a terrible transformation for her pride before the goddess.

The Story of Arachne, a Greek myth, retold by Harriet Cole

Arachne was the most talented of all the weavers in the rich and ancient kingdom of Lydia. So great was her skill that the nymphs crept from their vineyards and streams to gather around the loom and watch the dance of her slender fingers in the warp and the weft of the web. So beautiful was her work that it was said she must have learned her art from the goddess Athena herself.

When she heard that, Arachne lifted her pointed chin and replied: "No goddess taught me art or skill. If Athena thinks she can weave a finer web than mine, let her come here and do so."

One day a stranger, an old woman, appeared at Arachne's door. "Watch it girl. It is neither wise nor safe to challenge the goddess."

Arachne laughed. "I'll challenge who I wish. As for you, keep your advice for your daughters, who might appreciate your words. I do not. And tell the goddess to come and fill one of my looms with cloth that is finer than what I weave."

"There is no need to tell the goddess anything." The old woman lifted her head and was suddenly straight and tall. Her lank hair grew glossy and brown and an owl hooted from Arachne's roof. "She is here. Let us weave together, Arachne."

Arachne blushed under the gaze of Athena's steady grey eyes, but she did not flinch. "Set up the looms," she commanded the nymphs with a wave of her hand, "one for the goddess and one for me."

The nymphs scurried to obey, propping the uprights against the wall, lifting the beams into place, stringing the warp and tying the weights to the ends of the threads. They brought out brilliant rainbow baskets of yarn and prepared the shuttles. Athena stood at one loom and began to weave her victory over Poseidon. The salt water flowing from the spring that was his gift to the people of Greece bordered her work. The quivering leaves of her gift, the olive tree, flashed the grey of her eyes at the center of her work.

Saucy Arachne wove the misdeeds of Zeus, Athena's lordly father. Swan, shower of gold, eagle, bordered the panel. In the center Europa, princess of the Sea People, clung to the neck of the Divine Bull. Her pale hands trembled on his horns, her slender feet curled in fear away from the flash of the waves as he carried her into the ocean.

Athena looked at Arachne's loom and frowned. The girl lifted her chin, her defiance undimmed. Silently, the goddess drew the sharp end of her shuttle across the fabric, slashing it into shreds.

"No!" cried Arachne. She cast one end of a cord over the roof beam, wrapped the other around her neck and, mourning the destruction of her web, hung herself.

"Death is not for you, you silly girl." Athene touched her shuttle to Arachne's forehead and the girl shriveled until she was nothing more than a small round creature hanging from a thread with only a single shred of her beauty left; her slender skillful fingers, now the eight legs of a spider.

To this day, the sight of one of Arachne's many daughters is a reminder that it is neither wise nor safe to challenge a goddess.

Adapted by Harriet Cole

- **Trickster myths** relate the ambiguous exploits of semi-divine figures. Tricksters in myths are generally male, in animal form, and function to upset the social order. While acting to satisfy their own needs and desires, tricksters defy the gods for the benefit of humans, and sow the seeds of conflict that others must resolve. Trickster stories are often humorous, but just as often are stories of destruction and grief.

- **Myths of sacred places** tell how a certain feature of the landscape came to be created or became significant through the activities of a deity or hero. In traditional mythological settings, the landscape is alive with the stories of the deities and heroes who formed it.

- **Hero myths** tell of the birth of the hero, his testing and transformation, and ultimate return to his people. A discrete adventure may be told as a single story. When the hero's complete story is told, or his greatest adventure, the story may be called an epic, as in "The Epic of Gilgamesh," the great hero king of ancient Sumer. Hero stories have a distinctive structure that will be discussed later in the chapter.

Myth and Landscape

Throughout the world, the features of the landscape are connected to stories of the deities. Here are three examples:

 On the coast of the Mie Province in southeastern Japan are the *Meoto Iwa* or the Husband-and-Wife Rocks. They represent the union of the Shinto creator god and goddess, Izanagi and Izanami, and by extension the sacred nature of human marriage. The rice straw ropes connecting the sacred rocks are maintained by local people.

South Mountain Park in Phoenix, Arizona, is the largest municipal park in the nation. To the Tohono O'Odham people it is known as Greasy Mountain and is the home of I'itoi, or Elder Brother. Elder Brother's home is in the shape of a maze which confounds his enemies, while representing the life path good people follow to achieve their goals and purposes.

 Spanning three hills in Ireland's County Meath is a prehistoric megalithic site known as Loughcrew, or Slieve Na Calliagh, the "Hill of the Hag." The site contains dozens of passage tombs and stone circles made from huge boulders that were carried to the summits of the highest hills in that county. The story is that the Cailleach, a titanic (earth creating) goddess was carrying the boulders in her apron. As she hopped from hill to hill, the stones fell, creating the monuments.

What is a Legend?

Legends are stories about people who exist or have existed, or are believed to have existed long ago, even in the mythic past. Like myths, they are considered true stories even when they do not correspond to "the facts" as modern people may understand them. Whether they are literally true or not, legends, like myths, provide important information about the values and ideals associated with their protagonist and his or her culture and time in history. There are both sacred and secular legends, generally about three types of people:

- **Legends about important religious figures:** Stories about saints, rabbis, shamans – and even deities – are common fodder for legends. In all religious traditions, there are stories about the greatest practitioners' deeds.

- **Legends about great leaders:** Throughout time, important leaders have been the subject of legend. King Solomon, a biblical figure, is the subject of many legends. Similarly, the stories of King Arthur are legends, since he was most likely an actual ruler. In America legends are related about great presidents. In more recent history, important leaders like Martin Luther King and Cesar Chavez, for instance, are becoming the subject of legends.

- **Legends about important cultural figures:** Legends spring up around remarkable people. Johnny Appleseed is a legendary American figure, as are Betsy Ross, Daniel Boone and John Henry. Elvis, Princess Diana, and Tupac Shakur are the subjects of legends that are being created in our time.

What is a Hero Tale?

A hero tale may be a story from a particular mythology, a legend about a great hero, or a folktale whose primary character embarks on a quest or accomplishes risky tasks. Although many scholars have described and analyzed the elements of hero tales, the best known is Joseph Campbell who elaborated the structure in *The Hero with a Thousand Faces*. After analyzing hero myths from around the world, Campbell observed in them a three part structure of departure, initiation, and return. Within each stage he identified several steps typically found in myth. It's rare to find a story with every step, but to qualify as a hero story, each major stage must be represented. In hero folktales the return stage is often truncated; once the boon is achieved, the hero returns to live happily ever after.

Campbell realized that the structure he was discovering in myth paralleled the basic three-part ritual structure found by anthropologists as they studied rites of passage in cultures around the world. A rite of passage is an event in a person's life when a transition is made from one stage to the next. The ritual challenges faced in the rite of passage transform the person, whether male or female. Similarly, in hero tales, the quest taken on by the hero is transformative. In mythic stories, the transformation may be from youth to adulthood – becoming the hero in the process. In hero folktales, the successful achievement of the tasks often results in marriage. In such stories, marriage symbolizes the integrated personality.

Campbell's work has had an important impact on popular culture, including storytellers and other artists. Many storytellers have been influenced by him and rely on the hero's journey structure in some form. Below is Joseph Bruchac's version of the hero path from *Tell Me A Tale: A Book About Storytelling* (45):

- **Departure:** The hero or heroine leaves home.
- **Difficulty:** The hero or heroine faces great obstacles including evil people, threats by monsters, and abandonment.

- **Discovery:** The hero or heroine finds a way to overcome the obstacles. Doing this, he or she gains power or is given a special gift.
- **Return:** The hero or heroine goes back home, often using what he or she has gained, which may be include material or spiritual wealth and knowledge, to help the people.

Where do I find myths, legends, and hero tales?

The best place to start is with the library. Look for the section on mythology, and browse by culture area to find books with the words "myth" or "legend" in the title.

There are hundreds of sites on the internet that retell myths and legends. Start with *The Internet Sacred Text* archive (http://www.sacred-texts.com/) where you can also browse by culture and religion. Another good source is *Encyclopedia Mythica* at http://www.pantheon.org/.

Story Structure is Life Structure

The most basic story structure – beginning, middle end – is also the most basic life structure. We are born; we live; we die. A hero myth, or a folktale with the hero's journey structure, reveals the deeply ingrained physical and psychological patterns of human transformation. Hero stories in particular are metaphors for what it means to have a human body with all its needs and remarkable capabilities. Because we all have bodies that are constantly changing, we literally and physically experience the hero structure of departure, initiation, and return. And because our bodies house our minds and spirits, the stories our bodies live result in radical psychological and spiritual changes. Every person lives through times of change during which he or she responds to a call, encounters obstacles, receives help, engages in conflict, achieves goals and ultimately becomes a different person than he or she was before the journey began.

The heroes of mythology defeat terrifying, supernatural monsters and exhibit strengths and skills that most of us cannot imagine possessing. But think of the monster as a metaphor for a great personal challenge, drug addiction for example. Most of us have known someone who had to fight the monster of drug or alcohol addiction and know what a heroic battle that can be. The person who successfully defeats addiction is transformed in the process, as are mythological heroes. Or what about a person right out of high school, who joins the military, is stripped of his or her previous identity, goes to war, and survives to return home? He or she is undeniably transformed by the process. Giving birth is another heroic process: the woman who conceives, carries, and delivers a baby is utterly transformed by doing so. The person she was before is gone, replaced by a new person called mother.

Hero stories provide us with models for how to endure the challenges life presents us. They tell us that we will be called and challenged, but that with help, faith, and persistence we can succeed. Most importantly for storytellers, they provide us with a timeless and endlessly productive pattern for finding and shaping stories that are deeply relevant to tell and to hear. It doesn't get any better than that!

Not all internet sites are reliable – in fact, many are notoriously unreliable. Check with your instructor if you have any doubts about the validity of a myth or legend that you find on the internet. He or she will be able to direct you to other sources for the story if necessary.

Folktales with a hero's journey structure will be found in the folktale anthologies and sites you worked with in the last chapter. Your main concern when searching for a hero tale will be that it conforms to the overall structure of the hero's journey outlined above.

Foundations of Excellence

When the audience listens to a story they hear not only the words, but the rate at which they are spoken, and the spaces between them. Pacing is the rate at which the teller speaks as well as the spaces of silence utilized within the story. When used effectively, pacing is an important tool for engaging listeners.

Here are some suggestions for integrating pacing into your stories:

- Match your pace to the action of the story. If you are in an expository section, there is no need to speak quickly. In contrast, when the action is intense, your pacing could speed up to match it. However, even in the exciting parts, don't speak so rapidly that your audience can't understand you.

- Match your pace to the mood of the characters. Someone sad or injured will likely speak more slowly than someone excited or ecstatic.

- Various speakers in the story may speak faster or slower depending on their characteristics.

- Be aware of your pace at the key points in the story. You may want to extend the silence just briefly – long enough to turn your head or take a breath – to highlight a point of action, information, or humor. This allows the audience to savor the images and the moment. That small silence can also enhance the audience's anticipation of what will happen next.

- Attend to the pacing at the beginning and ending of your story. Your normal rate of speaking will usually suffice for the beginning. At the end of the story, slow your pace and be distinct in your enunciation. You might lower the pitch of your voice, but not the volume. This helps the audience anticipate and focus on the end of the story.

Use these techniques only to the extent that they support the story and feel natural to you. It is not necessary to layer them on for their own sake. If you have built a solid relationship with the story, your understanding of it will be reflected in your pacing. Remember that at whatever pace you are speaking, your voice must be supported by the energy of your body and by your focused intent to deliver the story to your listeners as well as you can.

Excellence and Ethics: There are several things to be aware of as you prepare to tell a myth or a legend, all of which have to do with respecting the story and the people who told or tell it.

- Be aware of the culture in which the story originates. Take the time to learn about the story and the culture. Is it part of a larger cycle of myths or stories? When was the story current? What part of the world does it come from? This information is usually available in the book or website where you found the story. If not, research further.

- Be sensitive to the language of the story, particularly the names of people and places. If you are unable to pronounce the names of the characters in the stories, describe them by their primary attribute. For example, if you were planning on telling the Japanese creation myth from Shinto mythology, you would encounter Izanagi and Izanami, the creator parents. But if you could not wrap your tongue around those names, you could refer to them as the Creator Father and the Creator Mother.

- If you do decide to use the proper names or place names as they appear in the story, be sure that you can correctly pronounce them. You can find pronunciation guides for classical myths online. If it is a story that you are serious about and plan to add to your repertoire, find a speaker of the language who can help you with pronunciation.

- Once you identify a story you'd like to tell, look for other versions of the story, especially if the first is a synopsis. You may prefer the other versions and you will certainly get more details on the story. This is a good opportunity for you to craft your own story based on the variants you find. The more variants you consider, the broader your knowledge will be about the story and the culture from which it comes.

- Take the time to ponder your own connection to the story and its meaning. It isn't necessary to understand everything about a myth or legend to tell it, but you should have some idea of the meaning of the major symbols and metaphors employed. Metaphor and symbol are the building blocks of myth; the stories are densely meaningful and the meaning often exists on several levels. The metaphors and symbols function to help us understand the stories.

The Epic Voice: Two Tellers

Olga Loya is a Latina storyteller who lives in San Jose, California. She pioneered the art of bilingual storytelling in America. Olga says that long before she was a professional storyteller, she was professional listener. She grew up listening to stories told by her grandmother and father amongst others. About discovering storytelling, Olga says:

I grew up in East Los Angeles, California. I have always told stories and, in 1980, I went to my first storytelling conference. It was like a thunderbolt to my heart. I knew I wanted to be a storyteller. I knew I had to pursue the art of storytelling. At first I told stories from books from many different cultures, and then I discovered the stories from Latin America. A little at a time all the stories of my childhood started coming back to me and brought me back to the beauty of my family, my ancestors. They brought me back to the beauty of the place where I grew up— East Los Angeles. They brought me back to my culture, my roots. Stories are and were that powerful for me. Soon I started remembering my family stories, and that just added another dimension to my evolution as a storyteller. (http://www.olgaloya.com/olgas_story.html)

Olga has worked with the legend of La Llorona, the weeping woman, since the beginning of her career as a storyteller. The version she tells is one she learned as a child from her grandmother, but as she has traveled throughout the southwest and Mexico telling stories, she has learned many others. "This story is a living entity. La Llorona is not just a character in a book. She is alive in the experiences and in the consciousness of many people. I've met many people who have encountered her, and I now tell some of those stories, too." Olga discovered that the archetype behind the character of La Llorona occurs in ancient and modern cultures. "La Llorona has an counterpart in the character of Medea in Greek myth, who killed her children when her husband rejected her for another woman. And we see the same story in modern life in the more recent story of Susan Smith, who drowned her children because she thought being childless would make her more attractive to her lover" (Interview).

In order to tell the epic length "Aztec Creation," Olga has spent years researching and reconstructing Aztec and Mayan myths for modern audiences. "When I tell the "Aztec Creation," I start by invoking the seven directions the way the old storytellers would have done. The seven directions for the Aztecs were north, south, east, west, above, below, and the present. I want to create a *lugar sagrado*, a sacred place, where the audience and the story can come together" (Interview). As a co-founder of *Going Deep: The Long Traditional Storytelling Festival*, she has been an important part of keeping the epic tradition of storytelling alive in our country. She tells these stories as part of her "impassioned quest to keep alive not only the fabric of her family, but the larger Latino culture, richly robed in folktales, ancient myths and history" (http://www.olgaloya.com/home.html).

Emil Wolfgramm says, "I'm just a water carrier, and these stories are pure water."

Emil is the master of the Tupaheo! style of traditional Tongan storytelling. He is the leading authority on the traditional poetic visions of the demi-gods Maui and the clan of Tangaloa gods. Born in Tonga and brought up in New Zealand, Emil raised his family and taught high school science in Hawaii, where he has lived for many years. Now retired, he is devoting his life to the preservation and perpetuation of the Tongan and Polynesian worldview as contained in the stories. As an elder in his community, Emil often finds himself providing the perspective of the ancient stories. He invokes the wisdom of gods like Maui in political and cultural processes. "If they try to move me I say, 'Who here is greater than Maui? I am Maui. I carry his water'."

Emil says you have to know the difference between plumbing and water. This is the foundation of his teaching as a storyteller and as an elder. In Western, science-based systems of values, he says we concentrate on the plumbing at the expense of the water. He reminds us, "Meaning making is more important than data collecting."

The genius of the Tongan Tupaheo! style of storytelling was to build in flexibility for the storyteller while retaining the essential outline of the story. Each telling starts with an honorific salutation, followed by a formulaic recitation of the story line in poetry which is fixed for that story and does not change. The poetic vision of the story is recited first and accepted by the audience, who signal their attention by clapping when asked. Then the storyteller – the water carrier – can give a unique performance of the story that fits that moment, adding and embellishing as he sees fit. Here is the honorific salutation that begins each story:

> All respect to the family of chiefs in our presence
> And to the clan masters of ceremonies
> While I recite this recitation.
> *Tupaheo!* (cupped-hands clap once quickly)
> This is a story from the very beginning of time,
> From our very first ancestors,

According to ancient customary ways.
These are the stories that build our land.
  Tupa! (clap once)

Emil says that the poetic imagery in the stories relates directly to the natural environment. The stories allowed his ancestors to predict and relate what would happen. "The poetry draws you into nature. It's mythology, history, instruction, and entertainment all in one. That's why we don't need Hollywood!" Everything a Tongan needs to know to survive is contained in the poetic visions supplied by the stories.

> I have such faith in the poetry my ancestors created. It's so straight, so powerful, it can handle any situation. I've never found a situation it couldn't handle. I'm so confident in the poetry because it's been refined through hundreds and hundreds of tellings over the generations. My only question is, "Am I good enough?" You can not kill the poetry. The poetry is perfect. The only problem is the teller. The teller is not perfect and never can be. (Interview)

Emil is training seven apprentices, mostly women, mostly his relatives. He has recruited them for their facility with language, and their willingness to learn and tell the mythic canon in both Tongan and English. He is sure that the ancestors will assist the new Tongan Tupaheo! Storytellers. "My ancestors are good. They are simple. They are *BAD*. They make the water flow. (Interview)"

He offers the following advice for storytellers raised in literacy who wish to understand and tell stories that come from oral cultures:

> Allow yourself to be shaped by the symbols of the oral tradition. Allow the old voices to sink into your soul and change it. It's a spiritual process. A storyteller has to access the old voices and tell from a place of spiritual authenticity. When you, as the literate person, are telling from an authentic oral tradition, you can still experience the power of orality. (Interview)

> When you do that, he says you can then understand the wisdom of the old Tongan proverb relevant to both story and life: `Alu`alu `i mala tau ki monū! [Treading from trouble to dilemma, arriving in blessedness!]

The Stories:

The Hungry Goddess, an Aztec Myth retold by Olga Loya

Once long, long ago the Aztec gods lived high up. In those days there was no sky and there was no earth. There was only water and water and water. There was water from nowhere to nowhere.

  Among the gods, there lived a goddess. She was called La Diosa Hambrienta, the Hungry Goddess, because she had eyes and mouths all over her body. She had mouths and eyes at her elbows, wrists, ankles, waist – everywhere. She was always hungrily trying to see what was happening. She was always trying to eat, and she was always crying out, *"Tengo hambre, tengo hambre."* [I'm hungry, I'm hungry.]

All day long she would wail, "*Tengo hambre.*"

All night long she would say, "*Tengoooo hambre!*"

Day in and day out, she called out, "*Tengo hambre.*"

Finally all the gods went to the two most powerful gods of all and said, "Por favor, can't you do something? The woman is always crying. We can't sleep. We can't think! She's always saying, '*Tengo hambre.*'"

Now the two most powerful gods were Quetzalcoatl and Tezcatlipoca. The gods called Quetzalcoatl the Plumed Serpent because he wore beautifully flowing feathers of many colors and he walked with a stick carved in the shape of a serpent. He dressed in white. He wore gold hoop earrings, bells around his legs, and pearls on his sandals. He also wore a mask shaped like a bird's head called the Wind Mask. With that mask, he could blow the wind for a long distance. Thus he was also known as the Wind God and the God of Light.

Tezcatlipoca dressed in black. He wore rattlesnake rattles around his legs. He was sometimes called the God of Smoking Mirror because he wore an obsidian mirror – made of black volcanic glass – on his foot, with which he could see everything that was happening in the world. Tezcatlipoca's other name was the God of Darkness.

Quetzalcoatl and Tezcatlipoca talked and talked. Finally they decided they would take La Diosa Hambrienta to the water; maybe the water would calm her. So they flew down to the water to see if there was anything there for the goddess to eat. Quetzalcoatl blew with his Wind Mask. He blew and blew, and the water went this way and that way. They could find nothing at all.

They flew up to La Diosa Hambrienta and carried her down to the water. On the way down, she continued to cry, "*Tengo hambre! Tengo hambre!*"

They put her on the water. She was silent. She was floating so quietly, so calmly.

The gods said, "Ah, she is now happy."

But no, she started to cry out again: "*Tengooo haaambreee.*"

Quetzalcoatl and Tezcatlipoca became quite upset. They transformed themselves into huge serpents and took hold of La Diosa Hambrienta. One god took her right hand and left foot and the other took her left hand and right foot. They started to pull and pull. But the goddess was very strong. She fought them long and hard. It was the most difficult fight the gods had ever fought. As they continued to struggle, they accidentally snapped her in half.

Quetzalcoatl and Tezcatlipoca were very surprised – and very sorry. They took the bottom half – from the waist to the feet – of La Diosa Hambrienta to the other gods and said, "Look what we have done!"

"What a shame," the other gods said. "Wait, we will use this half of the hungry woman and it shall be the sky." That is how the sky came to be.

The gods looked at the goddess's top half. "Poor thing," they said. "Look how unhappy she is. What can we do? Let us make her happy."

So they transformed her hair into the forest. Her skin became the pastures; her eyes became the lakes, the rivers and the ocean. Her mouth became the caves; her shoulders became the mountains. She became Mother Earth – the earth we live on to this day.

All the gods said, "Ah, now she will be happy!"

But no! She again started to wail, "*Tengooo haaambre, tengooo haaambree!*"

To this day La Diosa Hambrienta, Mother Earth, is still hungry and thirsty. When it rains, she swallows all the water. If a tree falls and dies, she eats it. If a flower wilts and dies, she eats it. When anything goes into the earth, she eats it. She is always hungry.

Sometimes when the wind is blowing late at night, if you listen very carefully, you might still hear her calling, "Tengo haaambree, tengo haaambreee."

(From *Momentos Magicos/Magic Moments* by Olga Loya)

Who is the Greatest Warrior? A Yoruba Myth from West Africa, retold by Marilyn Omifunke Torres

Among the stories of the Orisas, the gods and goddesses of the Yoruba, there is an ancient tale about a meeting between Ogun and Obatala. Ogun is the Orisa of war and the guardian of warriors. He is respected as the greatest warrior in heaven and on earth. Obatala is the eldest Orisa, the Orisa of all creation, and the father of all humans. In the holy *Odu* of *Egiogbe*, the story of all that is known and unknown, the meeting between Ogun and Obatala was recited like this:

Long ago Ogun was walking in his forest domain and he overheard Osun, the Orisa of Rivers, and Ochosi, the Orisa of the Hunt, speaking to each other about a great wise man and warrior from another region.

Ogun overheard Ochosi giving enthusiastic praise to this warrior who was believed to be even greater than Ogun. Ogun immediately stopped along his path, interrupted the conversation forcefully, and asked passionately and aggressively, "Who is this person you claim is a greater warrior than I?"

Osun looked at Ogun and laughed, "My dear, to find out, you will have to travel to a far distant place, to a very ancient land where this warrior lives." Osun continued, "It is said that he lives on a great mountain that reaches far into the clouds, even beyond the heavens."

Ogun responded indignantly to Osun's laughter saying, "I am the greatest warrior ever known. If there is one who is greater than I, then I will travel to the far reaches of heaven or earth to face this great one. I will see for myself the basis for this claim!" And so, Ogun set out for this ancient land. They say the journey was long and time stood still as he traveled.

Finally, when Ogun arrived, he looked and saw high up into the farthest reaches of the heavens, a great mountain just as Osun had described. On this mountain lived Obatala. Ogun thought to himself, "Ahh yes, I am here and up there in the heavens is this great warrior Obatala!" As he climbed higher, Ogun noticed that the mountain became more and more luminous.

When he reached the summit, he saw an opening on the side of the cliff. This was the opening to a old cave. Entering it was like walking through a door in time. Deep within, he saw a very, very, very old man. He noticed that his eyes glistened like the stars and his skin was dark like the night sky. He wore a silken white luminous robe. He sat there in a state of grace, tending to a mysterious circle of fire.

Ogun saw that in his right hand he held a beautiful and unusual staff with figures carved in every cardinal and non-cardinal direction. The staff had both male and female figures, all standing on each others shoulders. He noticed that this elder simply tended the fire with his left hand, never looking up to see who entered the cave. Ogun walked up to the circle of fire and sat across from Obatala. He faced this grandfather proud and unafraid.

Ogun said, "Obatala, it is said that you are the greatest warrior ever known. Yet, it is I, Ogun, who has held this place among my lands. I have come to see for myself what makes you such a great warrior as has been claimed. How can it be that such an old man as you could be regarded as the greatest warrior ever known? What did you do to achieve this honor?"

Obatala listened as Ogun spoke, and gently tossed the embers in the circle of fire. It is said that this circle of fire on the great luminous mountain was no ordinary fire. It was the *Opon Ifa*, the primordial divining tray and the center of the world, marking all the eight directions and containing all the stories of the past, present, and future.

Obatala held his eyes fixed on the flames and looked deep within them. Some time passed. Suddenly Obatala spoke, "Ogun, if you wish to understand why I have been proclaimed as the greatest warrior in these lands, then I will give you two tasks to fulfill and should you complete them, you will have your answer!"

Ogun immediately took up to the challenge given to him by Obatala and agreed. He said, "So be it! It is done!"

Obatala said, "Then as your first task, go back to your land and create everything you need to sustain life. Build everything, grow everything, and weave everything from beginning to end. For one year you must do this. At the end of the year, come back and we will speak again!"

Ogun stood up, emphatically gesturing and laughing, "This will be easy, old one." He turned and left. Obatala simply smiled and continued to tend to the circle of fire – the place of all stories. "Ah, yes," thought Obatala, "a new story is now being written."

The year passed and Ogun did all that was asked. He built a great city where many came to give him honor. He effortlessly grew all things in such surplus that he fed a nation. He wove all things with such precision and beauty that his reputation far exceeded his own lands. Many came to give him praise as the master artist. Ogun was so busy, working, working, working that time moved quickly. The day soon came for him to return to Obatala. Ogun was proud of all his great works and was ready to return to the ancient land, the great shining mountain, the house of Obatala, to seek his answer.

Ogun entered the cave and there Obatala sat, tending his fire of stories as if time had stood still. Ogun presented himself before Obatala, pronouncing in a thundering voice, "This was a very easy challenge, grandfather. Nonetheless, I have given it all my effort and completed it superbly!"

Obatala smiled, eyes fixed on the circle of fire. Suddenly, he looked up at Ogun for the very first time, "Ogun, please be seated."

Ogun immediately sat down before Obatala. Obatala raised his head, and looked deeply into the eyes of Ogun. Ogun saw time mirrored back – all that was, is and will be. Obatala said, "Ogun, now that you have done this effortless task, return to your land and for one year sit in one place. Sit. And there in the solitude of existence, you are to reflect on every detail of what you accomplished the year before."

Obatala continued, "Review every detail of every single step and decision that resulted in each outcome you achieved. Once you have done this, return to me. Be prepared to share all of what you have learned from what you created and your reflection upon it."

Obatala stood up swiftly like a bird in flight. Ogun was startled, for he did not see how this old man could move with such speed. Obatala said to Ogun, "This is your second and final task. Then you will have your answer!"

Ogun was puzzled. This was not what he had expected. He stood up immediately and said, "So be it! It is done!"

Ogun returned to his domain and sat. He sat and sat and sat. A sense of irritation began to move over his being. At first it was a just a slight inner tremble; then it rose up like a tidal wave with a roar that could not be held back. Ogun began to feel a sense of confusion and anger.

He did everything within his power to just sit in one place, but it was terribly difficult and he struggled.

He began to reflect on all that he had done. He reflected and reflected and reflected. Ogun struggled with this seemingly simple task: the task of reflection. He looked deep within to 're-member' his life's work, to put it together again in his mind bit by bit.

Ogun asked himself, "Why am I struggling with this task? Why should reflection on all I have done be so difficult? This does not have to be so hard!" But hard indeed it was. Remembering every step, every choice, every method, every effort, every idea that inspired him was no small task. It required a supreme effort to just sit and reflect. The hours felt like days, the days felt like months, the months felt like years, and the year felt like time had stopped.

Ogun was spent, simply exhausted. When the year ended, he came to the conclusion that what Osun and Ochosi had said was true. Obatala was the greatest warrior. To place oneself in a single position and sit for one year and reflect was like sitting for a thousand lifetimes. The power and the memories were more than he could bear. Any warrior that could do this was indeed the greatest!

Suddenly time moved. Ogun felt that this realization had brought his reflecting to an end. The year had finally passed. Ogun made his way to the land of Obatala. As he climbed the mountain, he surrendered.

The memory of that day in the forest when he interrupted Osun and Ochosi's dialogue flashed before him. As Ogun climbed the mountain, he began to remember his gestures and comments with embarrassment. How could he have known what was going to be asked of him and what would be shown to him over time? As Ogun reached the entrance of the cave he heard drums and music, singing and laughter. "What is this?"

Entering the cave, Ogun saw Obatala standing, holding his staff in the air, dancing and cheering. Obatala was singing praises and songs to Ogun. He was whirling in delight and laughing with a thunderous sound that echoed as if it was moving through a great gate in the universe.

Stunned, Ogun asked, "What are you celebrating, Obatala?"

Obatala laughed, clapped and waved his arms through the magnificent luminous robe. "You, Ogun! We are celebrating you as the greatest warrior in your land and ours!"

Ogun shook his head in disbelief, "How can this be, Obatala? I have come to tell you that this second task was the most difficult I have ever attempted. I am not even sure if I can claim success."

With great joy, Obatala said, "Ah, but you have succeeded, Ogun. It is indeed so, you *have* done it!"

Shocked Ogun responded, "But Obatala, what do you mean?" Obatala stopped, looked deep into Ogun's eyes and said, "My son, you are the greatest warrior ever known because you have not only done what you know well; you have also ventured into my world. And now, by reflecting for one whole year, you have done what I do well, too. You are the greatest warrior of all time, and from this day forward those who come to learn the way of the warrior must give praise to you first!"

In that moment, the realization of what Obatala was saying swept over Ogun like a great wave. He leaped into the stars, knowing his true place in heaven and on earth. *Maferefun* Ogun, *Maferefun* Obatala. Praises to the spiritual power and wisdom of Ogun. Praises to the great spiritual power and wisdom of Obatala.

Marilyn Omifunke Torres is an ordained Yoruba priestess. She is Chief Olumeto Agbomola of Imota and Chief Iyasale Egungun of Imota.

FIE PA'A, FIE FĀNAU?! : Wanting to be barren, yet wanting to bear a child – simultaneously! A Tongan Proverbial Story, retold by Emil Wolfgramm

Māui 'Ata-langa (Māui the Creator-of-Space) and his wife, Hina, relocate their family, including their teenage son, Māui Kisikisi (Māui the-Well-Proportioned-Youth) following adventures in which they domesticate the various mankind-devouring plants and sea creatures. That began the island hopping cycle of events from their home island of *Ha'afuluhao* (The Clan of Conquerors) through the Tongan archipelago, until we find them setting up a new home compound on the volcanic island of *'Eua*.

As you know, the project of establishing a home is a manifold and unending series of delegated tasks for all members of the family. The houses were built and duly outfitted as befitting an industrious immigrant family.

Once housing and amenities were completed, Maui and Hina focus their attention upon establishing a sustainable food farming system. The Māui family was renowned in this world life of *Maama* (the World of Light) and in *Lolo-fonua* (The Underworld) which was the birth realm of Māui 'Ata-langa for their farming.

One day Hina comes upon her son, Māui Kisikisi, who was napping after clearing a large plain of ground cover single-handedly that very morning for the purpose of planting the root crops, *kūmala* (sweet potato) and *talo*. To Hina, napping was a waste of precious and valuable time when so much work needed to be done while the sun was up. Do you know of anyone in your house like Hina?

Well, Hina berates her needlessly napping son and says, "Māui how can you sleep when there is so much more work to be done?" And she reaches out and shakes him.

Poor Māui Kisikisi rouses from his deserved nap to face his mother who says, "Quick, quick, Māui awake and plant the *kūmala* and *talo*!"

He feels an injustice in the commanding and badgering tone of her words. Is she insinuating that his efforts that very morning were a small matter? Has this ever happened to you in your family?

Māui feels his anger boiling at the false accusatory words from his mother, and he jumps up and fastens his work skirt of *lousī* leaves about his waist. Then, grabbing his *huo-keli* (digging implement) he stalks off into the plain, dragging his woven baskets full of *kūmala* clippings and *huli'i talo* (planting stems) until the plain ends near the sea cliffs. He puts his planting stocks down into a pile. Then he paces to the edge and he raises the *huo-keli* in his hands above his head, while stretching his frame upward and backward.

He then heaves the *huokeli* over his head and forcefully drives it securely into the ground so deeply that he pierces the foundation rock supporting the entire volcanic island of *'Eua*. Māui Kisikisi leans into the shaft of his digging implement, shoving it deeper under the surface. By this ferocious act, a magical thing happens to the *huo-keli*. The submerged portion of this powerful shaft grows in length in response to the will of its owner until it drills into the stratum of foundation rock beneath dirt and rock mantle which camouflages its existence.

Māui Kisikisi grabs the end of his *huo-keli* next to his chest with his left hand. With his right hand on the shaft below his waist, he spreads his thighs, and bends his knees. He leans his whole weight and pushes downward with all his strength while chanting an incantation to strengthen the tensile quality of his *huo-keli!* Slowly yet smoothly the shaft of the *huo-keli* flexes and moves down towards the ground – and so, we have the first lifting lever in the mythic era of space and beauty ever seen in *Maama*, the world of light!

This legendary action amplifies as our hero, Māui Kisikisi, pushes ever so smoothly and continuously, until a muffled rumble is heard from beneath everyone's feet as the foundation stratum responds to the wondrous power of the lifting shaft of the *huo-keli*! The entire section of the island lifts skyward towering over everyone's head and continues to gain elevation.

Hina, who observes this immediate rearrangement of her island neighborhood, raises her voice and says to her son, Māui Kisikisi, "Stop! Stop! Look at what you're doing! You're tearing up the island! Don't do that any more!"

Māui Kisikisi controls his efforts and stops raising the end of the plain. He withdraws his *huo-keli*, leaving behind a huge island feature that looks like an arch of rock and earth suspended in the air above the plain of 'Eua Island.

Still trembling with anger Māui Kisikisi says to his mother, "Hina 'oku ke fie pa'a, fie fānau?!" which translates into "Hina, you are of two minds at the same time! Hina, you cannot be barren and yet give birth simultaneously!"

In recognition of this event, this arch is called *Ko e Mata-langa 'a Māui* (The Raised Perimeter from the Huo-keli belonging to Māui) which is renowned as a geographic treasure to the inhabitants of The Kingdom of Tonga.

This proverbial story from the Tongan Oceanic world is a poetic treasure that has lasted for about 3,500 years. Tongan parents have told it for millennia to teach values about the cultural symbols and signs relative to successful living.

Saint Brigid's Cloak, a legend from Ireland, retold by Sharon Creeden

So it is said that Saint Brigid was the Abbess of Kildare who did great charitable works. When she wanted some land in Leinster to build a church, she took her nuns to the king's castle. The king was away hunting, so Saint Brigid waited by the gate. When the king rode up, he saw a blue flag waving. It wasn't a flag at all; it was Saint Brigid's cloak fluttering in the wind.

The tight-pursed king guessed that she was there for money for her charities. He cut her greetings short: "Don't be flying your cloak like a flag in front of my castle. I've neither silver nor gold to give you."

"It's not money I'm begging," Saint Brigid assured him, "just a wee bit of ground for a church."

"Bride of Kildare," the King of Leinster said, "where would I be getting this ground? I've none to spare."

"Just the barest bit of rock will do," she replied. "At least grant me as much land as my cloak will cover."

The king thought, *She'll wheedle me to death. I'd best give her what she wants.* He said, "Just what your cloak will cover. Not an inch more."

At that, Saint Brigid lifted her cloak to catch the wind. "Away with it," she called to her nuns. Four sisters caught the hem of the cloak and ran in the four directions of the compass. The cloak billowed and expanded. More sisters picked up the cloak and ran and ran until it covered almost a mile in every direction.

"Stop!" cried the king, for it seemed that her blue cloak would cover the whole of Leinster.

Stop she did – when she was ready, and when she was sure the king was convinced of her power. Of all the land her cloak had covered, Saint Brigid claimed only a few rocky acres to build a church. And afterward, she only had to mention her miraculous cloak for the king to freely open his purse to her charities.

(From *In Full Bloom: Tales of Women in Their Prime* by Sharon Creeden)

La LLorona, a legend from Mexico, retold by Guadalupe S. Angulo

The legend of La Llorona, the weeping woman, has been told to me many times. There are many different versions of La Llorona, but for this particular one, I called my Nana, who lives in Empalme, Sonora, Mexico. I knew she would know an extraordinary version. My Nana is by nature a wonderfully endowed storyteller. The story takes place a long time ago. No one really knows when.

There was once a beautiful girl by the name of Maria. Maria's family, like most families from pueblos in Mexico, was poor. When Maria turned a certain age, it was time for her to marry. Her father, being the man of the house, began to look for an honest, hardworking man for Maria. Although Maria knew it was time to get married and get out of the house, she wanted to wait for her true love. Her father brought man after man, but she did not like any of them. Maria wanted a man of a higher class than she was.

Time passed, and Maria was still not married. One day all the single women in the pueblo were excited because there was talk of a rich ranchero coming to town for supplies. Maria put on her best dress, even though it had holes and it was very old. She had nothing else, but she figured it didn't matter. She would win him over with her beauty. She went off in search of her ranchero, but by the time she got there, it was too late. He was surrounded by women of a better class than Maria. She saw this tall, handsome man and knew - she knew – this was the man she wanted to marry. She was very disappointed to see him with other women. Maria went back home and thought to herself, "Maybe I should marry one of the suitors my father has arranged. Maybe it is the best choice for me."

The next day Maria was sent to the market. She was wearing her old work clothing. But Maria was not the only one at the market. The ranchero was there, too, but this time he was alone. As she was gathering her things, she accidentally bumped into the ranchero and their eyes met. At that very moment, she knew she was in love.

When the ranchero started to apologize, he saw how beautiful Maria was. She was more beautiful than any of the other women in the pueblo. He, too, fell in love at that very moment. The ranchero did not hesitate to ask Maria to be his wife. Maria wanted to scream at the top of her lungs to everyone. As they both walked to her home, they were talking and getting to know one another. Of course, Maria's father was overjoyed that the ranchero wanted to marry his daughter.

The wedding was held immediately and everyone in the pueblo attended. After the big celebration, it was time to leave Maria's pueblo and go to the rancho where her new life was to begin. She and her ranchero were inseparable.

The years went by and they had three beautiful children. Maria, still as much in love as the first day she saw her husband, was saddened by the long trips he often took. On her rancho, many women were jealous of Maria for having such a handsome husband. Rumors spread around the rancho about Maria's husband being unfaithful while away on his long trips. Maria knew this was true, and it broke her heart. Even though she knew the truth, there was nothing she could do but share her husband with other women. He was like most Mexican men in those times; it was normal for husbands to cheat. Maria just figured she would put her happiness aside for the sake of her family.

The day came when Maria knew that her husband would be returning from one of his very long trips. She was so eager to be with him. It had been a long time since a kiss or even a kind word had passed between them. Maria and the children awaited his arrival at the gates to the rancho. But as his wagon approached, she noticed another person riding with him! She was confused and alarmed and she prayed that this was not what she feared most. "Can it be that my time here is done?"

She hurriedly took the children inside hoping it was just her imagination. As the door opened to their home, the ranchero asked Maria to come to him. As she walked towards him, she saw a very striking young woman standing next to him. Without a trace of regard or remorse in his face or voice, the ranchero told Maria, "This is my new wife. Pack your belongings, take the children, and go back to your family."

Maria was devastated! She wanted to die right there and then. Imagine the love of your life telling you to leave your home. I can only imagine the pain her heart must have felt in that horrible moment. There was no choice for Maria and her children. They had to leave, but they had nowhere to go.

Maria was going out of her mind and not thinking clearly. She decided to cause her husband the same pain he had caused her. Her children were cold and hungry and were beginning to cry. Some people say she did not want her children to suffer a life without a father. Other people say she was just being selfish and thought if she got rid of the children, it would all go back to normal. Maria hugged and kissed her three children on that cold night before she did the unthinkable. She took the children one by one and drowned them in the cold river that ran through the rancho.

Maria started to make her way back to her old home to tell her husband what she had done. Maybe it was the guilt she had inside her or maybe she honestly thought her husband would take her back. Instead, that night, her husband was so angry and hurt after she told him what she had done that he beat her until she was almost dead! After that Maria knew there was only one thing left to do. She had to be with her children. She crawled back to the river and drowned herself.

The legend goes that when she reached the gates of Heaven, God said, "I blessed you with three children. Where are they?"

Maria could only whisper, "I don't know."

God shook his head and said, "Maria, until you return with your children you will never be allowed to enter the gates of Heaven."

And so, to this very day, the spirit of Maria floats over the waters crying out for her children. "Mis hijos! Dónde están mis hijos?" Wailing and searching, always searching, for her lost children, so that they and she can gain entrance to Heaven.

That is where she gets her name, La LLorona, the crying woman. It is said if she finds children playing by the river at night, no matter whose children they are, she will take them to the gates of heaven and claim them as her own. If you ever hear the cries of La LLorona, you should run away until you hear her no more.

(c)2008 Guadalupe S. Angulo.

Guadalupe S. Angulo was a student in The Art of Storytelling in the Spring of 2008. About this story, she says, "I believe it was love at first sight for Maria because it happened to me at the age of nine. The very first time I laid eyes on the person who is today my husband, I knew that he was my partner in life and I fell madly in love."

5

How to Tell a Story in Public

"I went to tell a story in my daughter's kindergarten class. I was kind of scared when I got there, but she was so proud of me and her little classmates were excited that I was there. It was so fun I forgot to be nervous. Everything went really well. Her teacher asked me to come again next month! (Storytelling Student Fall 2006)"

Why is it important to tell stories in public?

Telling stories to other people is important for three reasons: stories need to be told, tellers need to tell them, and people need to hear them. All the preparation that you have invested in preparing yourself and your stories over the past few weeks has been for this purpose. You have been preparing to relate your stories to others. A story that remains in the teller's head is like a painting that never escapes the artist's easel.

Storytelling is a performance art. Storytellers perform in public for the enjoyment and benefit of others. Any performance involves successfully applying a set of skills. When you apply the knowledge of your language in speaking, you are performing a skill set. When you successfully drive your car from one place to another, you are performing those skills. Storytelling performance is similar, with the added element of an audience. That added element is the source of fear or discomfort for many people. It is, at the same time, a source of excitement and satisfaction. For a storytelling event to be whole, listeners are required. In their presence, magic often happens. When the story, the teller, and the listeners come together something new and dynamic is created that cannot exist when any of the three is missing. This is what makes telling your stories to others in performance so exciting and fulfilling.

For some people the word performance has a negative connotation. It can conjure images of flashy costumes, bright lights, and bigger than life personalities that seem antithetical to what many perceive as the folk art roots of storytelling. While certainly performance in general, and storytelling performance in particular, can include bright lights and flashy personalities, it need not be defined so narrowly. Remember, when storytellers perform, they are seeking to build a relationship with their listeners. They don't just perform; they relate.

How do I prepare to tell a story in public?

There are four primary factors to consider as you prepare to tell a story in public:

The people: Who are your listeners? Profiling your audience is an essential part of preparing to tell a story in public.

- Do you know the people who will be listening to your stories? For your first stories, select family members, friends, or co-workers who will be supportive of you, people who will listen to you attentively.

- If you do not know the people to whom you will be telling, find out as much as you can about them. How many are expected? What are their ages, ethnicities, native languages? Are there more males than females, more adults than children?

- Remember, it is your job to engage your listeners, to throw the net of the story over them and pull them in.

- Never talk down to your listeners, whatever their ages. Relate to your listeners as naturally and authentically as you can. The goal is to *be* the storyteller, not to portray your idea of what a storyteller is.

The stories: What stories will you tell?

- As a new teller, your repertoire of stories is developing and your choices of what to tell may be limited. Think about the stories you know and consider what kind of audience is most likely to appreciate them, or to whom you would feel most comfortable telling. The good news is that most people of any age and background can enjoy a well-told story of any type. If you are telling a simple, playful story you don't need to ask your audience to pretend they are five years old.

- If you have made arrangements to tell to a group of kindergartners or primary grade students and you only know long complicated folktales, you will want to learn something with interactive elements. (See "Mr. Wiggle and Mr. Waggle" at the end of the chapter.)

- Master your material to the best of your ability.

The place: Where will you be telling?

- The environment in which you will be performing is crucial to the success of the experience for you and your listeners. The more you know about the setting, the more comfortable you will be. As the teller, it is your responsibility to take charge of the environment to ensure that it will support you, the story, and your listeners. In general, you will need a quiet place where you can stand and move easily as you tell, where your listeners can sit comfortably, and where there won't be visual or auditory distractions.

- If you are telling at home, in your workplace, or in some other familiar location, you will know the best place to gather a group of people to listen to your story.

- If you are telling somewhere you've never been before, ask your contact for the details of the space. Plan to arrive at least half an hour before you are expected to tell so that you can assess the space. If it does not appear to be conducive to storytelling, ask to rearrange it so the experience is pleasant for all. A common exception to this is in a classroom setting where it is generally not convenient for you to arrive early.

Yourself: Preparing to give a story to others.

- The most important thing you can do to prepare yourself is to know your stories very well. Do not procrastinate on learning your stories and be sure to practice them by telling them to others as often as you can. Telling stories is the best way to prepare to tell stories. The better you know your stories, the more able you will be to relate to your listeners and to create a storytelling moment for them and yourself.

- As you are practicing your stories, remember why you like them. Allow yourself to connect deeply to the enjoyment that you experience in the story. Let the humor, emotion, excitement, satisfaction, whatever it is in the story that delights you, root itself deeply in your consciousness.

- On the day of the performance, dress in clothing that is comfortable and attractive. Avoid jewelry that clatters, rattles, or that will in any way distract your listeners. Even the most casual telling is still a performance. Remember that you will be the center of attention. Check your appearance in a full-length mirror before you leave the house. You honor your listeners by attending to your appearance and grooming, and it is also a reminder to yourself that you are doing something special.

- When the time has come to tell your story, take a moment before you start to ground yourself. Literally be aware of how your body is connected to the floor. Be sure that your feet are planted securely, even if you are seated in a chair. Then, take in the whole context. Feel yourself, your audience, and your story, all ready and waiting to be told. Reconnect with whatever it is in the story that delights you, the reason you want to tell the story to others. Scan your audience and make brief eye contact with them. Acknowledge to yourself that

Storytelling and Breath

Breathing and storytelling are intimately connected. Your story is carried to the waiting ears of your audience by your voice, and your voice is powered by your breath. It is important to become aware of your breathing so that your voice has the power it requires. In addition, effective deep belly breathing is a great tool for managing stress.

Follow these steps to take a deep breath:

- Stand or sit with your back straight and your shoulders relaxed. If your shoulders are tense, take a few moments to roll them backward and forward.

- Take a deep breath as slowly as you can. As you take the breath in, let your belly expand. This allows your diaphragm to lower and your lungs to completely fill. Your shoulders and chest should not move as you breathe in, or only very slightly. If they do move, especially up toward your ears, you are breathing shallowly and your lungs will not be filling completely.

- Let your breath out slowly, through pursed lips, and let your belly fall inward as you do. Once again, your shoulders should not be moving. The action is in the lower ribs and abdomen.

- Repeat this several times, ideally for 5-10 minutes.

Make deep breathing a regular part of your life beyond preparing for performance. Your blood will be fully oxygenated, your brain will be working better, and you will be less stressed. It's good for you!

this is your performance space, and begin your story. Don't wait until performance day to practice this step. Learn how it feels to take charge of the storytelling moment and to tell well.

Much of the above is part of your on-going development as a storyteller. On the actual day of the performance, remember the following:

Before the performance:

- I know I've said this before, but here it is again - master your stories. Learn them, know where they came from, and practice telling them so that you will not be nervous, at least not on that account.
- Drink plenty of water and practice your deep breathing.
- Know where you are going, what time you are supposed to be there, who you will be telling to, what the telling environment will be like, and who your host is.
- Be there at least half an hour before you are scheduled to tell.

During the performance:

- Remember to ground yourself before telling.
- Enjoy yourself. Let the story take over and do its work.

After the performance:

- Assess yourself. How did it go? What went well? What would you do differently next time?
- If someone else has given you the opportunity to tell, send a thank you note to that person.

What options do I have in performance?

Of all the performance art forms, storytelling offers one of the widest ranges of options to its practitioners. Storytellers routinely integrate music, poetry, props, and dance into their performances. Some storytellers tell with a partner. Others use puppets. It is important to remember that each one of these options requires another layer of preparation and expertise. If you choose to integrate such an element into your storytelling, be sure that it will serve the story and add value to the overall experience. For example, if you are going to integrate a piece of poetry or song into your performance, be sure that you have it completely memorized and can recite or sing it easily without referring to notes.

How do I find a place to tell a story?

One of the best ways to find specific venues for your storytelling is to brainstorm and network with your teacher and your fellow students. Find out what other students are doing and share your own ideas. Below are examples of the kinds of places you will want to consider:

Home and family: If you have a supportive family, tell to them. Students with children or younger brothers or sisters often rely on them for an audience. Holiday gatherings can be ideal, especially for sharing a personal or family story. You might even learn some more stories from your listeners. Just don't try to compete with the turkey or the football game.

Workplace: Is there a break room where you work? Consider telling to your co-workers or colleagues. Here are what some previous students have tried with success:

- One student worked as a waiter in a small Italian restaurant. He asked his boss if he could offer to tell a story to parties of six or more who had ordered dessert. He got permission and told all his stories on the job to tables of willing diners. He said that each time, the whole restaurant ended up listening to and enjoying the stories.

- Another student was teaching swimming to teenaged girls with self-esteem issues. She told stories to them before their lessons to help them bond and relax.

- Another worked as an aide in a hospital and told stories to her co-workers in the break room. When she had finished her class requirement, her colleagues still wanted to hear stories from her.

What about using dialects and accents?

As a storyteller, my interest has always been how to tell as authentically as I can by developing and using my own voice. And beyond the philosophical and ethical implications, using an accent or a dialect is very difficult to do well. I'm not talking about storytellers whose first language is other than English, and whose speech incorporates an accent from their native language. In such a case, that is their authentic speech in English. I'm talking about a native English speaker adopting an accent from another language or attempting a dialect of English when telling a story. It's risky and can easily end in failure and offense. Here is the bottom line: only use an accent or dialect if it is one that you have mastered and that you know you can use with integrity and without causing offense. Consider these questions:

If you want to use an accent or dialect in your story, how do you plan to do it? Would you switch back and forth between the accent and your natural voice? For example, if you are telling a French folktale, would you use a French accent when the characters are speaking and your own voice for the narration? Or would you use a French accent for the whole story? If the latter, then you would be portraying a storyteller with a French accent rather than being the storyteller yourself. This is, in fact, acting rather than storytelling. Having the right to use a French accent means you have mastered it and are authentically connected to it in some way. If you can keep it distinct from your natural voice as you tell the story, you might have success.

What is your connection to the dialect or accent? Is it part of your family or culture? Regardless of your connection to it, have you mastered it? Is it accurate? Are you sure you can use the accent without causing offense?

Why do you want to use the accent or dialect? For humor? To evoke the feeling of the culture or setting of the story? In either case, incorporating a little vocabulary from the language or culture can accomplish the same thing. For example, let's say you are telling a Mexican folktale. Rather than attempting the whole story with an accent, consider adding a few words of Spanish, providing you can pronounce them correctly, to enhance the connection to the cultural roots of the story.

Personally, I think it is hard enough to tell a story well without bringing in these issues. On the other hand, I'm not talented with accents and dialects. Some storytellers can use dialect effectively. You might be one of them. It is a special talent, honed with practice and experience. Be sure you have the talent and are willing to invest the effort in practice before you try integrating an accent into your story.

Elementary school classrooms: Do you have a child, a younger sibling, or a grandchild in school? Do you have a friend who is a teacher? If you have or can establish a connection with an elementary school teacher, seek permission to tell in his or her classroom. See the box below for details on telling in such an environment.

Telling stories to children in an elementary classroom

Many beginning storytellers have the opportunity to tell their first stories in elementary school classrooms. Telling to children can be profoundly satisfying. They already know they like stories and they are accepting and tolerant of beginners. This doesn't mean, however, that you can take anything less than your "A" game to them. Children, and listeners of any age, deserve the best story performance you can give. Here are some tips to be sure that you and the children in your audience all have a good experience.

Find out from the teacher what signals she uses to get the children's attention and to maintain order. Some teachers clap twice and the children respond by clapping twice. Some teachers hold up a hand and wait until all the children have a hand in the air. Others say, "Criss Cross," and the children respond by saying, "Applesauce!" Whatever the signal is, practice it with the children yourself before you start telling. This gives you a way to restore order, if necessary, that the children have already been trained to use. If the teacher does not use such a device, have one of your own ready to teach.

Greet the children warmly, and introduce yourself if the teacher has not already done so. Ask the children if they know what they are supposed to do when listening to a storyteller. Some will call out answers like, "Listen," or "Be quiet!" I always ask the children to listen with their ears, their eyes, their mouths, and their hands: ears open, eyes looking right at me, mouths shut, and hands in their lap. When there is a participative element in the story, I usually teach it before beginning the story so the children know what to do when the time comes.

Although I always prefer to stand while telling, if I am in a small space and the children are all sitting on the floor, I ask for a chair. This allows me to be closer to the children, and it means they don't have to bend their necks back to see me. This facilitates eye contact and makes it easier on everyone. Don't sit on the floor yourself because the children, especially kindergartners and pre-schoolers, will want to crawl on you. It is easiest if the children are in chairs, but this isn't always possible.

Plan your program with the stories requiring more concentration from your listeners at the beginning and the more active, participative stories at the end. This works because the focus of their attention tends to be stronger at the beginning. Remember, the younger the child, the shorter the attention span. If a child begins to fidget, or if a couple start talking to each other, direct your story right to them for a few moments. This will usually result in eye contact and restored attention. If a child continues to be disruptive, the teacher will often intervene by touching the child or removing him or her. Discuss this strategy with the teacher before you begin.

When your stories are over, thank the children and congratulate them on their listening. If there is time, answer any questions they may have. Thank the teacher and make your exit. Once you are home, send the teacher a thank you note for allowing you to tell to his or her class.

Wherever you choose to tell, remember to keep the environment safe for yourself and your listeners. If you have doubts about whether your potential listeners will respect and support you, choose different listeners. If the space where you are planning to tell is noisy or subject to interruption, choose a different space.

Telling a story is supposed to be an enjoyable experience, the giving of a gift. Do what you can to maximize the experience for yourself and your listeners.

Assessing your performance: Once your performance is done, assess it as honestly as possible. This is important so that you can savor your success, while at the same time making plans for improvement.

- What went well? Remember what felt right, what worked, where in the story your audience was most engaged.

- What feedback did you get at the time? What did your listeners tell you about your performance?

- What would you do differently next time?

Foundations of Excellence

Excellent storytellers, and those who are on the road to excellence, know that in the moment of telling a story they must achieve a dynamic balance between the needs of the audience, the imperatives of the story, and their own talents, skills, and capacities. The people who are able to achieve this consistently and effectively we call masters.

It is the storyteller's relationship to the audience that distinguishes storytelling from other art forms based in narrative, such as theatre or film. If, for some perverse reason, you had to choose between telling your story perfectly and relating to your audience, choose the audience. Your relationship to them is the key. Even experienced professional storytellers have moments when they do not feel as connected to their stories. When that happens they make sure their relationship to the audience doesn't suffer. The other thing that experienced tellers know is that the story has its own initiative, and in those moments when the teller may not be completely on top of her game, the story often has the power to carry both of them.

But the story can only assist you when you have learned it to the best of your ability. The better you know your story, the better able you will be to relate to your listeners. You will have the energy to give to them rather than to remembering the story. Attend also to your relationship with yourself as the teller. If you are giving energy to fear, you have less to give to the audience. Over time you will experience moments when all three elements – the story, the audience, and you as the teller – are in balance. When that happens, you will have achieved a significant milestone on the road to excellence.

Excellence and Ethics: Storytelling is an art form that relies absolutely on the authenticity and honesty of its practitioners and their habits of relating to themselves, their listeners, their material, and their hosts. When any of the storytellers' relationships are compromised, their ability to excel is also compromised.

Story: Be clear about the source of your story and your relationship to it. It is not necessary to invent a false source or provenance for your story and doing so can have a negative impact on your relationship to both the story and your audience.

Self: Know yourself. Pick stories that are right for you, that reflect your values and experiences. If someone asks you to tell a story, or genre of story, that you do not like, decline the offer.

Audience: Honor your listeners to the best of your ability. Seek to delight them with the stories you choose and the way you tell them. Do not imagine them naked, or in any other demeaning way to ease your own performance anxiety.

Hosts: Be honest about your needs and keep your commitments. If you have particular needs (e.g. avoiding foods and fragrances to which you are sensitive or allergic) let your sponsors know as soon as possible. If something occurs that prevents you from keeping a commitment, your first obligation is to notify the people who are expecting you. Be as flexible and sensitive to the needs of your hosts as you can be while still performing to the best of your ability. If you can't meet their needs, tell them right away.

Do I have to use a microphone?

The simple answer is yes. Using a microphone effectively is as important as mastering your repertoire. Even in the smallest venues a microphone is often needed and in any professional performance context you will be expected to use one. Here are some tips:

Be prepared. Get to your venue early enough to review the set up and do a sound check. That way you can assess all the factors below.

Check the height of the stand. Before you perform, make sure you know how to adjust the height of the microphone stand so the microphone is right at your mouth. If you are unfamiliar with using a microphone, do not plan to hold it in your hand. It takes practice to remember to hold it right in front of your mouth, and new tellers often let the microphone drop too low. Using the stand keeps your hands free and ensures that the microphone remains at the correct height. If you do not know how to adjust the stand, ask for help.

Check the directionality of the microphone. Some microphones require that you speak directly into the center in order to be heard. Others receive sounds from a range of directions, and can accommodate movement. Assess the microphone yourself, or ask the host or sound technician how best to use it.

Place wireless, lavaliere, and head-set microphones correctly. If you are using a lavaliere microphone, do not clip it right under your chin. The sound can't reach it there. Clip it approximately one hand width below the base of your neck, or at about the second button on a shirt. If you will be using a wireless microphone, be sure to wear something to which the unit can clip. Make sure that a head-set microphone is secure on your head, and that the mouthpiece is positioned correctly on your face.

Conduct a sound-check. First and foremost, determine the volume so the speakers can be turned up or down. Determine how close to stand to the microphone to assess not only that you are heard clearly, but also to check that plosive sounds, the sound "p" in particular, do not make the microphone pop. That means you will need to try a few sentences of your story where you are speaking more loudly and rapidly.

Get used to it. As with other skills required to become a storyteller, practice is the best way to become proficient with the microphone.

Supporting Storytellers and Storytelling: National and State Organizations

NATIONAL
STORYTELLING
NETWORK

The storytelling movement in our country is supported by the **National Storytelling Network** (http://www.storynet.org). The NSN hosts an annual conference, publishes a bi-monthly magazine, and maintains a directory of members. It also co-produces the National Storytelling Festival with the International Storytelling Center (http://www.storytellingfoundation.org/)http://www.storytellingfoundation.org/). This Festival is held annually on the first weekend in October in Jonesborough, Tennessee. These two organizations and their events are among the most visible and prominent, but in every state there are local organizations that support storyteller.

In Arizona, for example, the statewide Tellers of Tales organization, the Arizona Storytelling Guild, and South Mountain Community College's Storytelling Institute provide ongoing support and training for new and experienced tellers. Tellers of Tales has chapters in Phoenix and in Tucson and holds monthly meetings open to the public. The Arizona Storytelling Guild is an organization devoted to promoting excellence in storytelling. These groups periodically host concerts and workshops presented by professional storytellers.

The Storytelling Institute at South Mountain Community College offers a wide range of courses leading up to a 30-credit certificate in storytelling. In addition to coursework, the Institute hosts storytelling events throughout the year. It holds an annual spring storytelling festival which includes concerts and workshops by noted professional storytellers from around the world. The Institute also sponsors the Storytelling  Amigos, a volunteer group that gathers monthly for members to hone their craft. Members also assist with Institute events. Check out the Institute's website for detailed information on the certificate program, storytelling classes, and events (http://eport.mariopa.edu/storytelling).

Storyteller.net is the largest and most comprehensive directory of storytellers available on the internet. Created and maintained by storyteller K. Sean Buvala, the mission of Storyteller.net is to "help everyone find great stories and great storytellers. We help great storytellers find themselves through training and resources in the circles of artistic, technical and business excellence." (http://www.storyteller.net) Members of Storyteller.net establish web pages where potential clients can learn about them and where they can sell their products. Members are encouraged to submit articles to the site. Hundreds of articles are available on a wide range of subjects of for beginning and experienced tellers. Sean also offers telecourses, workshops, podcasts, and interviews with storytellers.

Students in The Art of Storytelling class at SMCC are required to tell stories outside of class. These are some of their self evaluations.

Which of the tellings went best? Why?

- The experience of doing the three previous tellings gave me more confidence in my last telling. I was telling stories to my family, and I know they support me. "Papa! Papa! Do it again like a lion," my little granddaughter told me. That little smile and her eyes full of happiness made my heart blow up with pleasure and tenderness.
- I work at a bank, so everyone in the room had either been in debt, was in debt, or on the verge of being in debt. The story I told was received positively.
- My third telling was my best because I was not nervous, I was not scared of forgetting the story, and most of all, I had fun!

What changes would you make if you had the opportunity to re-plan and re-do this project?

- I would take more time to plan the stories for my first telling.
- I would have gotten a clearer picture of who my audience was at the Adult Day Care Center and would have had stories to fit that audience.
- I would be more interactive with the audience.
- I would do more public tellings. I found I was more nervous telling in front of a small group of close friends than I was telling in front of a large less intimate audience.
- I would make time to learn more stories, so I could have a little more variety available when I told.
- I would try to get an earlier start on the project. It was tough trying to get three tellings done in a month's time.
- I will prepare more, especially when telling to an audience I don't know well.
- I will pre-rehearse my stories to feel comfortable with each story and my choice of words.
- I would tell to different audiences in different settings.

How would you evaluate your overall experience?

- I had a lot of fun being the center of attention on all of these occasions. I definitely had the most fun making my nieces giggle at my chicken noises.
- I learned a lot about storytelling and myself. I also learned a lot about people, what it takes to entertain them and hold their attention.

Can you see yourself telling stories in the future?

- I am planning to be a math teacher and I am going to tell stories to my students because stories fortify the imagination and help us store information.
- I have found great joy in telling to the elderly. If I can brighten up their lives for just one day with story, I have accomplished something.
- I will use stories in my personal life because I come from a large, loud family that likes to tell stories around the dinner table or over a couple of beers.
- I will incorporate storytelling to teach my children to listen carefully because truly learning to listen is an art.

The Stories:

The following story is a favorite of storytellers in America and beyond. I learned it from Jim May, and the version below is similar to his. The key to telling a story like this is consistency. Keep both your language and your actions consistent throughout the story. Encourage your listeners to join you. At the beginning of the story say, "Whenever you think you know what I'm going to do or say, do it and say it with me." Although this is a simple story, it is very fun and adults enjoy it as well as children.

The Story of Mr. Wiggle and Mr. Waggle—with instructions

Once upon a time, there were two best friends: Mr. Wiggle (Show right thumb and wiggle it.) and Mr. Waggle. (Show left thumb and waggle it.)

Mr. Wiggle and Mr. Waggle lived on either side of a great big mountain. Mr. Wiggle lived in a little house here. (Open right hand, lay thumb on palm of hand and close fingers.) Mr. Waggle lived in a little house over here. (Open left hand, lay thumb on palm and close fingers.)

One day Mr. Wiggle decided to visit his best friend, Mr. Waggle. He opened the door. (Open fingers on right hand.) He went outside. (Put thumb up.) He closed the door. (Close fingers again.)

Then he went up and down, and up and down, and up and down, over the mountain to Mr. Waggle's house. (Trace the path up and down the mountains with your thumb.)

He knocked on the door. (Knock on closed left fist with right fist.) No answer. He knocked again. (Knock on closed left fist with right fist.) Still no answer. He knocked one more time as loudly as he could. (Knock on closed left fist with right fist.)

No answer! So, Mr. Wiggle went up and down, and up and down, and up and down, 'til he got back home. (Trace the path up and down the mountains more slowly – he's tired and disappointed.) Then he opened the door, he went inside, and closed the door. (Open right hand, lay thumb on palm of hand and close fingers.)

The next day Mr. Waggle decided to visit Mr. Wiggle. (Repeat the whole sequence, reversing the hands and names).

The next day, simultaneously – and at the very same time – Mr. Wiggle and Mr. Waggle both decided to visit each other. They opened their doors.(Repeat the sequence with both hands simultaneously.)They went up and down, and up and down, and up and down. (Continue until your hands meet in front of you.) And they ran right into each other. They had so much to talk about! They talked and they talked and they talked and they talked. (Keep your fists together wiggling your thumbs as the friends talk. Invite the audience to join you in saying talk, talk, talk.) Are they done yet? No! They talked and they talked and they talked and they talked. (Keep wiggling as they talk. Let them talk, and wiggle with you as long as it is fun.)

Finally, the sun was going down. Mr. Wiggle was not afraid of the dark, but Mr. Waggle was, so they decided to go home. Because they were best friends, they gave each other a big hug. (Cross your thumbs in a hug.)

And then they both went up and down, and up and down, and up and down. (Move your hands up and down as before.)

When they got home, they opened their doors. (Open the fingers of both hands.) They went inside. (Put your thumbs in your palms.) They closed the doors. (Close your fingers over your thumbs.)

That night, as he was going to bed, Mr. Wiggle thought of his best friend and said, "Good night, Mr. Waggle." (Put your right hand behind your back as you say this.)

And when Mr. Waggle went to bed, he thought of *his* best friend and said, "Good night, Mr. Wiggle." (Put your left hand behind your back as you say this.)

And that is the true story of Mr. Wiggle and Mr. Waggle!

Three Zen Stories

Each of these stories provides a metaphor for facing fear and anxiety in performance.

No Fear, a Zen Tale retold by John Suler

A Taoist story tells of an old man who accidentally fell into the river rapids leading to a high and dangerous waterfall. Onlookers feared for his life. Miraculously, he came out alive and unharmed downstream at the bottom of the falls. People asked him how he managed to survive. "I accommodated myself to the water, not the water to me. Without thinking, I allowed myself to be shaped by it. Plunging into the swirl, I came out with the swirl. This is how I survived."

(http://www.rider.edu/~suler/zenstory/goflow.html)

Great Waves, a Zen Tale from Japan, retold by Paul Reps and Nyogen Senzaki

In the early days of the Meiji era there lived a well-known wrestler called O-nami, Great Waves.

O-nami was immensely strong and knew the art of wrestling. In his private bouts he defeated even his teacher, but in public he was so bashful that his own pupils threw him.

O-nami felt he should go to Zen master for help. Hakuju, a wandering teacher, was stopping in a little temple nearby, so O-nami went to see him and told him of his trouble.

"Great Waves is your name," the teacher advised, "so stay in this temple tonight. Imagine that you are those billows. You are no longer a wrestler who is afraid. You are those huge waves sweeping everything before them, swallowing all in their path. Do this and you will be the greatest wrestler in the land."

The teacher retired. O-nami sat in meditation trying to imagine himself as waves. He though of many different things. Then gradually he turned more and more to the feeling of the waves. As the night advanced the waves became larger and larger. They swept away the flowers in their vases. Even the Buddha in the shrine was inundated. Before dawn the temple was nothing but the ebb and flow of an immense sea.

In the morning the teacher found O-nami meditating, a faint smile on his face. He patted the wrestler's shoulder. "Now nothing can disturb you," he said. "You are those waves. You will sweep everything before you."

The same day O-nami entered the wrestling contests and won. After that, no one in Japan was able to defeat him.

(From *Zen Flesh, Zen Bones* by Paul Reps and Nyogen Senzaki)

A Zen Parable retold by Paul Reps and Nyogen Senzaki

Buddha told a parable in a sutra:

A man traveling across a field encountered a tiger. He fled, the tiger after him. Coming to a precipice, he caught hold of the root of a wild vine and swung himself down over the edge. The tiger sniffed at him from above. Trembling, the man looked down to where, far below, another tiger was waiting to eat him. Only the vine sustained him.

Two mice, one white and one black, little by little started to gnaw away at the vine. The man saw a luscious strawberry near him. Grasping the vine with one hand, he plucked the strawberry with the other. How sweet it tasted!

(From *Zen Flesh, Zen Bones* by Paul Reps and Nyogen Senzaki)

What Happens When You Really Listen, a folktale from India, retold by A. K. Ramanujan

A villager who had no sense of culture and no interest in it was married to a woman who was very cultured. She tried various ways of cultivating his taste for the higher things of life, but he just wasn't interested.

Once a great reciter of that grand epic, the Ramayana, came to the village. Every evening he would sing, recite, and explain the verses of the epic. The whole village went to this one-man performance as if it were a rare feast.

The woman who was married to the uncultured dolt tried to interest him in the performance. She nagged him and forced him to go and listen. This time, he grumbled as usual but decided to humor her. So he went in the evening and sat at the back. It was an all-night performance and he just couldn't keep awake. He slept through the night. Early in the morning, when a canto was over and the reciter sang the closing verses for the day, sweets were distributed according to custom. Someone put a few sweets into the mouth of the sleeping man. He woke up soon after and went home. His wife was delighted that her husband had stayed through the night and asked him eagerly how he had enjoyed the Ramayana. He said, "It was very sweet." The wife was happy to hear it.

The next day his wife again insisted on his listening to the epic. So he went to the enclosure where the reciter was performing, sat against a wall, and before long fell fast asleep. The place was crowded, and a young boy sat on his shoulders and made himself comfortable and listened open-mouthed to the fascinating story. In the morning, when the night's portion of the story came to an end, everyone got up and so did the husband. The boy had got off earlier, but the man felt aches and pains from the weight he had borne all night. When he went home and his wife asked him eagerly how it was, he said, "It got heavier and heavier by morning." The wife said, "That's the way that story is." She was happy that her husband was at last beginning to feel the emotions and greatness of the epic.

On the third day, he sat at the edge of the crowd and was so sleepy that he lay down on the ground and fell asleep with his mouth hanging open. When the performance was over, as the people left the enclosure, his mouth was filled with the dust of their passing. When his wife asked him how it was, he moved his mouth this way and that, made a face, and said, "Terrible.

It was so dry and gritty." His wife knew something was wrong, asked what exactly had happened, and didn't let up till he finally told her how he had been sleeping through the performance every night.

On the fourth day, his wife went with him. She sat him down in the very first row and told him sternly that he should keep awake no matter what happened. So he sat dutifully in the front row and began to listen. Very soon, he was caught up in the adventures and the characters of the great epic story. On that day, the reciter was enchanting the audience with the story of Hanuman the monkey and how he had to leap across the ocean to take Rama's signet ring to Sita, the abducted wife of Rama. When Hanuman was making his leap, the signet ring slipped from his hand and fell into the ocean. Hanuman didn't know what to do. He had to get the ring back quickly and take it to Sita in the demon's kingdom. While he was wringing his hands, the husband who was listening with rapt attention in the first row, said, "Hanuman, don't worry. I'll get it for you." Then he jumped up and dived into the ocean, found the ring in the ocean floor, and brought it back and gave it to Hanuman.

Everyone was astonished. They thought this man was someone special, really blessed by Rama and Hanuman. Ever since, he has been respected in the village as a wise elder, and he has also behaved like one. That's what happens when you really listen to a story, especially the Ramayana.

(Adapted from the story of the same name in *Folktales from India: A Selection of Oral Tales from Twenty-two Languages* by A.K. Ramanujan.)

The Story of the Arrowmaker, a Kiowa tale, retold by N. Scott Momaday

The Kiowas made fine arrows and straightened them in their teeth. Then they drew them to the bow to see that they were straight. Once there was a man and his wife. They were alone at night in their tipi. By the light of the fire the man was making arrows. After a while he caught sight of something. There was a small opening in the tipi where two hides had been sewn together. Someone was there on the outside, looking in. The man went on with his work, but he said to his wife, "Someone is standing outside. Do not be afraid. Let us talk easily, as of ordinary things." He took up an arrow and straightened it in his teeth: then, as it was right for him to do, he drew it to the bow and took aim, first in this direction and then in that. And all the while he was talking, as if to his wife. But this is how he spoke: "I know that you are there on the outside, for I can feel your eyes upon me. If you are a Kiowa, you will understand what I am saying, and you will speak your name." But there was no answer, and the man went on in the same way, pointing the arrow all around. At last his aim fell upon the place where his enemy stood, and he let go of the string. The arrow went straight to the enemy's heart.

About this story, N. Scott Momaday says: "When I was a child, my father told me the story of the arrowmaker, and he told it to me many times, for I fell in love with it. I have no memory that is older than of hearing it."

(From "The Story of the Arrowmaker" by N. Scott Momaday)

6

How to Tell a Fact-based Story
Historical, Biographical, and Family Stories

"I worked myself all up before telling...palms sweating, stomach doing all kinds of crazy flips, and mouth dry. I stood before my classmates and tried to tell the story and just hoped that at least half of them would enjoy it. And then, after taking my seat, I found that most, if not all of them, had enjoyed it and everything was cool!"
(Storytelling Student Fall 2001)

What are Fact-based Stories?

Historical, biographical, and family stories – all based in fact – are about events that really happened and people who really existed. Historical stories are about events from the past, or people who played parts in the events, and are often told in ways that highlight new or unknown perspectives. Biographical stories are about the famous, infamous, and influential: people who have had an impact on culture or history and whose lives have been documented by others. Family stories are about the people in your family, some of whom may be famous, may have witnessed history, or are unknown in the wider world, but worthy of a story nonetheless.

Your role as the crafter of the story comes to the forefront in telling stories based in fact. In any event or life there is far more information than needs to be told or can be told in a single story. The teller must select and shape the information to create the best story possible about the topic. Telling a fact-based story is not giving a lecture or reciting a set of facts, but rather telling something that will hold listeners' interest and move them in some way, whether emotionally, spiritually, or intellectually.

A story based in fact may fit into more than one category, as does the story about my grandfather that follows. It is a family story, as well as a historical story, set in a documented event from the past. In fact, although historical, biographical and family stories can be described as if they were separate types, they often overlap, and the processes of finding, crafting, and telling them are similar.

What is a historical story?

Most of us have sat through a history class or tried to read a history text and been bored to tears. History needn't be boring; it's about people's lives and all the magnificent, innovative, breathtaking, horrible things that have happened in the past. As is clear from their spelling, the words "history"

88

and "story" are related, yet so often history is presented in its barest bones – what happened when and where to whom. But it's the juicy details, the fascinating moments of serendipity, unknown heartbreaks, and the brushes with greatness that we remember. These are the things that bring history alive and they are also the best subjects for historical stories.

A historical story tells about events and the people who played parts In them. The best stories bring to light facts and perspectives that are not usually covered in large history survey texts.

Storyteller Elizabeth Ellis is known for her historical stories. She says that telling a historical story from a fresh point of view can allow us to hear voices from the past that have been neglected by others. Here are her recommendations for creating a story from history:

Carefully select the topic and sources: Your first step is to choose a topic that fascinates you. Whether you choose a person or an event in history, your passion for the subject is the key to creating a good story. Once you've identified the topic, you must find as much information about it as you can from both primary and secondary sources. Primary sources are first-person accounts, such as letters, journals, and reports by people who witnessed the event or knew the person you want to tell about. Secondary sources are one or more steps removed from the event or person, but they provide the wider context and perspective that is essential for crafting the story. In your research you may find a story that is close to being tellable, but you should still take the time to research the time period for yourself. Your efforts will pay off in a deeper understanding of the story you want to tell.

Identify the story's main character: Your choice here is to tell a story about a real historical figure or to tell about real events in history from a fictional character's point of view.

Dedication Day

When Roosevelt Dam was under construction, my grandfather, Grantley Warren was nine years old and growing up in nearby Globe, Arizona. He was fascinated by the dam and by the process of its building. The dam was to be dedicated on March 18, 1911, and former president Theodore Roosevelt himself was coming for the ceremony. My grandfather wanted desperately to meet President Roosevelt, but how would he get there? He hitched a ride on a neighbor's horse-drawn wagon for the 30-mile journey north-west on rutted dirt roads to the dam. Despite the difficulty of the ride and the dam's distance from most towns, there was quite a crowd – close to 1,000 people. Grantley wormed his way through the assembled well-wishers and managed to get right next to President Roosevelt. He said that the great man even shook his hand. In some of the official photographs of the day, the boy who became my grandfather is standing beside Teddy Roosevelt! He was there at 5:48 p.m. to witness the moment when President Roosevelt pushed the button that released water from the reservoir and that water came gushing out the spillways.

Roosevelt Dam was a great point of state pride for my grandfather. For all his life he loved to tell about it: how it was built, about the brave muleskinners, and the Italian stonemasons and engineers. He knew how much water it could hold and how much electricity it could produce. He knew the size and weight of the stones and what it took to feed a twenty-mule team.

But his favorite part of the story was to tell about how he stood right by President Roosevelt and had been a living witness to history on dedication day.

If you choose to tell about a real person, you must stick to the facts as they have been documented. Creating a fictional character, someone who might have witnessed the events you want to tell about, can allow you more flexibility to craft the story and to weave in events or perspectives that a single historical person could not have had. As with telling about an actual person, you must remain true to historical accuracy.

Determine possible points of conflict to shape the plot: The heart of any story is conflict. Without conflict there is no story. When formulating your story, keep asking yourself, "What are the points of conflict? How can I show them in the story? To whom can the story happen?" Answers to these questions provide the basic plot and the major characters. The points of conflict may be relationships between characters from different backgrounds, how the characters interact with the environment, or their responses to great challenges or tragedies.

Give the story "voice" (point of view): You must choose your story's voice. The story will differ according to its point of view. Events and people are described positively or negatively depending on who is telling the story. The Civil War, The War Between the States, and the Late Unpleasantness are all the same event, but seen through different eyes. The story of a runaway slave can be told by the slave, the slave owner, the child in the Big House who has been raised by the slave, the bounty hunter, or any number of other people. The story will be dramatically different in each case! In the past, history was most often told from the white, male perspective. Telling a story from a different point of view can allow us to hear from history's missing voices.

Create reality – focus listener attention: To make the story "real" for the listener, the characters must be believable. Beware of depicting a character as totally good or totally evil. Historical accuracy in a story is very important, but the story must also entertain. Don't shy away from story elements that will grab people and hold their interest. Find that theme to which people will relate – greed, betrayal, loyalty, lust or whatever it may be. Developing a theme helps the listeners relate to the story and to feel it. Incorporate limited amounts of description, focusing more on dialog which will hold the audience's attention for longer periods. Don't worry about costumes or props. Give the listener an aural experience. Because our world is saturated with visual experiences, give listeners opportunities to enter their imaginations and make the pictures themselves.

When I think about history, the first thing that pops into my head are huge dry tomes crammed with names and dates – the kind of book that can put me to sleep in five minutes flat even when I'm interested in the information they contain. But then I remember Dr. Richard Morales, who teaches history at South Mountain Community College. Dr. Morales doesn't just give lectures in his classes; he tells the stories of the past with such passion and energy that he brings history to life. Students in his classes have told me he is so absorbing that it can be hard to remember to take notes. And I know from having taught in the room next to him that the force of his commitment to his subject comes right through the walls. Dr. Morales is someone who truly knows how to give voice to history – to tell the stories of the past.

Bring the story to a satisfying conclusion: All stories need a satisfying conclusion, although that does not necessarily mean a happy ending. A satisfying conclusion is achieved by tying up all the loose ends and answering all the questions that may have been created in the listener's mind. A satisfying conclusion may be sad or unhappy if, because of the facts or circumstances, that is the **only** way it can end realistically. The listener will accept that, because – after all – life is like that at times!

Adapted from "Researching and Crafting the History Story", by Elizabeth Ellis, in *Storytelling World*, Winter/ Spring, 1997, Issue 11, page 7-8.

What is a Biographical Story?

In a historical story, the event is the context and people's lives are seen in relation to it. In a biographical story, an individual life provides the overall context. As with a story from history, there is always far more information than can be included in a single story. The storyteller's job is to find the elements of a person's life that will make a good story. All of Elizabeth Ellis' recommendations for a historical story also apply to a biographical story, even the one about the main character. A biographical story can be told from the point of view of someone close to the person, or someone who witnessed the person's life and times.

Who are my people and where did I come from?

Becoming interested in family stories can help to answer these questions. Perhaps you already know about your family and its history, but if you do not, now is the time to find out. Who in your family knows the stories? Find that person and sit him or her down (respectfully, of course) and start learning the stories of your ancestry. Here are some questions to get you going:

- What is your family's ethnic or cultural heritage? How did your people come to where they are living now?

- Do you have a famous relative, someone who did something remarkable? If so, research him or her and compare what you learn with family memory.

- Did someone in your family achieve something against great odds? Remember, this can be something known only to the family, such as keeping the family together during a crisis, or enduring the challenges of emigration to and surviving in a new country. Perhaps someone survived a great illness, tragedy, or injustice and lived to tell about it.

- Did someone in your family live through an interesting or challenging period in history? Did someone march with Martin Luther King or César Chavez? Did someone survive the war in Vietnam or Iraq? Did someone live through a natural disaster such as Hurricane Katrina?

- Is there someone in your family who is a character, someone with a big personality known for interesting exploits?

- Family stories can also include the funny, endearing, or poignant every day experiences. What are the stories that your family tell about each other when you get together for holidays, reunions or other occasions?

An elderly person in your family can be a goldmine of stories about the way things used to be and about persons long gone. If you want to ask your relatives about the past remember to start with concrete questions rather than general ones such as, "Tell me about the good old days." Here are some examples:

Ask a relative:

- to describe, or to draw, the house that he or she grew up in.

- about times he or she got in trouble or was frightened.

Continued

Who are my people and where did I come from? (continued)

Ask about:

- meal times: what they normally ate, who prepared it and how it was served.
- holidays and special occasions: who was there, what happened, what they ate, how they entertained themselves.
- the cars they drove and where they went in them.
- the way children played: where and with what.
- where the adults worked and what they did for a living.
- the seasons: what winter was like and what happened in the summer?
- school: where was it and how your relative got there?

Of course these questions needn't be limited to the very elderly. They should get almost anyone talking and thinking about the past, and that leads to stories.

If you are telling about a well known person, the key to the story will be to find and tell something about them that is not well known and that rounds-out or deepens our understanding of them. This is what Paul Harvey has done with his long-running radio program, *The Rest of the Story*. "The Boy," one of the stories at the end of the chapter, is written in this style. When telling about a less well known person, the challenge is to share the person's significance with the listeners without giving a lecture or overloading them with details. The story of Phillis Wheatley at the end of this chapter does just that.

What is a Family Story?

A family story is about the people in your family. The beautiful thing about telling a family story is that it deepens our relationship to our own history and heritage. The other advantage to a family story is that you may already know it, and with a little crafting it will be ready to tell. Perhaps a relative is the hero or mentor discussed in the previous section. Read "Who are my people and where did I come from?" on the previous page for tips on learning family stories from relatives.

How do I structure a historical, biographical or family story?

One of the key differences between telling a folktale or a myth and telling a story based in fact is that the storyteller must provide the structure of the story. Once the event or person is identified, crafting the information will give shape to the story.

The most basic story structure is beginning, middle, and end:

- **Beginning** sets the context (place, participants, time).
- **Middle** is where the action occurs (what happens, what problem is addressed, what changes occur).
- **End** provides the resolution (growth achieved, wisdom gained, problem solved).

Storyteller Donald Davis uses a mnemonic called "The Five Ps" for structuring a story. He says that to create distinct images for the listener, to make a Picture in a person's head, your story must include:

- Place: where and when did the story happen?
- People: who are the people in the story? What do they look like? How old are they? What are their personalities like?
- Problem: What is the problem facing the people in the story? What is the conflict in the story?
- Progress: Something must happen to improve the situation. How is the problem resolved? What do the people learn that allows for the resolution of the problem?

LynnAnn Wojciechowicz has added a sixth "P" to the equation. She says the story must also have a Point. There must be a reason for the listener to be interested in the story. It could be a lesson learned by the main character. It could be a universal truth revealed by the story.

Let's apply this process of creating a picture to "Dedication Day," the story of my grandfather at the beginning of the chapter.

- Place: Globe and Roosevelt Lake in Arizona, 1911.
- People: My grandfather, Grantley Warren, and President Theodore Roosevelt.
- Problem: How will my grandfather get to the dam for the dedication?
- Progress: He hitches a ride on his neighbor's wagon. He gets there and even gets to meet the great man.

Legendary Meanness

My great grandfather, Rudolph, was a legend in my family for his meanness. He was short, cross-eyed, and had a very short fuse. His family feared him. Stories about his cruelty were told long after his death. When one of his daughters disobeyed him, he put her out of the house. When she asked to return, he refused her. She died in the flu epidemic shortly thereafter, and some of her siblings never forgave him. Another story was that he was so mean that the miners who worked for him in Globe, Arizona, firebombed his house. That was the way I heard the story for years; the miners just up and bombed his house because they hated him so fiercely. "Who could blame them?" was the unstated subtext to the story.

The real story of the fire bombing is more complicated, however, and it took some research at the Globe Historical Society to unearth the truth. In 1918, miners all over the southwest were forming labor unions, and their bosses at the mines were resisting. Violence was common. Rudolph, staunchly anti-union, was the supervisor at the Old Dominion Mine in Globe, and as such, an obvious target for the miners' wrath.

Fortunately, someone warned my great grandmother, Florence, nine months pregnant at the time with her eighth child, and she got herself and her children out of the house before it was bombed. She found refuge for the family in the honeymoon suite of the Old Dominion Hotel, where they lived until the house was rebuilt. She later told of standing on the balcony and looking to the east to see the army marching in from Fort Apache to quell the violence. This was the last time troops were mustered from there. Those troops were being led by her brother-in-law, who waved up at her with grim determination as he passed.

The destruction of the Warren home in 1918 was part of a political struggle taking place throughout the state and the region. But I have to wonder. If my great grandfather hadn't been so mean, would they have bombed somebody else's house?

- **P**oint: Meeting President Roosevelt was an experience he remembered and told for the rest of his life. Beyond that, he always took great pride in Roosevelt Dam and its construction.

Donald Davis also recommends the following sequence to structure an effective story:

- There is a normal world of the character's experience.
- Trouble comes!
- The character's world is turned upside down.
- The character receives help from somewhere and/or learns something new that helps to restore balance.
- A new normal world is established as a result.

This sequence is especially useful for thinking through and structuring a story that is more complicated than "Dedication Day." Structuring your fact-based story is not an option. A strong story structure results in a satisfying story experience for the teller and listeners alike. It is an integral part of the storyteller's art.

Foundations of Excellence

Storyteller Susan Klein tells of witnessing a fellow teller, Michael Parent, wrestle with a family story, struggling to determine what to keep and what to let go. Finally Michael said, "I love you Uncle Joe, but you've got to go."

Determining the focus, the primary meaning or import of a story, and choosing only those elements that support that focus require artistic self-discipline and a touch of ruthlessness. In the process of researching and developing stories, lots of tantalizing details and interesting tidbits of information emerge, and we get emotionally attached to them. But regardless of our affection for a nice bit of gossip or a beloved character, if they do not serve the primary focus or move the story along, they are irrelevant and must be excluded from the story. Not doing so results in a self-indulgent mishmash that serves neither the story nor the audience.

In response to the question, "What is the story really about?" storyteller Beth Horner says:

This question pervades the entire process. Story creation would be so simple if the answer to this question appeared early on, but it rarely does. Instead, it is a process of sorting and experimenting, muddied by the many possible stories that could be told from the same source material. One must get in touch with one's heart when it comes to a family story.

Once I established my connection to Jane Harper and chose to craft the story about my name search, it became clear the story was *really* about my childhood search for identity: my realization that I was the sum of all who came before me. All that they had experienced and learned in life was mine to draw upon. "Through My Voice: Telling Family History," *Storytelling Magazine*, July/August 2004.

To get to the heart of the story you are developing, Susan Klein recommends taking the time to carefully ponder the following questions:

- What is this story about?
- What is my intent in telling this story?

- Why is it necessary to tell this story?
- Why should I be the voice for this story?

Answering these questions will help to focus and structure a story in development. These questions are useful when applied to all of the stories in your repertoire – including the folktales, myths, and legends. The process will illuminate the relationship between the stories and the teller. Over time you may learn that the stories you choose, your intent in telling them, and their big themes show many commonalities. These commonalities provide glimpses of the core of your emerging identity as a storyteller.

Excellence and Ethics: Fact-based stories are always more than facts. The storyteller must provide story structure for those facts. In addition, the teller must decide how to supplement or embellish the facts to create art. When the teller invents a character who speaks as witness to events or who fills in details not provided by history or memory, that character must reflect the inherent integrity of the facts. Crucial facts that are not convenient to the teller's evolving understanding of the story cannot be eliminated or altered.

When you create a story about a public person whose life has been documented in multiple sources, you generally do not need to seek permission. Creating a story from a single source, with the intent to tell it for pay, requires securing permission from the author or publisher of that source. Lack of response from the copyright holder upon seeking permission is as good as a "no." "No" means no, and no response also means "no." For more on the ethics of telling stories that belong to other people, consult Susan Klein's publication, *Ethics, Apprenticeship, Etiquette, Courtesy, and Copyright* at www.susanklein.net.

> When you are telling about your own family or friends, you should ask permission – especially if the story might embarrass them or cast them in a bad light. Sometimes when you seek information from family or friends to complete a story, they will remember events differently than you do. If you like their recommendations, keep them. If you do not, then honor your own memory and instincts in developing the story.

Bringing the Past to Life: An Authentic Voice

Rex Ellis is a storyteller. He is also Vice-President for the Historic Area at the Colonial Williamsburg Foundation in Williamsburg, Virginia. Throughout his adult life, he has intertwined storytelling and museum work to both educate and delight his listeners.

Rex grew up in Surry County, Virginia, and when he was a year old, his family moved to Williamsburg, home of Colonial Williamsburg, the world's largest living history museum. The museum loomed large in the lives of his family and friends, many of whom worked there. Of his early years near the museum he says:

Ironically, I never knew or even suspected that Colonial Williamsburg's significance had anything to do with me as an African American. To those of us who lived in the black community during the 'fifties and 'sixties, it was simply a place to work; it was our McDonalds; our Pizza

Hut. It was where you worked during the summer or after school to earn extra money. The significance of it as a place to visit was never even talked about, except by a few well-meaning teachers, who were careful not to mention that it was the capital of a slave-holding colony. http://www.weyanoke.org/6ellis.html

But the museum exacted a toll of shame on the African-Americans who worked there. Rex says that he was a full time employee at Colonial Williamsburg before he identified the source of that feeling: slavery. Williamsburg had flourished in colonial times because his ancestors had been slaves, and yet slavery was rarely, if ever, mentioned at the museum. There were black re-enactors, but they talked about the jobs they did, how they cooked, cleaned, or made candles, but not about the experience of slavery.

That began to change in the late 1970's, when a new vice-president at Colonial Williamsburg began to push for the inclusion of the slave's experiences. Rex was hired as a re-enactor and that began his career in museum education and also his career as a storyteller.

What brought me to storytelling was Colonial Williamsburg. When I began working here in 1979 part-time, I began with a desire to mention the unmentionable: slavery. I wanted to open up a door that the black and white community wanted to remain closed. And that was the story of colonial slavery. I learned very early on that if I wanted to persuade employees to discuss such a controversial topic, as well as, discuss it openly with visitors myself, I'd better do it in a way that humanized what history had dehumanized. There is no better way of humanizing people than by telling others their story.

And so, rather than talking about facts, figures, and statistics, I try to humanize people from the past and provide audiences with stories about actual people. So I talk to them about Betty Wallace. I talk to them about Sukey Hamilton and London Briggs. I talk to them about the people we know existed, and I give them the story of their lives. As much as I can, as much as we know the story of their lives. Those stories became so popular that it was not hard for me to then suggest a program of storytelling that introduced audiences to a variety of colonial characters, enslaved and free.

Somebody got wind of that at a place called Jonesborough, Tennessee. And in 1989, I was called by a man who was responsible for the storytelling renewal that took place in the mid seventies by the name of Jimmy Neil Smith. He called and said, "I hear that you use stories to teach history. Could you come to a conference we're going to have?" I came to the conference, shared a few stories with them, talked with them, and did a workshop on storytelling and teaching history. As a result they invited me to come to the National Storytelling Festival as a featured teller at Jonesborough, Tennessee. That was back in 1989. From that point to this, it has been a part of not only my life, but also my work here at Colonial Williamsburg. (adapted from http://www.history.org/media/podcasts_transcripts/StorytellingFestival.cfm)

Since then, Rex has been featured at festivals around the country as well as internationally. He has served as the president of the board of the National Storytelling Network, and received their highest honor, The Circle of Excellence Award in 2001. In 2005, he started an annual storytelling festival at Colonial Williamsburg. Through it all, he has dedicated himself to opening doors and building bridges with story. His often repeated quote, "It's hard to hate someone whose story you know," goes to the heart of the importance of storytelling. Rex writes about his intentions:

Throughout my years, I have tried to use my skills to tell and teach others about culture. I also have wanted not to just tell but also to help others realize how important we are to one another, that we sink or swim together. I have tried to suggest that there is more to African American history than meets the eye. Storytelling has given me the forum to do just that. It has allowed me to combine my interests in history, the performing arts, and education. (From *Beneath the Blazing Sun: Stories from the African-American Journey* by Rex Ellis)

The Stories:

The Boy by Michelle Mostaghim

I am going to tell you a story about a boy who through adversity found the strength to become the man he is today.

Born in Lake Wales, Florida in 1982, the boy was the first son of Carrie and Hazell. Even though Lake Wales is just an hour drive from Disney World, it seemed like a whole other planet. Things moved very slowly in this small town. The best thing that happened to this family in a long time was the birth of the baby boy. When the boy was a tall lanky six year old, the family welcomed another son.

Money was scarce and tensions were high in this once happy household. Carrie and Hazell decided to end their marriage. The young boy was bounced from his mom's house to his dad's house, never having a permanent home.

When the boy turned twelve, his dad suddenly died from a heart attack. His mom found it hard to provide for him and his brother, which resulted in her spending time in and out of prison. There were no other relatives, and the boys were all alone with no place to live. Because they had no home, the boy and his brother drifted from one neighbor's house to another.

As an outlet to cope with everything going on in his life, the boy decided to start playing football and baseball. At the age of fourteen, a local cop told the boy to play basketball because that was the best way to get into college. The boy thought about it and then decided he would go for it.

The boy attended many different schools, until at sixteen he ended up at Cypress High School, where he played basketball for two years. Standing 6' 6" by that time, he learned to do a mean jump-shot and was named MVP.

Word soon spread about how well the boy played, especially since he had never had any formal training. The television show *Real Sports* came to his high school to do an interview with him. He knew that he would have to share his past with everyone, so after thinking about it, he decided to go for it. He knew it would show off his basketball skills and highlight what he had achieved.

The once lanky young boy who struggled with the loss of his father, the pain of not having his mother around, the loneliness of having no home, and having to switch from school to school, finally graduated from Cypress Creek High School.

The *Real Sports* show was a success and viewed by many people. In the year 2002 at the age of 19, the boy was the second youngest player to be drafted by the NBA. He now stands 6' 10", wears an orange and purple jersey for the Phoenix Suns and goes by the name AMARE STOUDEMIRE.

© 2008 Michelle Mostaghim

The author was a student in The Art of Storytelling at South Mountain Community College in 2007.

Phillis Wheatley (1753 – 1784) by LynnAnn Wojciechowicz

"Going once, going twice, sold for $68,500 to the book dealer in the back of the room."

On Friday, May 29, 1998, a creased and yellowing three-page hand-written manuscript of a 70-line poem entitled "Ocean," written by Phillis Wheatley, fetched significantly more than its estimate of $18,000 to $25,000 at Christie's auction house in New York City.

Who was Phillis Wheatley, and why would a manuscript of one of her poems now be worth $68,500?

"Going once... going twice... an eight year-old female from Senegal, sold to Merchant John Wheatley."

The year was 1761, and the place was the Boston slave market. John Wheatley and his wife Susannah had come looking for a young girl who could be trained as a personal servant for Susannah, to help her as she grew older.

There were other more robust, healthy looking girls for sale that day, but something about the slender half-naked girl trembling on the auction platform attracted Susannah. "That one," she told her husband.

Susannah named her Phillis and put her eighteen-year-old daughter, Mary, in charge of teaching Phillis enough English to understand instructions and carry out household chores. Phillis caught on so quickly that Mary was soon teaching her to read and write.

In sixteen months, Phillis was a skilled writer, and she could read and understand the most complex sections of the Bible, along with the works of three English poets—Milton, Pope, and Gray. By the age of twelve, Phillis had mastered grammar, mathematics, history, astronomy, and enough Greek and Latin to read the classics. At thirteen she wrote her first poem.

The Wheatleys recognized Phillis' literary gifts, intelligence, and piety, and decided to nurture her genius. Susannah considered Phillis her protégée and kept her by her side, introducing Phillis to noted colonists and dignitaries, including clergymen and intellectuals.

In 1770, at the age of sixteen, Phillis was received as a member of the congregation worshipping in the Old South Meeting House. Phillis' poetry reflects the depths of her religious beliefs:

On Being Brought from Africa to America
'Twas mercy brought me from my Pagan land,
Taught my benighted soul to understand
That there's a God, that there's a Saviour too:
Once I redemption neither sought nor knew.
Some view our sable race with scornful eye
"Their colour is a diabolic die."
Remember, Christians, Negroes, black as Cain,
May be refin'd, and join th'angelic train. (1773)

At the age of nineteen, Phillis took an ocean cruise to England with the Wheatley's son Nathanial, in the hopes that this would improve her poor health. She was well received in England, and she was presented to many members of the nobility. While in London, Lady Huntingdon supervised the publishing of thirty-nine of Phillis' poems in a book entitled, *Poems on Various Subjects, Religious and Moral,* the first book to be published by an American black slave. At that time, women who were published usually used male pseudonyms. Phillis published under her own name – highly unusual among the few women writers of the time.

Because the publisher feared readers might not believe that a teenaged black slave could have written the poems in the book, he had eighteen Boston dignitaries sign a statement attesting to their belief that Phillis did indeed write the poems. Among the signers were the Governor of the Colony of Massachusetts, the Lieutenant Governor, seven ministers, three lawyers (including John Hancock), and her master, John Wheatley.

In 1776, after George Washington had been appointed General of the Armies of North America, Phillis sent him a letter of congratulation and a poem entitled "First in Peace," predicting that Washington would free the colonists from English tyranny and bring peace:

> *Proceed, great chief, with virtue on thy side,*
> *Thy ev'ry action let the goddess guide.*
> *A crown, a mansion, and a throne that shine,*
> *With gold unfading, WASHINGTON! Be thine.*

Washington was so impressed that he took the time to meet her when he was in Boston. Unfortunately, the deaths of the Wheatley family members and the Revolutionary War caused serious problems for Phillis. John Wheatley freed Phillis in his will when he died in 1778, but she had nowhere to go and no means of support. She married a black businessman named John Peters, but his grocery store failed soon after their marriage. During the war, Peters took Phillis to the little village of Wilmington outside of Boston, but they struggled even more there. In the course of these years, Phillis had three children who inherited her frail health.

When the British troops left, Phillis moved back to Boston with her children. She moved in with a widowed niece of Mrs. Wheatley and tried to get a manuscript of thirty-three poems published, but with no success. After six weeks, Peters came and took his family to a small apartment. Shortly thereafter, two of her children had died dead, and the third was gravely ill. Phillis Wheatley died; she and her third child were buried in a pauper's grave on December 5, 1784. She was thirty-one.

Phillis Wheatley was a remarkable woman who loved freedom in all its forms, and who felt most free in the Wheatley home and in the Christian church.

We remember her today as the first African American woman poet, an inspiring example of the triumph of human capacities over the circumstances of birth.

> *Should you, my lord, while you peruse my song,*
> *Wonder from Whence my love of Freedom sprung,*
> *Whence flow these wishes for the common good,*
> *By feeling, fears alone best understood,*
> *I, young in life, by seeming cruel fate*
> *Was snatched from Africa's fancy'd happy seat . . . .*
> *Such, such my case. And can I but pray*
> *Others may never feel tyrannics way*

"Going once... going twice...s old for $68,500 to the book dealer in the back of the room."

Wouldn't Phillis Wheatley be surprised to know that a manuscript of a 70-line poem she wrote in 1773 sold for $68,500 in 1998, 225 years later!

© 2008 LynnAnn Wojciechowicz

Escaping Pancho Villa by Liz Warren

My grandmother, Violet Milliken, was born in 1900 at her family's mining claim in Walker, Arizona, twenty miles south of Prescott, deep in the Bradshaw Mountains of Arizona. When she was ten years old, her father was hired to run a big copper mine in Mexico. He moved the family, including Violet, her mother, and her baby brother Charles, to Cananea, south of present day Douglas on Arizona's border, and he took charge of the mine there.

Now, this was at the time that Pancho Villa, the notorious Mexican bandit – or freedom-fighter, depending on your point of view – was active in the area. One day, as my grandmother told us many times, Pancho Villa walked into her father's office. I imagine Pancho Villa wearing a large sombrero, with a long moustache trailing down the sides of his mouth, and with his broad chest crisscrossed by bandoliers of bullets.

Pancho Villa walked right up to the broad desk, placed his hands on the edge and leaned menacingly toward James Milliken. He said, in Spanish, "I don't need to kill you. I don't even particularly want to kill you, but that is exactly what I will do if you and your family are not out of Cananea in 48 hours." Then he turned and left the room.

James knew Pancho Villa was not kidding. He and his wife Lucy planned to leave Mexico immediately. The best and fastest way to leave Cananea was to take the train to Nogales, and then get another train back up to Prescott. Lucy and the children would leave the next morning, and he would follow the day after. The only problem was that the train from Cananea to Nogales was routinely robbed. It was entirely likely that if Lucy was carrying any money or valuables, she would be robbed. That would leave her with no way to buy the tickets to get from Nogales back to Prescott.

This is what Lucy came up with. She had beautiful, long, thick, auburn hair which she wore up on her head. She took down her hair, took off her gold wedding band, and threaded it on a piece of her hair behind and above her ear until it nestled against her scalp. Then she arranged her hair so that the ring was completely hidden.

She and her two children, Violet and Charles, boarded the train and headed for Nogales. The train was stopped by robbers. When they got to Lucy, they insisted that she empty her purse and turn out her pockets, but there was nothing for them to take and they moved on.

When they arrived in Nogales, Lucy and her children went to a pawn shop. She took down her hair, slipped the ring from its auburn safe and hawked it. She then bought the tickets that would take her and the children back to the comfort and safety of their home in Prescott.

The next day, James got on the train to Nogales. I don't know where or how he hid his money or his valuables. I never thought to ask all those times I heard the story as a child and now my grandmother is gone. But he hid it somewhere because when he got to Nogales, he went to the pawn shop and bought the ring back. Then he made his own way home to his wife and family.

When I was younger, I loved to imagine what that reunion might have been like. Those were dangerous times. Lucy had to wonder if she would ever see James again. I had a romantic idea of him throwing open the door to their house, swooping her into his arms, and placing her wedding ring back on her finger.

The truth, regrettably, was nothing like that. This incident, escaping Pancho Villa with her two small children on a train beset by robbers, was the beginning of the end of the marriage. Within the year, Lucy had left with her young son Charles to begin a new life in Los Angeles.

Violet was left in the keeping of her paternal grandparents because her father was too devastated to care for her. The loss of her beloved brother and her mother's abandonment, dealt Violet a blow from which she never fully recovered.

Somehow though, my grandmother Violet ended up in possession of that wedding ring, and today I have both the ring and the story.

The Haunted Cuckoo Clock, a True Story by Shean R. Howlett

My mother, father and sister were living in England when I was born. My father was gone for long periods of time because he was an Air Force pilot. So my mother would travel and she acquired a taste for antiques. She got them from all over Europe, but mostly London and Germany.

We moved to Gilbert, Arizona, after my father died in 1991. My mother brought all her antiques with her. One of these antiques was a very nice late 1800's cuckoo clock. It was beautiful but it didn't work.

My mother wanted the clock to be restored, so she took it to a clock smith who lived in the greater Phoenix area. His workshop was his living room. I was about five at the time and it seemed to me that he had hundreds of clocks. There were clocks everywhere, including cuckoo clocks on every wall and tons more hanging from the ceiling. He had giant grandfather clocks in every corner. His house looked like the cluttered workshop of Merlin the Magician from the cartoon movie *The Sword in the Stone*.

We left the cuckoo clock with the clock smith for a while and then went back to pick it up. The clock smith said he was unable to fix it. He had taken it apart and fixed all the little gears and polished it up nicely, but he was still unable to do anything to get it to work. We brought it home with us and set it on my mother's antique buffet. At times we would fiddle with the clock, trying to make it work by sheer force of will – and maybe a little physical abuse – when mom was not around.

It was about this time that the trouble began. Everyone in the house began to have horrible nightmares. We were all dreaming all kinds of terrifying events, such as people dying and monsters looming. In one, I was even a girl! A most horrifying experience for a five year old boy!

Every morning we gathered in the kitchen to talk about our nightmares. We could not figure out why we were all having them. This went on for quite a while and we were all very tired of them. One day, all of us were in the family room where the clock sat on the buffet. We were all just talking and blabbing. While we were sitting on the floor, we started playing with the cuckoo clock again. My sister was fidgeting with it but as usual it wouldn't work and in disgust she put it back on the buffet. She didn't think about it, but she set it down backwards, so that it was facing the mirror of the buffet.

We began talking again, but something stopped us. We heard this tick, tick, tick, tick. We looked at the cuckoo clock and in the mirror we saw the second hand of the clock moving. It was working! My mom picked it up and it stopped. She set it back down the right way on the buffet, facing the room, but no sound, no movement. Together we puzzled at it. My sister grabbed the clock and spun it around towards the mirror and it went tick, tick, tick, tick.

Right then it clicked. We knew where the nightmares had come from. The cuckoo clock was haunted! My mom picked it up again and tried it in front of all the mirrors in the house. Each time, it only worked when it saw itself in the mirror.

My mom got on the phone and put an ad out in the local paper to find a buyer for it. Shortly after the ad appeared, a couple came to see the clock. They immediately fell in love with it. My mom sold it to them, they left, and we never heard from them again. After that, the nightmares stopped for all of us. From then on, Mom was a lot more careful about the antiques she bought. Never again did we buy an antique cuckoo clock, and every time we did see one, we walked away.

The author was a student in The Art of Storytelling in 2008.

7

How to Tell a Personal Story

"If I had had to tell a story about myself as my first story, I probably would have dropped the class. When we got to that story, I felt OK about it, though. I knew the other people in my class by then and telling the other stories helped, too. Actually, now whenever I listen to somebody else tell a story, it always makes me think of one of my own." (Storytelling Student Spring 2003)

What is a personal story?

A personal story is an autobiographical narrative, a story from your life and experience. It may be a funny story, or a story about learning something important, experiencing something unique and marvelous, surviving a great challenge, or making a transition from one stage of life to another.

When faced with telling a personal story, many people say, "Nothing interesting has ever happened to me! I have nothing to tell about." We are, however, united through the seemingly ordinary events and circumstances of our lives. The best personal stories reveal something of the universal human condition while being grounded in the particular details of one life. That is why almost anyone can tell a personal story. You don't have to be a hero or a star to tell an effective personal story – just human. And most of us, as humans, have plenty of experiences with accidents, failures, foibles, disobedience, misunderstandings, and hard-won successes – all of which are the ideal fodder for personal stories.

Personal stories are important because they allow us to revel in our common humanity from an entirely unique perspective – the point of view of the individual storyteller. When we listen to a personal story, we recognize the similarities in the human condition that transcend the barriers of human life. Storyteller Rex Ellis says that it is hard to hate someone whose story you know. This may be the most important reason to both tell and listen to stories. By telling stories we can learn to relate to each other with more understanding and compassion. Storytelling is a path to peace.

How do I move from memory and anecdote to story?

There is one thing beyond being human that is necessary to tell a personal story. As with fact-based stories, personal stories require a structure to contain the memory or life experience. Our memories and life experiences don't often come with a ready-to-tell story shape. Usually when we tell other people about something that has happened to us, we are telling anecdotes. An anecdote is a short account of an incident. For example, here is an anecdote from my life:

> Last November, my husband Mark and I were driving between Pine and Camp Verde on an icy road during a snow storm. I lost control of the car and we began sliding all over the road. I said to my husband, "What are we going to do?" Just at that moment, we went off the road, up a steep embankment, plowed through some pine saplings, and came to a stop with the left front wheel hanging off the edge of the embankment – all of which took about two seconds. Mark then said, "We're going to crash!"

Now, this is a good anecdote and I told it several times when telling about the wreck. I thought my husband's response was funny, and it allowed me to talk about the accident without dealing with the panic of it. But even though it is a good anecdote, it is not a story because it doesn't reveal what changed as a result of the incident. This is the key difference between a story and an anecdote. Anecdotes relate an event; stories place the same event in a larger context of meaning.

To turn this anecdote into a story, I would first have to decide what it means to me. I would need to determine what it reveals about my relationship to my husband, and how it fits into the broader pattern of my life. Maybe I would include how my husband is known as Mr. Literal for statements like, "We're going to crash." Or maybe I would make a frame to tell about how thankful we were not to be hurt and what this taught us about being grateful for every moment of life. Or maybe I would stick to the mundane and tell about how I realized that my tires were old, that I had neglected their maintenance, and vowed that I would never do anything so irresponsible again. Here's a story made from the same anecdote:

> Once, my husband Mark and I went up to Pine for the annual Tellabration storytelling concert where I would tell and he would take photographs. We'd both been busy the week before and we were tired and crabby with each other. The morning after the concert, I was annoyed with him because he didn't get out of bed to help me make breakfast for our hosts and the other guests. When we got in the car to leave, the air inside the car was as frosty as it was outside.
>
> Instead of going straight home to Phoenix, we had decided to go from Pine to Camp Verde to visit my aunt and uncle. The road between Pine and Camp Verde goes over the Mogollon Rim. It was already spitting snow in Pine, and when we got to the top of the rim, the road was icy and the snow was swirling in the air. I could feel my tires slipping on the road. I said to Mark, "I'd better slow down."
>
> I just touched the brake and the car began spinning and careening all over the road – completely out of my control. On the verge of panic, I said to my husband, "What are we going to do?" Just at that moment, we went off the road, up a steep embankment, plowed through some pine saplings, and came to a stop with the left front wheel hanging off the edge of the embankment – all of which took about two seconds. Mark then said, "We're going to crash!"
>
> There we sat, neither of us hurt, and I couldn't help but laugh! That was vintage Mark – to calmly state the obvious even in a crisis. No wonder he's known amongst our friends as Mr. Literal! We called AAA, and it didn't take long for them to get us off the embankment. The tow truck driver commented that the tread on my tires was very shallow, "Tread that worn is probably why you slipped off the road." I felt my heart sink to realize that I hadn't given the smallest thought to my tires before we left Phoenix. Fortunately, the car was drivable, and after stopping at my aunt and uncle's to calm our nerves, we drove home.

All our crabbiness with each other had completely evaporated. I felt engulfed in a glow of gratitude – both for my husband and for our safety. To survive a serious accident without a scratch surely gives perspective on what is important in life. It made my petty marital annoyances seem even more microscopic and irrelevant.

Well, the car was in the body shop for over a month. The first thing I did when I got it back was get a new set of tires. And now when we leave town I check my tires, *and* I check my attitude.

One of the first things you probably noticed about the story that I made from my anecdote is that it is longer; it has more details, more dialogue, and most importantly, it has been placed in a context of meaning. These are all natural consequences of crafting an anecdote into a story, and ideally result in something that will be more enjoyable to tell and to hear.

Providing Structure to an anecdote: The story structure rubric developed by Donald Davis discussed in the previous chapter is called "The 5 Ps." Donald says that to make a **P**icture in someone's head with your story you must tell the **P**eople, **P**lace, **P**roblem, and **P**rogress. LynnAnn Wojciechowicz added another 'P' for **P**oint. An anecdote usually focuses on the **P**roblem, whereas to be satisfying, a story must have all the elements. Let's apply it to my story:

- **The People:** my husband and me.
- **The Place:** on the road between Pine and Camp Verde on a snowy day.
- **The Problem:** quarreling with my husband, losing control of the car and crashing.
- **The Progress:** neither of us got hurt, we got rescued, I learned about my tires, and got a new perspective on what is important.
- **The Point** – I learned to remember gratitude for my husband and to keep up the maintenance on my car.

Another formula that Donald Davis devised is Character, Crisis, Discovery, and Lesson Learned. Applying these steps to my story yields a slightly different result:

- **Character:** Liz; the story is really about me.
- **Crisis:** crashing on an icy road.
- **Discovery:** I discovered that my grievances with my husband weren't really important and that my tires were almost shot.
- **Lesson learned:** It's all about the 'attitude of gratitude'.

Another easy way to move from an experience to a story is to add a phrase like, "From that day on. . . ." Then add what changed as a result of the experience. Other phrases to play with are:

- After that I never . . .
- After that I always . . .
- That experience taught me a big lesson . . .
- I learned . . .

As the story grows and develops, you may not want or need to use a formulaic phrase to convey what growth or change resulted from the experience. Or you may find that it is just the ticket to help you frame a story from an anecdote. Here is an example to consider. Several years ago, a student in

The Art of Storytelling wanted to tell about a time when she was learning to ride her bike. This is a brief retelling of her story:

> When I was five years old I was learning to ride a two-wheeled bike. My brother still had to run along beside me to keep me steady, but I was proud of my progress. One day my mother said that our relatives were coming over for a barbecue. I said, "I'm going to show everyone how I can ride my bike by myself."
>
> My mother said, "You are not really ready to ride that bike by yourself. I don't want you on that bike while our company is here."
>
> But I ignored her. Once everyone had arrived, I got on the bike. I started down the driveway, but I lost my balance and crashed into the rose bushes.
>
> I was scratched up and bleeding, but my mother wouldn't help me! She said, "I told you not to ride that bike."
>
> My brother felt sorry for me and he came and helped me out of the bushes.

Now this is clearly an anecdote, and one that gives us very clear images. We have the picture, people, place, and the problem, but no progress or point. We need to know what happened next. I asked her to add "From that day on . . ."

She then told the same story. We had been expecting her to say, "From that day on, I always listened to my mother." But she didn't say that. After her brother had helped her out of the bushes, she surprised us by adding, "From that day on, whenever I was really in trouble and needed help, I always went to my brother!" An even more effective ending because it was unexpected.

This is a good example of the unique perspective that each person brings to a story. The same basic incident, crashing a bike or disobeying a parent, will result in a completely different story and a distinct experience for the listeners. It's also a good reminder never to discount our own experiences, or our responses to them, no matter how small they may seem.

What should I do if I can't think of any stories about myself?

Review the box on the next page which includes some story prompts from Donald Davis. Here are some additional story prompts to consider as you are trying to decide what to tell:

- Think about the firsts in your life – first bike, first day at school, first car, first crush, first kiss, first job, first time sky-diving.

- Think about the people you have known – who are the memorable people in your life? Who are the troublemakers? Who are the angels?

- Think about the places you know – where did you grow up? Where did your grandparents live? What was it like there?

- Think about your scars, physical and otherwise – how did you get them? What did you learn as a result?

- Think about the transition points in your life – as you went from childhood to adulthood, graduation, moving to your own place, finding your career, finding a mate, or the loss of important family members.

- Look at old photographs of yourself and your family – what is the 'back story' of the image? What is going on that the photograph does not show?

- Ask your family members for their favorite memory or story about you.
- Think about holidays at your house – what were your family traditions? What are they now?

Foundations of Excellence

Through their own deep connections to the stories they tell, top-notch professional storytellers have the capacity to create vivid characters and intense sensory impressions for their listeners. They see and know their characters. They feel their stories with clarity and intensity, and therefore, so do their listeners. They can make our skin crawl and our mouth salivate. They can make us feel as if we would recognize their Aunt Emily on the street.

Personal stories are the perfect place to begin to experiment with characterization and building in sensory details because we are grounded in the people, experiences, and environments about which we speak. We don't include every detail we know about a person in our stories, but they should be clear to us as we relate the story. What should be known about a character includes:

- Gender, age, race, and ethnicity.
- Overall build, hair and eye color, posture and carriage.
- Orientation to life. Is the character an introvert or an extrovert; optimist or pessimist; quick or slow to anger; loving or distant; a trickster or a sage?
- Relationship to the teller and function in the story.

Once the person is established in a teller's own mind, it becomes easier to experiment with how to convey the character to listeners. Not all of the features of a character will be relevant to the story being told, so details must be chosen that serve the story. Then, with the essential features of the character in mind, the teller can describe a character verbally, as well as show the character to the audience using body and gestures.

Creating sensory impressions is another aspect of excellence, one that has great power to engage listeners. We must be aware of the places in the story that call on the senses, in order to integrate their expression into the telling:

A useful resource for story prompts is *Telling Your Own Stories for Family and Classroom Storytelling, Public Speaking, and Personal Journaling,* by Donald Davis. Here are a few gems from his book:

- Can you remember a time when you got a gift or a compliment which you did not at all deserve?
- Can you remember a night your parents never found out about?
- Can you remember a time when you got into trouble for something you had already been told not to do?
- Can you remember a time when you got sick at a very inconvenient moment?
- Can you remember a time when your first impression of someone turned out to be completely wrong?
- Can you remember a problem with a haircut? Makeup? An article of clothing?
- Can you remember a time when you almost won, but not quite?
- Take us on a visit to your childhood doctor's office.
- Can you remember the first person you ever had a crush on?

- **Sight:** What must listeners "see" to appreciate the story? What sizes, colors, shapes, and locations are crucial to the story? What does an Arizona sunset look like? How about the dappled shade under a eucalyptus tree?

107

As you develop your personal stories, as well as stories from other genres, make it a habit to integrate well-developed characters and sensory information. You will see the results in your listeners' reactions to you and your stories.

- **Sound:** What are the sounds of the story? What do the characters hear, and how do they sound when they speak? How does an angry child with laryngitis sound? How about the sound of a loaded suitcase hitting the ground and splitting open?

- **Touch:** What textures and temperatures must the listeners know about? What are the characters' tactile experiences? How does a homemade burlap shirt feel? How does it feel to be stuck in a downpour?

- **Taste:** What is being eaten and drunk in the story? What does lemonade taste like without sugar? How about fresh baked bread with melted butter?

- **Smell:** What fragrances occur in the story? Are there flowers, food, or perfume, and will knowing their distinct odors enhance our experience of the story? What does a freshly baked apple pie smell like? How about a dead fish?

Excellence and Ethics: The crafting and telling of personal stories present ethical issues that may not arise with other types of stories. Below are some considerations:

Do I have to tell the story exactly as it happened or can I change it a little? The obligation of the storyteller is to tell the best story possible. That often means that the facts may have to be altered slightly in service to the effectiveness of the story. Read the profile of Donald Davis for his thoughts on bridging non-fiction and fiction in personal stories.

The Fourth "D"

"I did not realize how much of my real self I would have to be putting into my storytelling. For me, the three D's (Delight, Desire, and Delivery) need a fourth D, and that is Disclosure, because I will have to communicate to the audience certain things about myself that I normally wouldn't." (Storytelling Student, Spring 2007)

Whenever you stand up to tell a story, your listeners learn about you. Even when you tell a folktale, myth, legend, or a story based in fact, the story you choose, how you craft it, and how you tell it reveals something about you. Of course, when you tell a personal story, the content of the story is about you. But this does not mean that you have to tell your deepest, darkest secret, or something that is intimate or private. A small incident from your life that has stuck with you for some reason is often the best choice. It could be an event that made you laugh, touched your heart, or from which you learned something. Sharing an everyday experience is a very effective way to connect with listeners.

If you want to tell an important, pivotal story from your life, consider using the hero's journey structure from the "How to Tell a Myth, Legend, or Hero Tale" chapter. The structure of a hero's journey story takes you from the "Call to Adventure", through "The Road of Trials", "The Atonement", and back to "The Freedom to Live." It is the narrative structure of the rites of passage we all endure. As such, it can be especially useful in crafting stories that represent major transition points in our lives.

How do I deal with the emotions the story brings up? Stories are meant to convey and evoke images and emotions, so it is to be expected that they will surface when crafting and telling a story. The emotions bring power to the experience, and as the teller feels them, so will the audience. The emotions should be worked through completely before telling the story. This is more serious when the emotions are sadness or fear, because if the teller begins to cry or lose control in the middle of the story the listeners will become distressed and worried, and will no longer be in the story. The result will be the same if the teller is laughing and falls out of the story. The teller has the obligation to be in charge of the story and its emotions so listeners feel safe.

What if people laugh at me? What if *they* start to cry? Personal stories do tend to have lots of potential for humor. If a story is funny, the audience will laugh. But, as my dad used to say, "They aren't laughing *at* you – they're laughing *with* you." Don't worry. It feels great to make people laugh. But the response of the listeners must not throw you out of the story.

Similarly, if the story is sad, listeners are going to respond to that as well. It's positive for people to experience the emotion of a story. The important thing is for the teller to have a handle on the emotions and to bring the story to its resolved conclusion. That way the audience is secure on the journey of the story.

What about the other people in my story? Is it okay to talk about them? As with fact-based stories, when a personal story includes living people it is simple courtesy to ask their permission. When I am preparing a story that I am going to tell in public, and it includes characters who are my friends or relatives, I always ask their permission. If the story is written out, I send them a copy to review. If it isn't written, I tell them about it to get their approval. I've never had anyone deny permission, although sometimes people correct inaccuracies or provide more details.

Once when I was learning to be a storyteller, I took a workshop from a master storyteller at the national storytelling conference. One of the participants got up to tell a story that was difficult to tell and difficult to hear. About half way through the story, the teller burst into tears and had to sit down. The rest of us were confused. We didn't know what to do. Should we comfort the teller? Should we go on to the next person? What were we to do about our own feelings and questions about the story?

Later the workshop leader told us that when a storyteller stands up to tell a story, he or she is just like the driver of a bus and the listeners are the passengers. She told us that abandoning a story, especially an emotionally challenging one, in the middle of the telling was just like driving the bus over the cliff. The story crashes and so do the listeners. She said that our primary responsibility was to make sure that the story and the listeners all finish up in one piece. That is why it is important to take the time to craft personal stories, to work through the emotions they evoke, and to rehearse them with trusted colleagues before telling them to other people. Given that, storytellers must always be mindful of what is appropriate for any given audience. There is some material that is simply not appropriate for telling in public and no amount of crafting and rehearsal will make it so – whether the emotions have been worked through or not.

The storyteller must remain in control of emotions during a telling. Sometimes the emotions become manageable in the process of crafting and rehearsing. Sometimes they don't. If you don't think you can remain in control of your emotions while you tell your story, you should choose another. It doesn't mean you have to reject the story permanently; just set it aside and continue to work on it until you can tell it and remain in charge.

People are usually pleased to be included in a story. On the other hand, if you have sought permission from someone to include him or her in a personal story and that permission was not granted, the denial for "permission to use" must be honored. "No" means "no."

If the story you are going to tell is primarily about you and other people have small roles, and those roles are flattering or neutral, you usually don't have to get permission. If there is a person in your story who has a big role, or who might not want you to talk about the incident, you should discuss it with him or her first. If you are telling a story in which a living person is the villain or the heavy, you might want to use a different name, or alter the particulars of the character to reduce the risk of recognition.

This is not to say that permission is necessary to tell your version of a story. Family members and friends will always have different versions of the same story. Sometimes valuable details can be gathered from their versions, but if not, just go ahead and tell it your way. As long as your relatives and friends are not portrayed in a way that could give offense to them, you are within your rights as the teller of the story.

Telling Your Story

One of the most rewarding things about taking the time to find and develop a personal story is the telling of it. When a story is ready, it's time to share it with trusted family and friends. After you tell, you may hear other stories about yourself from them, and you will probably hear stories from their lives. Developing personal stories helps us to deepen our understanding of the events in our own lives. Telling them allows us to communicate who we are to others. Community is built and sustained when we understand ourselves, communicate that understanding with others, and then listen to them in return. Tell your story and witness the connective tissue of your life become stronger and more satisfying.

Personal Stories: Two Masters

The job of the storyteller has always been to entertain and inform by telling the stories that carried the collective wisdom and experience of the people. But what is a storyteller supposed to tell if he or she lives in a culture where there is no collective set of stories, no single canon of wisdom that is shared by all the people? This is the problem that storytellers face in our country and a big part of why so many modern storytellers have turned to telling personal and family stories. In a large, multicultural society like ours, the common ground is found in the experience of being human, in the stories of negotiating life that simultaneously underpin and transcend culture and heritage. The artists profiled below are just two of the many modern storytellers who have mastered the form.

 **Michael Lacapa** was of Hopi, Tewa, and Apache heritage and lived most of his life in north-eastern Arizona. His first passion was for art, specifically drawing and painting. After college, he became a high school teacher and then worked for the Apache Tribe to develop multicultural curricula for native children. Storytelling was a tool for this process which led to the opportunity for his first children's book. By the end of his life, Michael was renowned as a storyteller and as an author/illustrator.

Michael told stories, especially coyote stores, from his traditions with matchless energy, delight, humor, and verve. He also told personal and family stories, each one crafted like a small jewel. He was a master at using folktale elements like repetition in his personal and family stories. In one of his stories, he talks about mornings at his grandmother's house with each tender vignette punctuated by the refrain, "Because you see, she wasn't like other people." By the end of the story the listener learns that his grandmother was blind, which recasts the story in a new light.

Michael's personal stories were based on the small details of everyday life. He told about the trauma of having the principal at his elementary school personally deliver a note to his desk. He told about walking home from school and riding in a truck. He told with tongue in cheek about the awe and wonder the opening of a giant can of spam could evoke in his relatives.

Michael subtly educated his listeners about Native American family, culture, and values by hooking them with common and often humorous experiences. In one moment Michael could make his listeners laugh like crazy, in the next he could bring them to tears, all with "small," carefully observed and poignantly told stories.

 **Donald Davis** was born and raised on land in western North Carolina inhabited by his family since 1781. He grew up hearing his grandmother's Welsh and Scottish folktales and hearing his Uncle Frank's stories of the adventures of daily life. He says, "I didn't learn stories, I just absorbed them" (http://www.ddavis-storyteller.com). After college, divinity school, and twenty years serving as a United Methodist minister, Donald became a full time storyteller. He travels from his home on Ocracoke Island off the coast of North Carolina for ten out of twelve months, giving over 300 performances and presentations a year. Featured annually at the National Storytelling Festival in Jonesborough, Tennessee, Donald is the best known storyteller currently working in our country.

With his depth of understanding of storytelling and his masterful ability to teach what he knows with great efficiency and effectiveness, Donald is highly valued as a teacher of both new and seasoned storytellers. You have already encountered him through his story structure rubrics included in this chapter and the previous one.

Although he is being profiled in the personal stories chapter, his stories are actually a blend of personal, family, and original stories. He often teaches about the necessity of filling out a memory or an anecdote creatively in a way that makes a complete and satisfying story with its own authenticity and truth, whether it could ultimately be labeled fiction or nonfiction.

What this means is that honestly stepping over into fiction may be the answer to dealing with and handling some of those stories which are either too incomplete in memory or too sensitive in nature to be told straightforwardly as family history.

When we have large gaps in memory or when we want to protect the innocent, this does not necessarily mean that the richness of such material must be either deliberately buried or forever lost. Rather, consider making use of such strong fragments as beginning places or seeds for what we truthfully label as fiction *(Telling Your Own Stories*, p. 26-27).

A Donald Davis story always includes humor. That's because Donald says humor is the way to make an opening through story. "When you make people laugh, it opens their hearts. Then they are ready to experience the other emotions the story may have to offer."

The Stories:

Pie of Peace by Doug Bland

When I was in the fifth grade, I was a pretty good high jumper—for a short kid. Every day at recess we gathered at the high jump pit for practice. This was in the days before foam rubber mats and fiberglass poles. We dug a hole in the ground and filled the hole with sand. Then we put wooden standards up on the front two corners of the pit. Each standard had nails pounded halfway in at one inch intervals all the way up to five feet. A bamboo pole ran from one standard to the other as the high jump crossbar.

Once or twice I earned a blue ribbon in the school track meet. Most of the kids took their winning ribbons home to pin on the bulletin board behind their desk or tape to the wall above their bed. Not me. I was so proud of that ribbon that I pinned it to my favorite t-shirt and wore it to school.

I liked the way the blue ribbon danced on my chest as I approached the high jump bar. My specialty was the western roll. You start on the left foot, right, left, right, gaining speed as you approach the bar. Then plant your left foot and kick your right leg up as high as you can above the crossbar. As you roll over the bar, pull in your chest and watch your trailing leg, or you'll knock the crossbar down every time. That's the western roll!

One day we were out at the high jump pit during recess. I looked up to see a crowd of kids watching us. There, in the front row, was Debbie Talbot—the most beautiful woman in the fifth grade! Then there were two more rows of kids and, towering two heads above everyone else, I could see the massive jowls, the giant crew cut hairdo, the little beady eyes of Glen McManus, the biggest, meanest bully in the school.

I was so intent on impressing Debbie Talbot that, without thinking it through, I put my life in mortal danger. I heard myself yelling, "Hey, McManus, how about you and me have a high jump contest right here, right now!" Then I went up to the high jump standards, took the crossbar off the standard, put it on the ground, and dared him, "You can start here if you want."

An audible gasp of shock erupted from the crowd of kids. They separated like the Red Sea, and, walking through them, came the Pharaoh of the playground, Glen McManus. Glen McManus was not a jumper. He was a thumper. He was a basher. He was a crusher, but he was not a jumper. He lumbered up to me and grabbed me by the blue ribbon. He ripped the ribbon off my chest, leaving a big hole in my t-shirt. Then he said, "I've got a better idea, Bland. Let's see which one of us can bury our heads deepest in the sand pit. You go first!"

With that, he turned me upside down and, like a javelin, he jammed me, headfirst, into the sandpit, burying my head clear up to the shoulders. That was bad, but, even worse, Glen McManus came back the next day, and the next day, and the next day, to challenge me to another bury my head in the sand contest. I kept winning!

I didn't know what to do. Finally, I went to my mother and I said, "Mom, there's this bully at school. He keeps picking on me. And I didn't do anything!"

My mother said, "Oh, Doug, you shouldn't fight."

"Well, it's not really much of a fight," I said. "He just keeps burying my head in the sand."

She said, "It takes a friend to make a friend. You need to be nice to Glen McManus."

112

I tried being nice to Glen McManus. My mother packed me a lunch most days, and, out of the kindness of my heart, and the fear in my soul, I gave Glen McManus my sandwich. And he took my Twinkie too!

I tried smiling at Glen McManus—and it just got sand in my teeth. I tried walking away from Glen McManus. I tried running away from Glen McManus! Nothing worked. He just kept burying my head in the sand.

So, I went to my dad. "Dad, there's this bully at school. He keeps picking on me, and I didn't do nothin'."

"Son," said my dad, "You need to stand up for yourself. You need to fight back!" My dad taught me "The Hammerlock Hold." What you do is wrap your "dominant arm" (that's what he called it, "your dominant arm") around your opponent's neck. Then, using the leverage of your hip, you throw them over your hip and onto the ground. When they hit the ground – wham! – it will knock the wind out of them. If not, when you land on top of them – fomp! – it will knock the wind out of them.

I wasn't too sure about The Hammerlock Hold, so I tried it out on my two best friends. It worked great! The Hammerlock Hold was the thing! I could hardly sleep that night in anticipation of trying out The Hammerlock Hold on Glen McManus.

The next day at recess we were out at the high jump pit when I looked up to see Glen McManus coming my way. I didn't even wait for him to get to the high jump pit. I ran out to meet him. I jumped up on the chest of Glen McManus and wrapped my "dominant arm" around . . . It was about that time that I found out my dominant arm wasn't that dominant. I couldn't even reach all the way around Glen McManus' neck. It was the size of a tree trunk. Pressing on, I tried to throw Glen McManus over my hip and onto the ground. At this point, I learned that in order to throw your opponent to the ground, you've got to have at least one foot on the ground. I wasn't even close. I just sort of dangled there, like a little necklace, around Glen McManus' neck.

The only thing that The Hammerlock Hold did to Glen McManus was make him meaner and madder than ever. This time, instead of turning me upside down and jamming my head into the sandpit as if I was a javelin, he crumpled me up into a ball about the size of a shot-put and shoved me deep into the sand. Then he rolled over the top of me three or four times, just to make sure that I was buried real deep.

Now I was desperate! I really didn't know what to do. Neither my mother's advice—"be nice"— nor my father's advice—"fight back"—had worked. I didn't want to have to go to my grandmother to ask advice for a couple reasons. First, I knew she'd suggest something real dumb. Second, I knew she'd make me tell the whole story. But now, I had no choice.

"Grandma," I said, "There's this bully at school. He keeps pickin' on me, and . . . He just keeps pickin' on me!"

"What did you do to him?" grandma wanted to know.

So I had to tell her the whole story about how I had teased Glen McManus in front of the kids at school in order to try to impress Debbie Talbot.

"Well, in that case," she said, "there's only one thing to do: You need to invite Glen McManus over to my house next Sunday afternoon for a piece of my apple pie."

I tried to spare her feelings. I said, "Grandma, that's the stupidest idea I've ever heard in my life!"

"Oh," she said, "So you think my apple pie is stupid?"

"No Grandma, your apple pie is the best!"

It was. Grandma was famous for her apple pie. The crust was so flaky and light and buttery, that it just melted on your tongue. The apples were always done to perfection, never too crunchy, never too mushy. She made it *a la mode*. That's French. I asked my Grandma what *a la mode* meant and she said that, in English, it means "Doug Bland's Grandma makes the best apple pie in the whole wide world." It was the truth!

Grandma said, "Well good. I'm glad you like my apple pie because the next time you get a bite of my apple pie, it will be with that McManus boy."

I didn't have a choice. I wrote out an invitation and gave it to a friend, who gave it to a friend, who gave it to a friend, who gave to some kid we didn't even know who gave it to Glen McManus and ran. I didn't know whether Glen McManus would show up or not.

But at two o'clock Sunday afternoon there was a knock on the door that rattled the china in the cupboard and made the panes of glass in the windows vibrate. Glen McManus!

Grandma greeted him at the door and showed him into the dining room. She had this big dining table with giant brass claw feet clutching large round glass balls. The table had enough leaves to expand it to about the size of a football field for Thanksgiving and Christmas and other special occasions. Now all the leaves were stored in the closet and there were just three places set. On each plate sat a generous slice of grandma's apple pie, steam rising up in tiny spirals and ice cream melting down to form a creamy sweet puddle on the plate.

We sat down at the table and grandma just started asking Glen McManus questions. I found out things about Glen McManus that I didn't know. I found out that his favorite subject at school was the same as mine: Recess! I found out that his favorite dessert was the same as mine: apple pie *a la mode*. I found out that his mother wasn't home much because she worked two, sometimes three jobs. And his daddy was either dead or in prison. He wasn't sure which.

I started feeling bad about teasing Glen McManus in front of the other kids at school. We finished up our pie, and grandma said, "Well, I guess that will about do it. Doug, why don't you walk Glen to the door."

We got up and I walked about ten paces behind him. At the door, he turned around. I cringed, ducked, and put my hands up to protect myself.

Glen said, "Your grandma makes real good apple pie." Then he turned and was gone.

I thought, "What a waste of time and apple pie this has been!"

Sure enough, next day, at the high jump pit, here came Glen McManus. I just stood at attention, straight as a javelin, waiting for him to bury my head in the sand pit. He looked at me. I looked at him. Then he walked right on by! The same thing happened the next day, and the next day!

I went to my grandma and asked, "What's going on? Glen McManus is not picking on me anymore!"

She said, "It's that apple pie."

"What do you mean," I demanded, "It's that apple pie?"

She said, "Lots of people know how to make a good piece of pie. But I know how to make a 'Pie of Peace'."

"What's a Pie of Peace?"

"Well," she explained, "if two people are mad at each other, but they are willing to sit down at my table long enough to have a piece of my apple pie, generally when they get up from the table, they aren't nearly so mad at each other as when they first sat down. That's why I call it my "Pie of Peace."

I wasn't so sure about this "Pie of Peace" thing. So I tried it out on my two former best friends—the ones on whom I learned The Hammerlock Hold. I invited them over for some of my grandma's "Pie of Peace." It worked great!

Ever since then, I've been telling everyone I know about grandma's "Pie of Peace." And now you know about it too.

© 2008 Doug Bland

The author is a storyteller and pastor at Community Christian Church in Tempe, which hosts a series of annual storytelling events. He teaches storytelling at South Mountain Community College.

Ballerina Eyelashes by Liz Warren

When I was born the universe had an official new center because I was the first grandchild born on either side of my family. I had two grandparents in Miami, Arizona, and another two in Skull Valley, Arizona, and I lived with my Mom and Dad on a dairy farm in Gilbert. By the time I was four years old, I had come to rely on the fact that whatever I wanted for my birthday or for Christmas I would get. So by July of my fourth year I was already telling my parents and grandparents what I wanted for Christmas that year.

I was completely smitten with the idea of being a ballerina and I knew everything that I needed to become one. First, I needed a pink tutu made out of stacks and stacks of pink netting. Then I needed a fairy wand and a jeweled tiara – I had evidently merged the ideas of fairy princess and ballerina. Finally, I needed a pair of those flat pink shoes with the pink ribbons that laced around your ankle and up your leg. Every chance I got I told them all about everything I would need to become a ballerina.

But in November of that year a terrible, terrible thing happened to me. My baby brother was born. I could not believe how much attention one tiny, red, squalling creature could get! There was a new sun in the heavens and I had been displaced.

He was getting all of the attention that was usually given to me. And if you can believe this, he had them all convinced that he could not talk. Whenever I got the chance I'd go over to his crib and grab his little t-shirt, and say, "You may have fooled the rest of them, but not me. I'm your sister and I know you can talk." Then my mother would come in and I'd have to let him go.

Well, eventually I found a way to get some of that attention back for myself. I started pulling out my eyelashes. I went to my mother; I grabbed the eyelashes on my top lid; I pulled my eye lid away from my eyeball and out came an eyelash as my eyelid flapped up against my eyeball.

My mother said "O-o-o-o-o-o-oh – don't do that!"

Then I went to find my father and I repeated the whole thing over again. I grabbed my eyelashes, pulled my eyelid away from my eyeball and out came my eyelash and my eyelid flapped up against my eyeball.

My father said, "Elizabeth Ann Warren you stop that right now!"

Well, some attention is better than no attention. The only problem was that eyelashes are a finite resource and it wasn't too long before it was looking pretty sparse up there on my eyelid.

One day my grandmother, Dora Warren, came to see me and when she saw the state of my eyelids, she said, "Do I remember you saying that you wanted to be a ballerina for Christmas?"

I said, yes, and I told her again everything that I wanted for Christmas – the pink tutu, the fairy wand, the tiara, the flat pink shoes with the ribbons – and she listened carefully.

When I was done, she said, "There's just one thing I think you should know. Ballerinas have eyelashes and if you want to be a ballerina, I suggest you let your eyelashes grow back."

Now my grandmother carried a lot of weight with me and I really tried to stop pulling out my eyelashes, but my baby brother wasn't getting less cute. He was getting cuter every day and if anything he was getting even more attention than he had before, so I kept pulling out my eyelashes.

A couple of weeks later my mother came to me and said, "Your grandmother is coming for a visit." I went into the bathroom and looked at my eyelids in the mirror – there were only two or three eyelashes left on each one and I knew I had to do something.

Now, I lived on a dairy farm. Have you ever seen the eyelashes on a cow? I took my little round-ended scissors, slipped them into the pocket of my jeans, went out to the corrals where the cows were. I waited until it was time for my father to feed the cows. As he drove the tractor down the side of the corral, his helper put the food into the troughs. The troughs were made of cinder blocks, just the right size for me to climb up on.

When the cows came to eat, they put their heads in the space between V-shaped slats of wood so they wouldn't crowd each other. Once my father had driven his tractor around the corner and I was pretty sure he couldn't see me anymore, I climbed up on the edge of the trough right next to my favorite cow.

I put my left hand under her left eye and then I took those little round-ended scissors and I trimmed her eyelashes off right into the palm of my hand. I have no idea how I thought I was going to attach those eyelashes to my own eyelids. I was just concerned with gathering the raw materials at that point.

I was studying the eyelashes in my hand, trying to decide if I should harvest the lashes on the other eye, when I heard my father bellowing from the other end of the corral, "Elizabeth Ann Warren!" All the cows turned to look at my father. He took two steps and was right beside me and the cows turned their big heads to follow as he did.

He looked at my hand. He looked at the cow. He looked back at my hand. Then he smacked my hand and all my beautiful eyelashes fell into the dirt. He said, "This is not how we treat cows! Why do you think we want you to have *your* eyelashes? She *needs* her eyelashes. Are *you* going to stand out here with an umbrella to keep the sun out of her eyes? Are *you* going to fan the dirt out of her face so that she doesn't get an eye infection?"

Well, I didn't have answers to those questions. I got in a lot of trouble for cutting the cow's eyelashes. And at Christmas that year? I got a stuffed lion and some socks and books and board games, but – I did not get a pink tutu made from stacks and stacks of pink netting. I did not get a fairy wand or a tiara. I did not get those flat pink shoes with the long pink ribbons to lace up around my ankles.

The good news is that both the cow's eyelashes and my eyelashes grew back. Time passed and my little brother started making his own trouble and I found other ways to get attention. But my dreams of being a dairy farm ballerina – well, they were never ever realized.

"Me llamo Ricardo" by Ricardo Provencio

"Cuando estés más grande, mijito."

Cuando era un muchachito me acuerdo de mis hermanos y hermanas preparándose para ir a la escuela.

When I was a very small boy I remember my older brothers and sisters each morning getting ready to go to school...Jesus, Raymundo, Gertudes, Jenny, and José all excited and running around our small home, yelling at each other to get out of our tiny bathroom, getting dressed, and making their way into our small kitchen. Mamá was standing in front of the stove, rolling the tortilla dough, shaping the tortillas, and pat-pat-patting them out between her beautiful hands before placing them on the *comal* to cook. Then she cooked bacon, eggs, and beans for our breakfast. Mmmmmm...the smell of breakfast took me to the breakfast table.

Jesus, Raymundo, Gertudes, Jenny y José siempre estaban muy emocionándose, vistiéndose, gritando uno a otro que salgan de nuestro baño pequeño, y mi Mamá en la cocina preparando un almuerzo y el olor de tortillas frescas, jamón, huevos y frijoles...mmmmmm!

Grabbing a tortilla from the *olla* covered with a small cloth to keep them warm and fresh, I spread on a huge glob of butter and watched it melt over the warm tortilla as I rolled it into a burrito to eat....mmmmmmm!

"Mamá, ¿cuándo voy a ir a la escuela?"

"Cuando estés mas grande Ricardo!"

"Mamá when am I going to school?"

"When you're bigger, *mijito*," and then she put her outstretched hand a few inches above my head as I stretched up to reach the top of my head to her hand.

"*Cuando estés más grande mijito*, you will go to school."

"*Yo quiero ir a la escuela Mamá!*" I said.

"*Cuando estés mas grande, mijo* - when you are bigger."

Mamá would go on fixing breakfast and telling each one of us to sit down and eat. Then she would pack each one a lunch, lovingly wrapping a burrito, an apple or banana and a Twinkie!!!! Then, everything went into a brown paper bag. My brothers and sisters would run out of the white screen door and it would slam behind them.

Raymundo, my brother six years older but closest to me in age, was always the last one out of bed and the last one out of the house, *era muy travieso* – he was mischievous. One day as he hurriedly grabbed his brown paper lunch bag and ran out of door, I snuck out and followed him.

Raymundo saw me and yelled out, "Go back home! *Vete a la casa!*"

I responded back, "*Pero yo quiero ir a la escuela!*"

"*Vete a la casa!*" Raymundo yelled back to me.

As he turned around, I followed him. He saw me again and this time Raymundo picked up a rock, threatened to throw it, and again said, "Go home!"

Again I turned around sadly, my head and shoulders slumped, and pretended to start walking home. As soon as he turned around, I started to follow him again. This time when he saw me, Raymundo really did throw a rock at me – not to hit me, just to scare me.

I went home and dejectedly asked Mamá when I was going to get to go to school.

"*Cuando estés mas grande mijo!*" she said.

I knew I was finally bigger and was going to go to school when Mamá took me to get new shoes, pants, shirts, and socks!

"Mamá, am I bigger now?"

"*Sí, mijo.* You are going to school!"

As my first day of school approached, I was so excited and happy. *"Yo voy a la escuela! Yo voy a la escuela!"* I shouted and sang out. *"Yo voy a la escuela! Yo voy a la escuela! La, la, la, la."*

I was up early for my first day of *escuela.* I put on my new blue pants, my new white shirt, my new black socks and shoes, and ran into the kitchen where Mamá greeted me with a warm *abrazo* – kiss – on the cheek and told me to sit down *para mi almuerzo de tortillas calientitas, huevos revueltos, frijoles y papas fritas.*

Mamá served me and as she packed each of the brown paper bags with a *burrito de frijol* wrapped with Saran Wrap – and a Twinkie. She pointed out the bag for me – mmmmm! I couldn't wait for lunch to get my Twinkie!

As Raymundo walked into the kitchen, Mamá told him, *"Raymundo lleva a Ricardo a la escuela.* Take Ricardo to school today, his first day at school."

"O-o-o-o-o-o-h, n-o-o-o-o! Mamá!" Raymundo wailed. *"No quiero llevar a Ricardo.* I don't want to take him!" Mamá firmly told him to make sure I got to school and to leave me off in front of the first grade classroom.

Raymundo made another groan and glared at me. I quickly grabbed his hand and headed out the rickety white screen door. As we went out the door, Raymundo took the lead and with a big smile on my face, I started to do a little hop, skip, and jump, and sang out my little ditty, *"Yo voy a la escuela! Yo voy a la escuela!* Raymundo jerked my arm to stay up with him and told me to stop singing so loud.

As we approached the corner, hopping and skipping, I turned around to wave *adiós* to Mamá. As she waved back, even though I was so excited, I also felt a twinge of fear about going to school. But I quickly recovered and went back to hopping, skipping and singing my off-to-school song.

As we approached *la escuela* and the large dirt playground, I started to search for my amigos del barrio – Arturo, Alberto, Elena, and Maria – but with all the other kids on the playground I didn't see them.

When we got to the front of the first grade classroom, Raymundo told me to go on and get in line. I looked at the line of kids forming and didn't see any familiar faces. I grabbed Raymundo's leg and started to cry, *"Yo quiero ir a la casa! Yo quiero ir a la casa!* I want to go home! Wa-a-a-a-ah!"

As Raymundo tried to pry my arms and hands from his leg, I squeezed tighter and cried louder. Then a gentle woman with a very friendly smile and kind eyes came to me, squatted beside me, and put her arms around me. I looked at her, she looked at me, and then I grabbed onto her leg! With me still hanging on to her, she walked me to my place in line.

I got in line and there in front of me was a girl with long, long, blonde hair! I had never seen such blonde hair up close! I stared at her hair, and I guess the girl in front of me felt me staring at her because she turned around to face me. She had the bluest eyes and the fairest skin. I had never seen any like that in my barrio!

She looked into my eyes and said with a smile, "My name is Stephanie Drakovich. Do you want to be my friend?"

A little stunned I said, "*Sí*, I will be your friend".

"What's your name?" Stephanie asked.

"My name is Ricardo Pedro Tellez Buttner Provencio," I blurted back.

We started to file into the classroom and sat down. There in front was our teacher. She was a little older lady, with white, white hair, a big, big nose, and big, big ears! Next to her on the wall behind her was a picture of George Washington. She looked just like George Washington! And that is what we used to call her in the playground behind her back.

Mrs. Washington, oops – I mean Mrs. Tapager, then started calling out the names on the enrollment roster.

"José?" she said with a heavy English accent. José raised his hand. I looked back at him in the back of the classroom. "José, from now on your name is 'Joey'," Mrs. Tapager said. "Elena?" she shouted out in her heavy English accent that sounded foreign to me, and Elena raised her hand. "Elena, your name is 'Helen' from now on," Mrs. Tapager said. "Alberto?" Again, she called out loud and Alberto raised his hand. "From now on your name is 'Albert'...Arturo? From now on your name is 'Arthur'."

"REECHardo?" she shouted out in her heavy English accent. No one raised a hand. Was that supposed to be my name? Again she shouted out looking for a hand in the air. "REECHARDO!" I slowly raised my little arm, not sure if that was my name. Her eyes focused straight at me and said, "Your name is 'Ricky' from now on!"

When I got home, I asked, "Mamá, is my name 'Ricky'? The teacher said my name is 'Ricky'."

"No, *mijo*, your name is Ricardo. Those teachers don't know Spanish *muy bien*, so they changed your name." And that was my name in the first grade.

The next year, I was again ready to go to school on first day and was so happy to be going back, and there I was in line behind Stephanie, too! We walked into the classroom, found our chairs, and there was the teacher in front of the classroom. She was a huge woman – as big and wide as two double doors! When she walked down the school classroom hallway she took up the whole thing! People would have to move themselves against the wall and make themselves skinny to give her room to pass.

Mrs. Moody was her name and she had a small round face, with a tiny mouth, tiny eyes and ears. With her cheeks dropping down on the side of her face, she looked just like a big bulldog? And that is what we called her, 'Mrs. Bulldog.'

Mrs. Bulldog, oops Mrs. Moody, started to call out the student roll. "José?" José raised his hand and she said, "Your name is 'Joey' in my class."

"Elena?" she called out. Elena raised her hand. "Your name is 'Helen' in my class."
"Alberto?" she yelled out, and he raised his hand. "Your name is 'Albert' in my class."

"Arturo?" she said. Arturo raised his hand, "Your name is 'Arthur' in my class."

"Reechardo?" she said. "Reechardo, are you here?" I slowly raised my hand. She said, "Your name is 'Dick' in my class."

I cringed and made a sad face as my classmates giggled and squeaked out "Dick!" under their breath.

When I got home, the first thing I wailed was, "Mamá is my name 'DICK?' The teacher said my name is 'Dick'!"

"No *mijo*, your name is Ricardo. Those teachers don't know how to speak Spanish," she said to me *en español*.

My name was 'Dick' for the whole year in the second grade. I got into a lot of fights that year on the playground as the kids teased me all the time.

The next year I was back in line, in front of the third grade classroom with Stephanie Drakovich in front of me. We filed into the classroom, found our seats and there in front of us was our teacher. He was a skinny man, as skinny as my little finger! He had a tiny face with a small pointed nose and his eyes were blood shot! With his red eyes, he was scary looking, and his name was Mr. Blood! Of course, we called him 'Dracula' on the playground!

Mr. Blood starting calling out his class roster, and just like in the first and second grades, each person with a Spanish name had his or her name changed to an English equivalent. When he got to me he stuttered, "Ree, Ree, Reechardo?" I slowly raised my hand, "Your name is 'Richard' in my class."

Back home I asked, "Mamá is my name 'Richard'?"

"No, mijo your name is Ricardo. Those teachers don't know any Spanish! *Pero, mijo* – it's better than 'Dick'!"

From the third grade all the way through the twelfth grade my name stayed 'Richard.' On into adulthood I remained 'Richard.' After one year of college and two years of Army service (one of those years in Vietnam), I came back after my discharge and was in my little *casita* on Pinal Street in Superior, Arizona. I was sitting in the *cocina* at the table with Mamá in front of the stove. She was making me some *tortillas, huevos, chorizo y frijoles*.

"*Pues, mijo*. What are you going to do now?" she asked.

"Mamá, I'm going back to school. I'm going to be a teacher like my big brother, Harvey."

"*Muy bien, mijo*," she said.

"Mamá, I need my birth certificate and other important papers to get registered."

Mamá said, "*Pues, están abajo de la cama*. All that stuff is under the bed in the cardboard box with the other important papers."

I pulled the box out from under her bed and looked for my papers.

"Mamá, I'm not sure if these are my papers. They all say 'Ricardo'."

"*Pues, mijo*! That is your name – not 'Ricky' – not 'Dick' – not 'Richard.' Your name is Ricardo."

Ever since that day, whenever someone asks what my name is, I proudly tell them, "My name is Ricardo! "

"*Me llamo Ricardo*."

© 2008 Ricardo Provencio
The author is a bilingual storyteller, college professor and counselor. He was one of the founders of the SMCC Storytelling Institute.

Bribing the Babysitter by LynnAnn Lauder Wojciechowicz

"Tell me a story, tell me a story, tell me a story before I go to bed. You promised me, you said you would, you've got to do it so I'll be good. Tell me a story and then I'll go to sleep."

That was my favorite song when I was little. I grew up with the radio, and that song was sung on my favorite radio program "Baby Snooks." She was always getting into mischief, sometimes getting away with her pranks, but more often getting caught and doing what she could to wriggle out of her punishments.

I loved stories so much when I was little, my mother used to say that after supper, I would tug on the hem of her dress, saying "Bed-time Mummy, bed-time." It wasn't that I wanted to go to sleep, I just wanted a story.

The time that stands out strongest in my memory occurred when I was six years old. My parents and sister were getting ready to go to a church supper, and they wanted me to get ready for bed.

"Dad, will you read me a story?"

"Not tonight, LynnAnn, I need to get cleaned up for the supper."

"Mom, will you read me a story?"

"Can't you see I'm in the middle of making this salad? I have to finish it, and then we need to leave."

"Doreen, will you read me a story?"

"I've got to make sure that I look just perfect. You never know which young men might be at this supper. I'll read you a story tomorrow night."

As I crawled into bed, I was not happy. My father had told me that he had spoken to Mrs. Passmore, the woman who lived in our basement apartment with her teen-aged daughter Lois. Mrs. Passmore planned to be home that evening, so my parents were leaving me in bed with the understanding that I could go downstairs to Mrs. Passmore if I had any problems.

"Good night, LynnAnn. Sleep tight." My parents gave me kisses and hugs as they left. But I was not tired, and I was not ready to go to sleep. I wanted a story! As I lay in bed, I formed a plan. My sister and I shared a bedroom with twin beds, but one closet. She is eight years older than I am, and I knew that sometimes she would leave change in her sweater and jacket pockets. I got out of bed and started rifling through her clothes. Sure enough, I found two quarters. I slipped my feet into my slippers and donned my robe.

Our house had been flooded out the year before, and the city moved us to higher ground. My father took advantage of this move to build a full basement, including a small one-bedroom apartment, storage space for us, and an open area where my mother did her washing and I could play with my India rubber ball. The Passmores could enter the basement from the outside back door, but I could also go down our kitchen stairs, past the shelves with all our canned and bottled food, through a little door to the open part of the basement, and then around the corner to their apartment door. And that is what I did. I knocked on the door to the apartment. Mrs. Passmore opened the door.

"LynnAnn, what's wrong?"

"Mrs. Passmore, could Lois come and read me a story?"

"I don't know. Your father told me he was putting you to bed. I don't think he would like it if Lois kept you up later than he wanted."

"He gave me two quarters to pay her."

"Well, if he gave you money to pay her, I guess it would be alright. Lois, would you like to go and read LynnAnn a story?"

So I led Lois through the open part of the basement, through the little door to our storage area and up the kitchen stairs past our bookcase with the *Encyclopedia Britannica* to the children's books that were part of the collection. I picked out my favorite, and as I climbed into bed, I turned to the story I wanted Lois to read:

121

Once upon a time there lived a little old man and a little old woman. Their children had grown up and left home, so it was just the two of them, and sometimes they got bored. One day the little old woman said to her husband, 'I'm going to make a gingerbread man. So she got out the flour, sugar, butter, cinnamon and ginger and mixed them together. When her dough was ready, she rolled it out and formed a man. She placed raisins for the eyes, nose, mouth, and buttons. Then she popped it into her hot oven. After about fifteen minutes, her husband said, "MMMM, I smell something good. Maybe you should check on your gingerbread man." So the little old woman opened the oven door, and pulled out the rack. That gingerbread man was golden brown. As the little old woman was admiring how good he looked, he popped up off the cookie sheet, jumped down onto the floor, singing "Run, Run, fast as you can. Can't catch me, I'm the gingerbread man."

Just then, I heard our front door open and footsteps coming down the hall. My bedroom door opened, and my father said "LynnAnn, what is going on here?"

Lois explained and showed him the quarters. She was allowed to keep the money, but she was sent back to her apartment with instructions NOT to listen to my requests after I'd been put to bed at night. I was punished and told I would have to work to repay my sister. Then, I was once again put to bed for the night.

It turned out that my father had forgotten to take his violin, and as he was the fiddler for the dance they were having after the supper, he had come home to retrieve it.

Well, I never did anything like that again, but my love for stories is just as strong today as it was when I was six.

"Tell me a story, tell me a story, tell me a story, and then I'll go to sleep."

© 2008 LynnAnn Wojciechowicz

8

Applications of Storytelling

"Today, while performance storytelling is largely featured at rural festivals, the medium is also used to great effect by practitioners in non-entertainment venues. In the same way that storytelling played a part in the regeneration and maintenance of community in pre-literate societies, it is back at work as a mode of organizational and community development, healing and motivation." (Caren Neile)

What do you do?

Here's a scenario most storytellers encounter at one time or another: A storyteller is at a party (or in line at the pharmacy, or at a friend's house for dinner, or at a meeting) when he meets someone new. Mr. New asks, "What do you do?" The storyteller answers, "I'm a storyteller." Mr. New responds with a quizzical look on his face, "What's that?" thereby providing the storyteller with an opportunity to educate another person in our culture about storytelling. A common follow-up question is, "Where do you do that?" To which the storyteller might respond, "Everywhere!" And it's true. Many people know little or nothing about storytelling, but storytellers are everywhere.

This chapter is dedicated to describing some of the ways in which storytellers apply their skill and knowledge beyond festival and stage performance. You'll also learn how people working in other professions use story to enhance the effectiveness of their work. Although storytellers work throughout our culture in many more ways than will be described here, these four are amongst the primary settings.

Educational Settings

Working in education, especially in the elementary grades, is the mainstay of many storytellers. Storytellers are hired to perform in classrooms and assemblies, to train teachers, and to conduct residencies. In a residency, the storyteller is hired to work over a period of time, anywhere from one to several weeks. The storyteller teaches the children, the teachers, and sometimes the families and community the basic skills of storytelling. A storytelling residency often culminates in a performance by the children and the teller.

Story and storytelling are used by teachers at every level within the educational system. As Martha Hamilton and Mitch Weiss say below, story is the oldest form of education, and is still relevant and effective for teaching all kinds of content.

Stories are the way we store information in the brain. If teachers fill their students' brains with miscellaneous facts and data without any connection, the brain becomes like a catchall closet into which items are tossed and hopelessly lost. But stories help us to organize and remember information and tie content together.

Stories go straight to the heart. As the Irish poet and philosopher James Stephens wrote, "The head does not hear anything until the heart has listened. The heart knows today what the head will understand tomorrow" (1929, 128). Because class members and teachers are emotionally involved and usually enjoy storytelling, it can help students develop a positive attitude toward the learning process. It also produces a sense of joy in language and words that is so often missing in the classroom setting.

Research backs up the idea that "even students with low motivation and weak academic skills are more likely to listen, read, write and work hard in the context of storytelling" (U.S. Department of Education, 1986, 23). Any point that is made in telling or any teaching that is done afterward is likely to be much more effective.

Above all else, stories are perhaps the best presents teachers can give their students, for stories are beyond the power of money to buy or the world to take away. Stories belong to the students forever – from the first listening. As far as we are concerned, there need be no other reason for sharing stories in the classroom. Even better, the educational benefits are many.

(Martha Hamilton and Mitch Weiss, *Children Tell Stories,* excerpted in *Storytelling Magazine*
   May/June 2007)

Engaging children in storytelling is extremely satisfying. Involving young people in storytelling is crucial to the growth and acceptance of the art form. When children participate in a storytelling program, their parents and teachers are involved, too. This extends the reach of storytelling throughout our culture. There is a drawback. People who are exposed to storytelling through elementary education often assume that storytelling is only for children. Storytellers frequently find themselves in the situation of having to explain that storytelling is for all ages.

The Gift of Story: Nine Reasons for Infusing Storytelling into the Curriculum

by LynnAnn Wojciechowicz

1. **Storytelling stimulates learning:**

   We learn what we attend to. Students pay attention to stories, and they retain what they hear. Stories provide language experiences that enable listeners to think about and to comprehend their environment. Stories affect language development and mental capacity. When students hear stories, they develop a repertoire of abstract symbols (words) that correspond to their internal experience of things. Listening and repeating, listening and repeating—that is the natural rhythm children use to develop language skills. Storytelling enhances that rhythm, and through stories language and content intertwine.

   Continued

The Gift of Story: Nine Reasons for Infusing Storytelling. . . (continued)

2. **Storytelling builds literacy skills:**

   Storytelling provides a natural bridge between the spoken and written word. Listening to a story requires the listener to focus on only one thing—the storyteller. Attention and memory are enhanced when we listen to stories.

   Storytelling enhances all areas of language: Our vocabulary expands when a story contains a word that is unfamiliar. The repetition and narrative context help us understand and remember the new word.

   Listening to stories improves understanding of grammar and literary devices. Some stories use formal language, similes, and metaphors.. Listeners develop a sense of story structure. Listeners also learn story comprehension and the ability to formulate narrative.

3. **Listening to stories encourages critical thinking:**

   Problem Solving: A story cannot exist without a conflict at its center. Stories explore ways to solve these problems, promote critical thinking skills, and improve listeners' ability to resolve conflicts creatively.

   Decision-Making: The stories we tell and hear influence our thinking and decision-making. When we hear about a character's decision, we instinctively evaluate it: Was it a good choice? What consequences will it bring? How would we react in similar circumstances?

   Organization and Boundaries: In telling or creating an oral story, we need to use our organizational skills to sequence the images that we want to relate to our listeners. Our stories, both personal and traditional, begin at the moment when old boundaries are about to change. Story structure becomes scaffolding experiences in life and in story.

4. **Listening to stories encourages creative thinking and strengthens the imagination:**

   Improvisation: A storyteller improvises, using traditional language and images to shape a story for one particular moment. The characters in the story, likewise, improvise solutions to their problems, often failing several times before passing a test.

   Inventiveness: Storytelling encourages spontaneity and self-expression. A storyteller innovates and weaves new relationships as the story emerges from the teller's unique perceptions.

   Imagination: The perceptions a person receives through sensory attention are stored and worked with as images. A person who has difficulty with imagery has trouble listening, speaking, reading, and writing, as well as other developmental and critical thinking skills.

   To be able to create our own images is essential to development and learning. If we can visualize a scene as we hear about it, it will be imprinted on our memories. It is through imagination that connections are made—to people, to disciplines, to all kinds of subject matter.

   Continued

125

The Gift of Story: Nine Reasons for Infusing Storytelling. . . (continued)

5. Storytelling enhances communication and promotes emotional development:

When we provide opportunities for people to tell stories, we are providing an opportunity for them to feel good. In storytelling, more than half of the story is communicated with facial expressions, gestures, and vocal inflections. As students tell stories their shoulders move back, their eyes sparkle, their muscles relax, and their voices become stronger. Everybody likes being listened to. Telling stories builds self-esteem and self-confidence.

As the listener is drawn into the drama, both the storyteller and the listener can "become" the character for a time. This enhances understanding of another's point of view and promotes empathy. Through story, listeners can encounter danger, overcome obstacles, and share adventures – all at a safe distance. This helps people gain confidence in their ability to handle frightening and difficult situations.

6. Storytelling creates classroom community:

Stories both create and emerge out of community. Classrooms are not always places of security or cohesiveness for all students. Storytelling unites the attention of those who come to share in the pleasure of the story, whose emotions and aspirations are touched in very different ways. When a group listens to a story, they share a common experience and develop a sense of community. This contributes to the group's identity and builds a sense of cooperation. Storytelling stimulates interactive and cooperative learning. In addition, a well-told story can be the springboard for curriculum integration. Activities from storytelling can span the entire curriculum, creating interdisciplinary bridges.

7. Storytelling builds cultural awareness and understanding:

Storytelling enables students to interact with culture, past and present, through narrative. Story is the way people make sense of the world around them. Storytelling provides opportunities to explore diverse cultural heritages and the values important to the people in those cultures.

Every time we tell a story we vary it. The stories we tell—and what we take from them—reflect what is important to us. Storytelling informs us of the roles we play within our culture. Stories provide a framework for experiencing and defining the world. Stories help people develop an understanding and appreciation of aesthetic principles.

8. Storytelling helps build character:

Teachers today are expected to incorporate character-building values into their lessons. For example, the Arizona program Character Counts asks for lessons on Trust, Respect, Responsibility, Fairness, Caring, and Citizenship. Stories, folktales and fables in particular, are one of the best tools for teaching these values in a meaningful way that students will remember.

9. Storytelling is a fun way to learn!

Storytelling captures the imagination of students and makes learning fun. Storytelling can also release tension and can provide relaxation. In addition, storytelling promotes different learning styles.

"Storytelling is the way we learn naturally. It's the way lessons and information get transmitted. I can't imagine how we'd communicate without it." Gay Ducey, storyteller, college teacher, librarian.

Healing Settings

Storytelling is becoming widely recognized as a vehicle of healing. Stories have proved to be powerful in promoting psychological as well as physical health. Professional storytellers train mental-health practitioners and lay people in ways to use storytelling. Here are some of the healing settings in which story is incorporated:

Psychotherapy and counseling:

According to the theories of narrative psychology, we establish and define our individuality by the stories we tell ourselves about who we are. Using narrative in therapy, individuals take an active role in the creation of their own stories, rather being victims of circumstance. By discovering the stories that shape them, these individuals create new stories and establish healthier patterns in life.

Universities and medical schools are now training doctors and nurses in the use of narrative as a way of putting the patient's own story at the heart of the healing process. Medical students are also taught to reflect on their own roles and reactions, in other words, their own stories. One of the first books about this new approach is *Narrative Medicine: Honoring the Stories of Illness* by Rita Charon.

Jungian psychologists incorporate folktales and myths into therapy. This helps clients identify the ancient archetypal symbols and patterns that influence their behavior and well-being. The ancient wisdom carried by those symbols and patterns moves them toward health.

Many people who have suffered trauma or abuse find it powerful and healing to tell the story of what happened to them. As they tell their story again and again, the story changes from one of victimization to one of triumph. Finally, they are no longer burdened by the trauma, and they can proceed with their lives.

Recovering from addiction: Storytelling is an integral part of Alcoholics Anonymous and related organizations such as Narcotics Anonymous. In fact, AA may be one of the few places left in which there is a vibrant oral tradition, since members' stories are passed on primarily in person rather than in writing. Patricia Mary Walsh, an addictions counselor, describes the role of storytelling in AA:

> Much of AA is unwritten and rests in an oral tradition to be passed down from one alcoholic to another. The oral tradition rests on the transmission of "THE story." Three basic tenets or core beliefs are expected to be in every story:
>
> - powerlessness over alcohol;
> - reliance on a Higher Power and
> - action through the Twelve Steps (Makela, 1996).
>
> Every alcoholic is expected to tell his or her own story, which is from personal experiences and no one else's, yet adhering to the template of the model story. Regardless of the daily topic at AA meetings, this story is to be told. The topic will merely put more emphasis and time on one of the three sections. In addition to the core format, its perceived depth of honesty is the criterion by which the story will be judged. (Patricia Mary Walsh, C.A.D.C. http://www.addictionrecov.org/paradigm/P_PR_F99/WALSH.HTM)

End of Life: Stories become very important at the end of life to both the person dying and to the relatives and friends. Hospice workers are often trained in techniques to help the dying and their families share and preserve stories. The excerpt below from *Good Lives and Goodbyes* highlights the power of stories when death is imminent.

Meaning at the end of life often comes through life review or storytelling. Telling a life story can have many dimensions. The storyteller needs to speak and be heard, to be assured the story will be preserved and passed on, and have the opportunity to share the wisdom gleaned from living a life. That sharing is a major part of the letting go that allows the dying to die in peace and dignity.

Story gatherers will find value in asking questions about life experience and actively listening to the answers. Tried and true questions include:

- "What do you think are the most important events of your life?"
- "What have you learned from your experience?"
- "Who have been the important persons in your life? And, why?"
- "What values do you want to pass on to your grandchildren?"

To make the story lasting, record it on either video- or audiotape. Or, write the story for the storyteller and then read it aloud.

Through this life exploration a storyteller may become awed by the adventures life has presented, the obstacles overcome, and the people who shared the journey. The storyteller may discover who needs to hear the important words: "I'm sorry." "Forgive me." "I forgive you." "Thank you." "I love you." And, "Goodbye."

(From *Good Lives and Goodbyes,* a Missoulian/Missoula Demonstration Project Special Section, http://www.missoulian.com/specials/dying/meaning.html)

To learn more about storytelling in healing settings, visit the Healing Story Alliance, a special interest group of the National Storytelling Network, http://www.healingstory.org/.

Organizational Settings

Storytelling is used in many organizational settings, from major corporations to non-profit foundations, as well as small businesses and service providers. Storytellers are hired to help corporations and other organizations identify and establish the "story" of the entity and what it stands for. The storyteller works with leaders and employees to develop and disseminate the story throughout the company. The National Storytelling Network has a special interest group devoted to storytelling in organizations. They describe their rationale as follows:

As the whole of human history shows and storytellers have always known, stories are a wellspring of communal life. Stories inspire, support, and sustain all types of human communities. Think of the patriotic tales that stir the national soul or the traditional holiday stories recounted at family gatherings. Consider the ancestral sagas of tribes and clans or the religious narratives that unite a congregation.

In her book *Around the Corporate Campfire: How Great Leaders Use Stories to Inspire Success,* Evelyn Clark describes how Jim Sinegal, co-founder, CEO and president of Costco Wholesale uses stories to reinforce the company's core values:

He smiles as he launches into another legendary tale. "But probably no story tells what we do relative to the products and value better than the salmon story." Jumping up to get a copy of a management presentation illustrating the story, Sinegal begins thumbing through the pages as he excitedly launches into the retelling.

"In 1996 we were selling between $150,000 and $200,000 worth of salmon filets company wide every week at $5.99 a pound. Then our buyers were able to get an improved product, with belly fat, back fins, and collarbones removed, at a better price. As a result, we reduced our retail price to $5.29. So they improved the product and lowered the price!"

The buyers weren't finished with the improvements, though. "Next our buyers negotiated for a product with the pin bone out and all of the skin removed, and it was at an even better price, which enabled us to lower our price to $4.99 a pound. Then, because we had continued to grow and had increased our sales volume, we were able to buy direct from Canadian and Chilean farms, which resulted in an even lower price of $4.79.

"Over a five-year period, a significantly enhanced product was lowered from $5.99 a pound to $4.79." and still the story kept getting better. "The final improvement was that the belly was removed, and customers get the top filet, and the price further reduced to $3.99 a pound."

Customers have shown their appreciation for this genuine fish story. Salmon sales over the same five-year period increased more than ten-fold, from $150,000-$200,000 per week to almost $2 million per week.

Sinegal says, "We've used that story so much as a teaching tool that I've had other buyers in the company, such as a clothing buyer in Canada, come up to me and say, 'Hey, I've got a salmon story to tell you.' That story explains the essence of what we do." And it's become part of Costco lore. Pages 65-66)

Having a story in common brings people together because stories cultivate the communion of hearts and minds that creates community. By playing a role in communal stories, people participate in a shared identity and engage in mutual interests. Stories provide a community with the common ground and shared vision needed to inspire collective striving.

(From the home page of the Storytelling in Organizations Special Interest Group of the National Storytelling Network http://storytellinginorganizations.com/).

Interpretive Settings

Interpretive settings include museums, parks, gardens and other institutions where the collections or exhibits require guidance and interpretation to be fully appreciated. Docents, guides, rangers, and museum educators often use storytelling to engage their visitors. Stories provide context for the exhibits, and transmit scientific, historical, or highly technical information with maximum comprehensibility. The docent or guide must have mastery of the subject matter, and he must also know how to shape information into a story. Then, he must be able to adapt that story for a wide range of ages, or develop multiple versions that will suit different needs. Alternately, he can look for folktales that serve to draw the visitors' attention to some aspect of the museum or its exhibits. Storytellers are hired to train docents in these techniques.

Two of my colleagues and I once conducted such training for docents and museum educators in the Phoenix area. Over a two year period we held a series of story circles and workshops at fifteen institutions. Our goal was to provide docents with the opportunity to experience story first hand.

Sandy Oglesby facilitated one of our first story circles at Pueblo Grande Museum. This museum is devoted to the Hohokam people who lived in the Phoenix area about a thousand years ago and who designed the canal system still in use today. Sandy demonstrated how to use story to engage visitors with the objects on a touch cart. The most provocative object on the cart was a large stone hand axe. She told three different types of stories each with the axe as its focus.

The first was the story of the object's discovery, told from the archaeological point of view. In the second brief story, Sandy made a personal connection to the object by describing how her brother had used just such an axe to chop down a tree at a wilderness survival camp. She recreated a dialogue between her brother and herself that detailed how effective the object was. "Sissy, I cut down a whole tree with an axe just like that. It was hard work, and it really helped me understand how skilled the Hohokam had to be to survive."

The third story was Sandy's research-based, imaginative, two minute re-creation of an event in the life of a boy who might have used the axe:

Our family had been walking for days. We carried only those things that were most precious and powerful. A dry wind stung our faces and sapped our energy as we trudged through the desert. Our goal was to find relatives and a new home. At the top of Greasy Mountain*, we saw the beautiful valley below and the green snake of trees that promised water and a new life. When we finally reached the river, we drank and splashed our faces with relief and joy. But suddenly Father straightened himself and raised a hand to silence us. A large man was approaching us on the opposite bank. Mother and the girls retreated quickly up the bank and into a shelter of trees. I stood with Father and reached for a mesquite limb floating near us. Just as suddenly, I felt my father relax as he and the other man shouted a family greeting. The large man came into the river where we were standing. He and father spoke their clan names and their father's names, too. Mother and my sisters rejoined us just as our relative handed my father a beautiful stone axe head. "We have been waiting for you and offer you this gift as a sign of welcome." Father accepted it, and then laughed as he saw I was still holding the branch like a weapon. "That will be the handle of our new axe."(*Greasy Mountain is the original name of South Mountain in Phoenix, Arizona)

When Sandy finished this story there was a moment of shared silence before the spell broke and we all came back to the real world. The participants had experienced for themselves how quickly they could be brought into the sphere of the object and the powerful emotions that could be evoked. (Adapted from "Storytelling: Invoking the Muse at the Museum" by Liz Warren, Sandy Oglesby, and Kathy Eastman, in *The Docent Educator*, Vol. 13, No. 1, Autumn 2003).

Stories in Action: Two Tellers

Washington storyteller and health educator **Allison M. Cox** has been at the forefront of working with stories in a wide range of contexts, especially those having to do with health and wholeness. She has applied her expertise in storytelling while working as a mental health therapist, a social worker, a health educator, and a prevention specialist.

Allison encountered storytelling in the mid-eighties when she was in graduate school. Her work with neurolinguistic programming, hypnotherapy, and therapeutic metaphor awakened her to the power of storytelling. A weekend workshop with famous poet and speaker Robert Bly clinched it. She began to tell stories in therapeutic contexts.

Allison was working as a counselor for pregnant women in the early 1990s, when a new director was hired at the health department where she worked. He immediately announced cutbacks and said that one-on-one services could no longer be sustained. He said that their efforts had to be "population based"; in other words, services had to be delivered to groups rather individuals. In addition, those services had to be "prevention oriented" and "tested and proven effective". Allison couldn't get his phrases out of her head. She remembered how her teachers in counseling psychology had always stressed the power of metaphor to help people change their lives. That's when a life-changing idea hit her.

I quickly wrote up a proposal and waited impatiently for a requested meeting with the director. When we finally met, I took a deep breath and proposed, "You say that you want our work to be population based, prevention oriented, and tested to prove effectiveness — then what you really want is storytelling!

"*Storytelling is population based.* I can tell stories to many people at the same time and each one will have their own personal interaction with the tale while sharing in the group experience as well.

"*Storytelling is prevention oriented.* The audience can try on new behaviors and adopt fresh ways of perceiving the world when listening to stories. The 'cautionary' tale is a standard story motif used around the world to warn others of what could happen.

"*Storytelling has been tested through time and proven to be effective* not only in getting a message across, but also in keeping the message in the minds of the listeners, which is why the shamans, healers, and great leaders through time have told stories (Muhammad, Buddha, Jesus, Mahatma Gandhi, Martin Luther King...). People relax into the safe and known environment of story, while they often raise their defenses when they listen to a lecture." (from

The Healing Heart – Families: Storytelling to Encourage Caring and Healthy Families by Allison M. Cox and David H. Albert, 6)

Allison was laid off, but she was awarded a two-month contract to find a repertoire of stories that could be used by the health department. They also gave her a list of subjects, such as violence, substance abuse, and many, many others to further define her story search. Surrounded by stacks of books, she "wandered through an ancient forest of folktales, myths, legends, and literary tales", looking for stories that met her criteria.

At the end of my allotted time, I had collected and gained permission to use 112 versions of folktales and literary stories on a myriad of health-related subjects. I was amazed at the generosity of others. Storytellers called me long distance and sent me their tapes. Authors sent lists of other books they had written that I might want to use as well. One publisher sent an entire catalogue and said, "Let us know what else interests you." I had told them all that the health department wanted to tell these stories to the people in the community who most needed to hear them, and they had opened their hearts and given freely. (7)

Within a year she was hired back by the agency and she has worked in health related fields and as a storyteller ever since. Building on her initial story search, she and co-author David Albert have produced two anthologies, *The Healing Heart – Families: Storytelling To Encourage Caring and Healthy Families* and *The Healing Heart - Communities: Storytelling To Build Strong and Healthy Communities.*

Joining with storytellers across the nation who are passionate about the power of story to heal, she went on to become one of the founding board members of the Healing Story Alliance Special Interest Group of the National Storytelling Network.

Allison is also known for her work with environmental stories. Below she describes how finding just the right story placed a community's environmental work in a larger context. She was asked by The Institute for Environmental Research and Education (IERE) to kick off a major reclamation project. Vashon Island near Seattle had been contaminated by the cadmium from an old copper smelter. Residents couldn't plant gardens until the heavy metals had been removed from the soil. The IERE was planting different varieties of foxglove, known for its ability to leach cadmium from the soil. They asked Allison, "Would you tell a story that will make a pretty dry (but important) topic interesting and memorable?"

I found a nugget of the story I developed in Candace Miller's *Tales from the Plant Kingdom* about a woman who befriends the hobgoblins by growing "goblin gloves" (foxgloves) and in turn, how these hobgoblins help her. The IERE staff explained that when they had a Shaman come out to bless the land at the beginning of their project, they were told to have this celebration to wake up or revive the local nature spirits who felt neglected and overlooked. This was an interesting expansion on who my audience would be! After the story was shared, IERE staff members said "this was the perfect way for our work to begin!"

(Adapted from http://www.dancingleaves.com/allison/environment/soil_reclamation.html)

Don Doyle had been a professor of theater for 26 years at Arizona State University when what he describes as a "minor miracle" led him to leave the university and become a full-time, professional storyteller. During his years at the university, he had always integrated story into his creative drama, directing, and acting classes. Don also taught storytelling and worked part time as a storyteller. All of this developed within him a great appreciation of storytelling as its own art form, distinct from theater. That in turn led to his involvement with the National Association for the Preservation and Perpetuation of Storytelling, the precursor of the National Storytelling Network. He went to his first national storytelling conference in 1986 and felt as if he had found another home in the arts with the people he met there.

In 1988, when Don was 58 years old, he had a serious heart-attack. His doctors said he needed triple by-pass surgery. For the six weeks before the surgery, Don devoted all his energy to visualizing a healthy circulatory system. He applied a technique he had taught and used in both theater and storytelling to his own healing. "I imaged cylinders full of liquid flowing smoothly, straws full of purple Kool-Aid, garden hoses full of my favorite drink, no blockages of any kind, my own red blood flowing feely throughout my whole body. I visualized that the whole time."

Just before the surgery Don had a scan that showed his circulatory system. That's when the minor miracle became apparent. The doctor called the whole family in to show them the pictures and said, "This has never happened before. All his arteries are open. I've never seen anything like it in all my years as a surgeon."

Don says, "I just knew that I had done that myself by seeing my blood vessels and arteries running smoothly, by telling myself the story of my health and seeing it clearly."

The surgeon recommended going ahead with the bypass as a precaution against the blockages recurring. The prognosis was very good, but nonetheless, the night before the surgery he lay awake.

> I couldn't sleep the night before the surgery. The nurse offered me something to help me sleep, but it didn't work. Like King Arthur the night before he met the Black Knight in the forest, I didn't know whether I was going to live or die. I thought about my life and what was special about what I'd done. I remembered one of my favorite stories from my own life in which one of my childhood worlds was destroyed. My grandma said, "Sometimes it's important to go back and do some rebuilding with your life when it seems like it's been destroyed." And that's what I decided to do. There were more things I wanted to do, and some things I wanted to change. I loved the university and my theater work, but I decided it was time to do some rebuilding and changing. Right there I decided that if I came through the surgery, I wanted to be a storyteller for the rest of my life. (Interview)

The surgery was a success, and for the twenty years since he's been the picture of heart-health, a far better result than was expected at the time. After his recovery Don began to invest more time in storytelling and when he became eligible in 1991, he retired from the university and became a professional storyteller.

Don has performed all over the country and has served his adopted art form very well. He served a three-year term on the National Board of the National Storytelling Network and has been a mentor to many storytellers all over the nation. He was the artistic director of the Mesa Storytelling Festival for the first six years of its existence, and he has produced Tellabration events almost every year since his retirement. In addition to many national theater awards, he has received both the Western Region Leadership Award, and the Oracle Lifetime Achievement Award from the National Storytelling Network.

One of his passions is encouraging young people to become involved with storytelling because, as with all things, the future of the arts rests with the youth. "It's wonderful to see an old folktale come to life in the mouth of a young person. Storytelling is especially powerful for young people when telling their own personal stories because it helps them realize who they are and where they've come from." (Interview)

The Future of Storytelling

The rapidly changing technological landscape has proved to be fertile for storytellers. Some of the new tools are websites, aggregate and directory sites, blogs, social networking sites, and digital storytelling. Some storytellers view the internet and other new technologies as a threat to the oral tradition. However, new information technologies are essential to the maintenance and survival of large diverse cultures. We will never lose the oral tradition. It is part of being human – an essential, defining feature of our species.

Rather than being a threat, new media has sparked interest in storytelling, even if it isn't being called that. YouTube, blogs, and personal websites function as forums for people – whether professional storytellers or not – to tell their stories and find the people who want to hear them. Beyond that, experts speculate that the digital age will move us to a "post-literate" state, when oral communication may become more important than written. Perhaps we are already there. Those who have the skills to tell stories well and in a variety of formats will always be needed and valued.

As humans, we are story creators, story tellers, and story listeners. We don't have any choice. Story is as intrinsic, inherent, and essential to our species as language or walking upright. It is our most primal mode of entertainment, and ultimately the most satisfying, too. We cannot escape the omnipresence and importance of story in our lives. Storytelling gives us moments of beauty, magic, joy, and profound emotion that do not occur, maybe cannot occur, in any other way. Those experiences are worth cultivating, promoting, cherishing, and preserving.

The future of storytelling lies with you. It lies with all of us. Go forth and tell. Tell folktales and myths, tell your own stories, and tell others about storytelling. There will always be a need for the true storyteller, someone who can tell a story to other people, face-to-face, in real time and make a difference by doing so.

The Stories:

A *Jataka* Tale of Friendship, retold by Laura Simms

There was once a King in India who kept a royal elephant in a stable made of gold. The elephant's food was carefully prepared, and his saddle had been painted by the best of artists. The King rode the elephant at the head of every procession and considered it to be a holy creature. But, the elephant was lonely.

One day a small and starving dog wandered into the stable and fell against the elephant's huge leg. Feeling sorry for the puppy, the large animal pushed his golden food bowl gently toward him. The little animal, barely able to lift his head, slowly took sustenance and then fell asleep. The elephant was careful not to harm the dog. He waited patiently, hoping that it would not die.

When the dog awoke, the elephant's heart rejoiced. He scooped him up from the ground and placed him behind his ears on his soft back. The dog nestled close to the elephant. In time, with food and love, the little puppy became well. And the elephant and the dog became the best of friends.

When the elephant returned from his royal processions, the dog waited, tail wagging, for his friend. And the elephant delighted in the dog's antics as he rolled and scratched, bit gently, and settled against the elephant's back. The little barks of the animal were like music to the lonely elephant, while the warmth of the elephant and his kindness were a salve to the dog.

But few human beings understand the feelings of animals and, when a merchant saw the plump dog, he offered to buy it from the elephant keeper. Unknowingly, the keeper sold the dog.

Within moments, the elephant grew weak with sorrow. He missed his friend. And after several days the elephant was heartbroken. He refused to eat or allow the King to ride on his back. The King sought the advice of doctors, but no one could find the cause of the elephant's illness. Finally, one doctor announced that the elephant had lost a friend.

The King ordered an investigation and heard, at last, about the dog. It was announced throughout the country; *the dog must be returned.* Fearful of the King, the merchant simply let the dog loose. The faithful creature traveled long and far and one day found his way back to the royal stable. When the elephant saw his tiny friend, he lifted his trunk in celebration and scooped the dog off the earth. The elephant's companion lay in silence against his friend's soft back. And, only when he was placed on the ground and had drunk his fill of water, did he begin to bark for joy. The elephant roared his affection with lifted head, swaying back and forth for happiness.

The King decreed that the feelings of animals should be respected – for they were as strong as those of human beings, and the love shared between the dog and the elephant should be a model to all in his kingdom who sought true happiness and friendship. And in that kingdom, no animal was harmed or chained again.

As for the faithful dog, a small throne was made for him, so he rode in processions on the elephant's back. He was rightfully named the Most Excellent Royal Best Friend.

This story was included as the epilogue to the issue of *Storytelling, Self, Society* devoted to healing stories, published in Spring 2005. About this story, Laura Simms wrote: I read this story in many versions and have since enjoyed telling it to young people and to adults. Not only do I visualize the events, but investigate and enliven within myself the feelings of all characters, including my own poignant associations of love and loss. It is not only the happy and satisfying conclusion that is healing, but the chance to feel the deep emotions of loneliness, happiness, compassion, selfishness, loss, misery, reunion, and celebration that is the true transformative medicine for the listener. The journey of emotions taken, which awakens and strengthens the capacity for a diversity of feelings and inner tenderness, serves to bring us closer to a sense of meaning and belonging to the world. A broken heart is an open heart, and this tale lets us break open, remain open and caring, without fear. Exposure, again and again to this sort of imagined journey allows the heart to become accustomed to being tender and receptive.

© 2005 Laura Simms

Mike's Moment by Don Doyle, PhD

When I was a theater professor at Arizona State University, two of my colleagues and I conducted a longitudinal study at an elementary school. We were studying the effect of consistent exposure to drama on three classes of children over a six year period, from kindergarten through fifth grade. We were each working with one class and we each met with our class twice a week during the school year. We engaged them in a variety of theater techniques, including improvisation, creative thinking, and character development and experimentation. They were also exposed to formal theater at least twice a year during the study.

The early sessions were devoted to introducing the elements of making a play, either from the ideas of the children or from a story that was told to them for the purpose of dramatizing. They did a lot of trying on roles to see how they felt in relation to what was going on and to the other characters in the story. Once the children were familiar with the basics, they knew what to expect when I came to the classroom. They were always eager to play. I called it playing the story, not acting the story. They would meet me at the door and say, "What are we going to play today?" or "What kind of play are we going to make today?"

I used my time with the children as a lab for my college students who came to the school to observe me working with improvisational activities, including story dramatization. I was teaching university classes in creative drama, which is a non-audience dramatic activity, benefiting the creative imagination and self-confidence of the participants. The research project was the perfect opportunity to demonstrate the procedures and techniques they were learning in their college class. I was teaching the children and college students how to motivate dramatic action that might originate from a story they had heard or from an aspect of the story such as place, character, time, or plot. I then taught them how to analyze the story and divide it so that it could be dramatized.

One particular day, the children were very excited and ready to play. The room was full of creative drama students from the university, all eager to see what would happen, all with their notebooks ready to observe and take notes. We wanted to do something that everyone could participate in. It wasn't effective, especially for kindergartners, to do something with only two or three children participating. I decided on 'The Three Billy Goats Gruff'. Some of the children didn't know it, so I told it with as much animation, excitement, and enthusiasm as I could muster. They were all anxious to try on some of the characters, and of course the most popular were the trolls because they were the most mysterious, spooky, and angry characters in the story. Plus, they could make strange noises and move in strange ways. They all tried on being trolls of different kinds before anyone else was cast. I emphasized that trolls were just like people; no two were alike and all were different and special in their own way. This was always part of my message for children, to take pride in being themselves.

After everyone got a turn being a troll, most of them also wanted to try on the billy goats. They tried on being a papa, a mama, or a baby billy goat and experimented with how each would come across the bridge. And of course the goats could talk to each other. They discussed why they wanted to go across to the greener grass. Sometimes they had to be persuaded to go across to the greener grass or convince the others. Finally, after we'd tried on all the roles, I cast it initially from volunteers. I knew that everyone would want to be a troll, so I had to talk up the billy goats and their importance in telling the story.

The story was actually cast and played many times, evaluating and recasting after each playing during a session. This insured that everyone got to experiment with different kinds of goats and trolls. Each time, I cast the goats first and there were always more than just three goats – several mamas, papas, and babies all crossed at different times. The bridge was represented by a long work table with a chair on either end. That gave the goats something to go over and the trolls something to be under – plus it was fun to crawl on all fours across the table like a goat. The many trolls couldn't actually all fit under the table and extended on either side which gave them more freedom to move and express their unique troll-ness.

As it happened there was a bully in this kindergarten class that most of the boys and even some of the girls were afraid of. Mike bullied the boys on the playground during recess, and before and after school, and he was very disruptive in the classroom. The college students were very aware of Mike. His behavior was a frequent topic of discussion in the college creative drama classes back at the university. The college students asked how I planned to deal with him. They wondered how I would manage him during the creative drama sessions. I wondered about that myself. Mike was always a problem – for his classmates and his teacher. How could I prepare myself to discipline someone when I was trying to bring out not only his, but his classmates' creativity.

Of course, Mike wanted to be the biggest and gruffest of the big billy goats. During the playing, I cast Mike as one of the big billy goats. In the story, the big billy goat goes across the bridge last. Mike was indeed the last of the big billy goats to cross, and I could feel the tension in the room mounting. The trolls knew that he was going to come across and they didn't know what to expect. Neither did the college students, because it was rare for him to play a role as important as that. Everyone thought that when the trolls said, "I'm coming up there to eat you up" that Mike would respond aggressively, maybe even violently.

When Mike got to the middle of the bridge with his trip-trap, trip-trap, the trolls all began to wake up and be angry that they were awakened. They said, "We're coming up there to eat you up!" At that point, I stopped the play as I often did and said, "Now we have a problem. How will we solve this problem?" I stopped it to avoid any fighting or violence, since the play would be over once he reached the other side. From under the bridge, the trolls said, "We should fight him and knock him off the bridge!" Others said, "We should kill him!" Then I asked Mike, "How should we solve this problem without having a big fight?" Mike said, "I think we should sing the trolls back to sleep." All the college students began writing furiously, and the teacher looked surprised at his solution.

I said, "What a wonderful idea! That sounds like a lullaby. What lullaby should we sing?

Mike thought awhile and then he said, "I'm going to sing 'Rock-a-bye Baby' to put them to sleep."

We were all astonished. The teacher, the other kids, the college students, none of us could believe that such a solution was coming from this child. When he began to sing, all the college students, all the goats who had reached the other side, the teacher, and I all joined in singing 'Rock-a-bye Baby'. I said to the trolls, "Let's see how the trolls go to sleep in slow motion", so as we sang, the trolls all slowly drifted to sleep under their bridge and Mike, the biggest billy goat, trip-trapped to the other side safely.

When Mike got to the other side, the whole room was silent – there wasn't a sound except for some sniffling here and there from the college students. Then, as we always did, we gathered together on the floor to talk about what was believable in the playing and what needed work. Everyone gave Mike positive comments about his playing, but especially about his solution to the problem in the story.

I can assure you that no one who witnessed that session will ever forget it. I'd like to tell you that Mike went on to have a better life after that moment; unfortunately, that wasn't the case. But for that moment, that one special moment, by playing an honest, heroic role in a story, Mike was able to step out of the role he normally played in life and create something beautiful. I hope he remembered it all his life.

© 2008 Don Doyle

Goblin's Gloves, a Welsh folktale, retold by Allison Cox

In Wales, foxglove was called Goblin's Gloves and was said to attract the hobgoblins who wore the long bells on their fingers as gloves that imparted magical properties. This story from my Welsh heritage is a favorite.

Garth didn't like it - no not one bit and told Gwen so every chance he got. "Anybody coming through our patch of the woods will be thinking that you're a witch, growing all those goblin gloves," he'd tell her.

But Gwen just laughed at him. "No one ever comes out here to our wood and they are such lovely flowers. How could I not grow them?"

"Well they don't call them goblin gloves for nothing! They draw them here Gwen - to dance and sing and who knows what kind of other mischief. Just not wise, I tell you; we should pull them all up."

"You just keep your nose out of my flower beds!" Gwen warned him and called over her shoulder, "Do not let me find any of my flowers missing."

Garth was already heading toward the forest path, so he just waved over his free arm and slung his axe over his shoulder with his other as he headed up Llanhiddel Mountain to cut firewood to sell in town. He always left early to be sure to be back before dusk, when the mountain spirits were said to walk about.

Gwen knew that Garth would indulge her and leave the flowers alone. He just liked to grumble about some things now and then, just so she would know that he was keeping an eye out.

What she didn't tell him was that she had been, over the years, transplanting all the goblin gloves that she would come across growing into the forest pathways on the way to back from town. She knew the flowers were only seeking more light and that they would get trampled underfoot as Garth carried wood to town to sell at market. In her gardens and the surrounding meadows, the long beautiful spikes of purple, pink and white bells sometimes grew up to eight feet tall - no other flower in her garden stood so tall for so long.

As Gwen weeded in her garden that morning she kept stopping and listening and looking around, for she felt that she was not alone. As she was weeding around the base of one of her favorite stands of goblin gloves, she straightened her back to look to see if perhaps some-one was behind her and then turned back around and - oh! - she made such a jump for there was a hobgoblin standing there where a tall stand of goblins gloves had been just a moment before.

The hob looked up at her with bright eyes. He had a long thick dark beard and copper-colored skin. Gwen figured he was about an ell high (2 feet) and though of the smallest stature, she thought he was very well proportioned. He was dressed in woven cloth of earthen colors and wore boots and a belt of leathers.

"Well, excuse me - I did na' see you standing there."

The little man bowed and spoke in a low voice, "Well it is me who is asking your forgive-ness for I have startled you who cares for our flowers and protects them from the one who cuts the trees,"

"Protect your flowers? Oh you mean the goblin gloves. Well now, it is my pleasure to have them grow here," Gwen said, secretly delighted that the hob appeared to her, and then real-ized what he had said. "And oh, do not pay any mind to my man's talk about pulling up the flowers. He really does love flowers too. He is just like an old bear and must grumble and growl a bit now and then. Truth to tell, he just worries when he leaves me home alone while he cuts wood up in the mountains. He's heard that you hobs are attracted to the goblin gloves and, well, he fears that you hobs will play tricks on me while he is gone."

"Tell your man that we hobs watch over you while he works and would never let any harm come to you. And we want to do more to thank you for growing our flowers here."

Gwen closed her eyes against the glare of the sun for a moment, smiling. "Oh there's no need. I am happy to grow these flowers here and..." She shaded her eyes to discover the little hob was gone and the goblin gloves reappeared in that same spot, shivering a bit as though a gentle breeze had blown across the little meadow. "Well, imagine that - a hob, talking to me... and wanting to help me none-the-less! Hmmm."

But that night when Garth was home, Gwen never did tell him about her visitor. Nor did she mention that before she went to bed, she had left some fresh cream in a bowl on the back step for the hob. In the morning the bowl of cream was empty but someone had worked the churn she had left filled with cream beside the hearth that night. All she had to do was but give it a thump or two to bring out the butter in a great lump.

One night Gwen and Garth had fallen asleep, forgetting to blow out the candle and when they arose in the morning Gwen found that someone had swept the hearth. The following nights, she left a mug of ale on the back step and didn't she find someone had done her other chores those nights too? Sometimes it would be her baking and brewing, other times her washing and mending. Garth never seemed to notice the extra help; he just complimented Gwen on her good bread and good beer. And Gwen noticed that after eating and drinking the food and ale that the hobs had left them, Garth seemed livelier and happier than he had in years. One morning he even jumped out of bed and hugged her, first thing in the morning - before tea even, and told her that he felt like a new man. "Well," Gwen thought, "Ya certainly act like one!" Gwen made sure to leave an extra bowl of cream on the back step that night. Their little farm prospered as never before.

But then one late afternoon, stretched into one long evening, Gwen was sure that any minute Garth would come home calling "I'm back, Gwen" and would be lowering the bundle of wood from his back, for he never stayed out so late. By long past bedtime, Gwen was worried sick. She went outside in her shawl, standing in the moonlight in her garden, looking toward the woods and calling, "Gaaaarth! Garth, are you out there love?" but she heard only the night crickets sing back.

Gwen clutched at her shawl and turned to go back inside when she heard, "He won't be coming home tonight." She spun around to find the same small hob, with the long dark beard and bright eyes staring up at her where she was just about to step. And rather than be surprised at this sudden appearance, Gwen thought only of Garth.

"And where might he be?" she asked the little man.

"The old woman of the mountain has a glamour on him and will not let him go." The hob said, looking steadily into her eyes.

Gwen cried "No!" for all who grew up in the shadow of the mountains knew of the old woman of the mountain, an evil spirit that sat amongst the rocks along the mountain trails, waiting to lure travelers off the path to their death.

Gwen dropped to her knees, and looking at the little man eye to eye, pleaded, "Please sir, if there is any power that you have to help him, I ask you to bring my Garth back home to me!"

"You wish us to protect the killer of trees who would have you pull up our flowers?" the hob asked.

"Yes, please! You know that he has never pulled up any goblin gloves and he cares for me who cares for your flowers. If anything ever happens to him then — it would be the end of me." The hob looked at her solemnly.

"Will you help him?" Gwen asked again. He nodded slowly.

"But can you really help him? Can one hob stop the magic of the old woman of the mountains?"

At this, the hob's face broke into merry smile. "We are more in number than one hob! Look around you my lady."

Gwen heard soft laughter echoing around the meadow and looked up to see, in every place where the tall spires of pink and purple bells of the goblins gloves had been growing, there now was standing the hobs themselves, dozens and dozens of them.

"And," he continued, "We hobs have powerful magic of our own." With that said, the hob-goblins all disappeared.

"Thanks to you all," whispered Gwen as she sat back down on the cool earth to wait. "Bring my Garth back home to me."

As he was walking up the mountain trail, the last thing Garth remembered was that he was thinking "If I could just get a little more wood, I will not need to come up the mountain at all tomorrow. I could spend the day with Gwen, maybe even take her to town to see some friends — she would like that." And wouldn't you know, just then he had come around a curve in the trail and that's when he saw her — a brooding, silent figure that seemed to step from the shadows themselves, and slowly pull back her dark hood to reveal a hag's face, wild eyes shining, and chanting...

> By my tongue do as I bid
> A curse on you thru power of stone
> A veil upon your mind I weave
> Dance o'er the cliff and break your bones!

Laughing, she pointed up the trail with long fingers and commanded him to "Climb!"

The spirit woman had complete control of Garth. He dropped the bundle of wood that he had been gathering all day as well as his axe and began to trudge further up the trail, where the hag had pointed. The old woman of the mountain floated after him, her black shredded cloak and gown flying about her in the winds that followed her. She cackled to herself as she guided the poor man higher up the trail to the cliffs that overlooked the valley and his little farm below. There, the trail widened out to a long rocky ledge. The old woman of the mountains was playing with him just as a child would dance a puppet on a string... taunting him before she walked the woodcutter over the edge.

Suddenly, the empty mountain ledge was filled with little men. They appeared in a circle around the hag who began to shriek at them, "Get out of my way!"

Garth came back to his senses but could not understand what his eyes then beheld. For there was the hag of the mountain — he remembered seeing her before all the world went dark. Only now she was surrounded by hobgoblins who stood in multiple rings around her, holding her imprisoned simply by pointing their fingers at her. Garth stared, trying to make sense of the scene before him. He took a step closer and saw that the fingers of every hob were covered with the flowers of goblin gloves and that the Old Woman of the mountain seemed to fear that they might touch her with these flowery gloves. He took a step closer still but a hob suddenly appeared before him, scaring him out of his wits. The hob simply looked into his eyes and said, "RUN!"

And Garth did exactly that! He darted past the hag and hobs, dashed down the mountain, and ran as long as his lungs would allow and then hurried on as fast as his legs would carry him until he reached the meadow surrounding his little farm. There, he was greeted by cries of relief as Gwen rose from her garden where she had been waiting ever since the hobs had disappeared.

That night Garth told Gwen all that he could remember that happened on the mountain, and Gwen told Garth about the appearance and disappearance of the hobs in the garden. Garth stayed close to home for several weeks. During these days, he scouted the forest paths for more goblin's gloves. He would dig these up and take them to Gwen who would exchange them with any other varieties of flowers she had growing and give these to Garth to transplant out in the woods until the only flowers that grew in their flower beds and around the edges of the meadow were goblin's gloves.

From that day on both Garth and Gwen made sure that there was a mug of ale or basin of cream left on the back step each night. Though they never saw the little men again, sometimes as Gwen and Garth lay in each other's arms in bed together, they would hear the light laughter and voices of the hobs as they danced and sang under the soft moonlight in the meadow outside.

(http://www.dancingleaves.com/allison/stories/foxglove/foxglove_stories.html)
© 2004 Allison M. Cox

Works Cited

Ashliman, D.L. *The Folklore and Mythology Electronic Texts*. http://www.pitt.edu/~dash/folk-texts.html

Baldwin, Jackie. Post to the STORYTELL Discussion List, April 16, 2008. Texas Woman's University School of Library and Information Studies, http://www.twu.edu/COPE/slis/storytell.htm

Baltuck, Naomi. *Apples from Heaven: Multicultural Folk Tales About Stories and Storytellers*. Linnet Books, 1995.

Bruchac, Joseph. *Tell Me A Tale: A Book About Storytelling*. Harcourt Children's Books, 1997.

Campbell, Joseph. *The Hero with A Thousand Faces*. Princeton University Press, 1972.

Charon, Rita. *Narrative Medicine: Honoring the Stories of Illness*. Oxford University Press USA, 2008.

Clark, Evelyn. *Around the Corporate Campfire: "How Great Leaders Use Stories to Inspire Success."* C&C Publishing, 2004.

Clayton, Sally Pomme. Tales *Told in Tents: Stories from Central Asia*. Frances Lincoln, 2004.

Cole, Joanna. *Best Loved Folktales of the World*. New York: Anchor Books, 1983

Cordi, Kevin. *Unlocking the World of Youth Storytelling*. http://youthstorytelling.com/youth_spot.html

Cox, Allison M. and David H. Albert. *The Healing Heart - Communities: Storytelling To Build Strong and Healthy Communities*. New Society Publishers, 2003.

Cox, Allison M. and David H. Albert. *The Healing Heart – Families: Storytelling To Encourage Caring and Healthy Families*. New Society Publishers, 2003.

Cox, Allison M. *Allison Cox: Storyteller, Author, and Health Professional*. http://www.dancingleaves.com/allison/index.html

Creeden, Sharon. *Fair is Fair: World Folktales of Justice*. August House, 1996.

Creeden, Sharon. *In Full Bloom: Stories of Women in Their Prime*. August House, 1999.

Davis, Donald. *Donald Davis Storyteller*. http://www.ddavisstoryteller.com/

Davis, Donald. *Telling Your Own Stories for Family and Classroom Storytelling, Public Speaking, and Personal Journaling*. August House, 1993.

Doniger, Wendy. *Other Peoples' Myths: The Cave of Echoes*. The University of Chicago Press, 1995.

Doyle, Don. Interview conducted April 22, 2008.

Ellis, Elizabeth. "Researching and Crafting the History Story", *Storytelling World,* Winter/Spring, 1997, Issue 11, page 7-8.

Ellis, Rex. "Colonial Williamsburg's Storytelling Festival," Colonial Williamsburg. http://www.history.org/media/podcasts_transcripts/StorytellingFestival.cfm

Ellis, Rex. "Symposium Speech #6," *The WEYANOKE Association: telling our own story*. http://www.weyanoke.org/6ellis.html

Ellis, Rex. *Beneath the Blazing Sun: Stories from the African-American Journey.* August House, 1997.

Encyclopedia Mythica. http://www.pantheon.org/

Forest, Heather. *Story Arts Online.* http://www.storyarts.org/library/index.html

Forest, Heather. *Wisdom Tales from Around the World.* August House, 1996.

Fujita, Hiroko. *Folktales from the Japanese Countryside,* Edited by Fran Stallings. Libraries Unlimited, 2008.

Fujita, Hiroko. *Stories to Play With: Kids' Tales Told with Puppets, Paper, Toys, and Imagination.* Adapted and edited by Fran Stallings. August House, 1999.

"Good Lives and Goodbyes, a Missoulian/Missoula Demonstration Project Special Section," http://www.missoulian.com/specials/dying/meaning.html

Grimm, Jacob and Wilhelm, *The Peasant's Clever Daughter.* Margaret Taylor, trans. http://classiclit.about.com/library/bl-etexts/grimm/bl-grimm-pcleverd.htm

Hamilton, Martha and Mitch Weiss. Excerpt from *Children Tell Stories,* in *Storytelling Magazine,* May/June 2007.

Hamilton, Virginia. *The People Could Fly: American Black Folktales.* Knopf Books for Young Readers, 2000.

Heiner, Heidi Anne. *Sur La Lune Fairy Tales.* http://www.surlalunefairytales.com/

Holt, David and Bill Mooney. *Ready-to-Tell Tales: Sure Fire Stories from America's Favorite Storytellers.* August House, 1995.

Horner, Beth. "Through My Voice: Telling Family History," *Storytelling Magazine,* July/August 2004.

International Storytelling Center. http://www.storytellingfoundation.org/)http://www.storytellingfoundation.org/

Jeffers, Herrick. *Once Upon a Time They Lived Happily Ever After.* 1997

Jones, Raymond E. and Jon C. Stott, eds. *A World of Stories: Traditional Tales for Children.* Oxford University Press, 2006.

Klein, Susan. ETHICS, Apprenticeship, Etiquette, Courtesy, and Copyright. Edited by C.Birch and M. Heckler. 4th ed. Oak Bluffs, MA: Ruby Window Productions, 2008.

Klein, Susan. *Susan Klein: Ruby Window Productions.* http://www.susanklein.net/

Klein, Susan. Telephone interview conducted April 21, 2008.

Leach, Maria. *How the People Sang the Mountains Up: How and Why Stories.* Viking Juvenile, 1967.

Lenihan, Eddie and Carolyn Eve Green. *Meeting the Other Crowd: the fairy stories of hidden Ireland.* Tarcher, 2004.

Lenihan, Eddie. *The Good People: Authentic Irish Fairy Tales.* (Audio Tape) Sounds True, 2001.

Lipman, Doug. *The Storytelling Coach: How to Listen, Praise, and Bring out People's Best.* August House, 1995.

Lopez, Barry. *Crow and Weasel.* Century, 1990.

Loya, Olga. Interview conducted November 8, 2006.

Loya, Olga. *Momentos Magicos/Magic Moments.* August House, 1997.

Loya, Olga. *Storyteller Olga Loya.* www.olgaloya.com

MacDonald, Margaret Read. *Tell the World: Storytelling Across Language Barriers.* Libraries Unlimited, 2008.

MacDonald, Margaret Read. *Three Minute Tales: Stories from Around the World to Tell or Read When Time is Short.* August House, 2004.

Maguire, Jack. *Creative Storytelling.* Yellow Moon Press, 1985.

Martin, Rafe. "Why Folktales?" http://rafemartin.com/articles.htm#folk

Mellon, Nancy. *The Art of Storytelling.* Element Books Limited, 1992.

Momaday, N. Scott. "The Story of the Arrowmaker: Transmitting the traditions of speech." Parabola: The Magazine of Myth and Tradition. Vol. XX, No. 3.

National Storytelling Network. http://www.storynet.org

Neile, Caren S. "A Place at the Hearth: Storytelling, Subversion and the U.S. Culture Industry," http://web.mit.edu/comm-forum/mit4/papers/neile.pdf .

Norfolk, Bobby and Sherry Norfolk. "Truth and Story." *The Moral of the Story: Folktales for Character Development.* August House, 1999.

Ramanujan, A. K. *A Flowering Tree and Other Oral Tales from India.* University of California Press, 1997.

Ramanujan, A.K. *Folktales from India: A Selection of Oral Tales from Twenty-two Languages.* Pantheon, 1994.

Reps, Paul and Nyogen Senzaki. *Zen Flesh, Zen Bones: A Collection of Zen and Pre-Zen Writings.* Tuttle Publishing, 1998.

Ristow, Bill. "What is narrative?" (http://poynter.org/column.asp?id=52&aid=49550)

Rubalcava, Kassandra. Interview conducted April 25, 2008.

Sawyer, Ruth. The Way of the Storyteller. Penguin, 1977.

Scheub, Harold. *Story.* University of Wisconsin Press, 1998.

Schwartz, Howard. *Gabriel's Palace: Jewish Mystical Tales.* Oxford University Press, 1994.

Sheppard, Tim. "Frequently Asked Questions." *The Storytelling FAQ.* www.timsheppard.co.uk/story/faq.html#Introduction.

Sheppard, Tim. "The Story of Truth and a Story about Truth." http://www.henshall.com/blog/archives/000156.html. August 13, 2007.

Sherman, Josepha. *Trickster Tales: Forty Folk Stories from Around the World.* August House, 1996.

Simms, Laura. "A *Jataka* Tale of Friendship," in *Storytelling, Self, Society: An Interdisciplinary Journal of Storytelling Studies.* Vol. 1, No. 2, Spring, 2005.

South Mountain Community College Storytelling Institute. http://eport.mariopa.edu/storytelling

Storyteller.net. http://www.storyteller.net/

Storytelling in Organizations Special Interest Group of the National Storytelling Network, http://storytellinginorganizations.com/

Suler, John. "No Fear." http://www.rider.edu/~suler/zenstory/goflow.html

The Call of Story. www.callofstory.org/en/storytelling

The Healing Story Alliance, a special interest group of the National Storytelling Network, http://www.healingstory.org/

The Internet Sacred Text Archive. http://www.sacred-texts.com/

"The Story of Truth & Parable." *Yiddish Folktales.* Pantheon Books, 1977.

Thomason, Dovie. Telephone interview conducted April 24, 2008.

Thompson, Stith. *The Folktale.* University of California Press, 1977.

Thorpe, Benjamin. *Northern Mythology.* London: Edward Lumley, 1985 http://books.google.com/books?id=6YkAAAAAMAAJ&pg=PA113&lpg=PA113&dq=aslaug+kraka&source=web&ots=FWIf9ohcm-&sig=bJ4I6b98YkREImx9Bam_gKE_fJQ&hl=en#PPA110,M1

Torres, Marilyn. Interview conducted February 26, 2007, Phoenix, Arizona.

Walsh, Patricia Mary. "Storytelling in AA." http://www.addictionrecov.org/paradigm/P_PR_F99/WALSH.HTM)

Warren, Sandy Oglesby, and Kathy Eastman. "Storytelling: Invoking the Muse at the Museum," *The Docent Educator*, Vol. 13, No. 1, Autumn 2003.

Wolfgramm, Emil. Interview conducted March 17, 2007.

Wolkstein, Diane. *The Magic Orange Tree and Other Haitian Folktales.* Schocken, 1997.

Zipes, Jack. *Fairy Tale as Myth: Myth as Fairy Tale.* University Press of Kentucky, 1994.

List of Stories

Chapter 1: What is Storytelling?

- "Truth and Story" a Yiddish tale from Europe
- "Anansi and the Sky God's Stories" a folktale from Ghana
- "A Whole Brain" a folktale from Kazakhstan

Chapter 2: Getting Started

- "Why Frogs Croak in Wet Weather" a Korean folktale
- "A Story and a Song" a folktale from India
- "Stone Soup" a folktale from Europe
- "The Gossiping Clams" a Suquamish (Native American) legend

Chapter 3: How to Tell a Folktale

- "The Magic Orange Tree" a folktale from Haiti
- "Aslaug the Deep-Minded" a Norse folktale
- "Paca and Beetle" a folktale from Brazil
- "The Tale of the Lizards' Tails" a folktale from Japan
- "The Monkey and the Crocodile" a folktale from Mexico

Chapter 4: How to Tell a Myth, a Legend, or a Hero Tale

- "The Story of Arachne" a Greek myth
- "The Hungry Goddess" an Aztec myth
- "Who is the Greatest Warrior" a Yoruba myth from West Africa
- "FIE PA'A, FIE FĀNAU?!: Wanting to be barren, yet wanting to bear a child – simultaneously!" a proverbial story from Tonga
- "Saint Brigid's Cloak" a legend from Ireland
- "La Llorona" a legend from Mexico

Chapter 5: How to Tell a Story in Public

- "The Story of Mr. Wiggle and Mr. Waggle" a participation story
- "No Fear," "Great Waves," and "A Parable" three Zen stories from Asia
- "What Happens When You Really Listen" a folktale from India
- "The Story of the Arrowmaker" a Kiowa (Native American) tale

Chapter 6: How to Tell a Fact-based Story

- "Dedication Day"
- "Legendary Meanness"
- "The Boy"
- "Phillis Wheatley (1753 – 1784)"
- "Escaping Pancho Villa"
- "The Haunted Cuckoo Clock"

Chapter 7: How to Tell a Personal Story

- "Pie of Peace"
- "Ballerina Eyelashes"
- "*Me Llamo Ricardo*"
- "Bribing the Babysitter"

Chapter 8: Applications of Storytelling

- "A *Jataka* Tale of Friendship" a folktale from India
- "Mike's Moment" a personal story
- "Goblin's Gloves" a folktale from Wales

Appendix A

Chapter Questions

Chapter 1: What is Storytelling

Name _____

Reflection:

1. What is the most important thing you've learned in this chapter?

2. What questions do you have? Is there a topic on which you need more information or further clarification?

3. Which of the quotes above best captures your emerging understanding of storytelling, and why?

Study Questions:

1. Name the four elements that help define storytelling as an art form.

2. What is the importance of images in storytelling?

3. What is the purpose of the audience?

4. What is the relationship between the story, the teller, and the audience?

5. How does the analogy of "Story as Floor Plan" work to help explain what storytellers do when they tell stories?

6. Where do storytellers get their stories?

7. Where do storytellers tell stories?

8. How are storytelling and story writing different?

9. What are the differences between storytelling and theatre?

10. What three aspects of storytelling has an "excellent" storyteller mastered?

11. How do Eddie Lenihan and Marilyn Torres bridge traditional and modern storytelling?

The Stories:

1. Explain how these three stories deepened your understanding of storytelling and its role in human life.

Chapter 2: Getting Started

Name _____

Reflection:

1. What is the most important thing you've learned in this chapter?

2. What questions do you have? Is there a topic on which you need more information or further clarification?

3. How do you feel about preparing your first story to tell?

Study Questions:

1. What are the three elements of storytelling?

2. What four kinds of stories will you be telling this semester?

3. What are the keys to combating nerves?

4. What are the three "Ds" of choosing a story?

5. What is a good way to jumpstart the process of finding stories that are right for you?

6. What is the first rule of learning a story from a book? Why is memorization not effective for storytelling?

7. Why are appreciations a good place to start when giving feedback?

8. What are the ongoing creative tasks of the storyteller?

9. What should you do if you forget your story while telling it?

10. What is the storyteller's minimal ethical standard?

11. How did Susan Klein get started in storytelling?

12. According to Susan, what is your responsibility after a folktale "resonates with your own story?"

Name _____

13. What two pieces of advice does Dustin Loehr offer to beginning storytellers?

14. What did Kassandra Rubalcava learn from Peter Cook?

The Stories:

1. Stories rely on metaphor to make meaning. How do you interpret the metaphor of revenge in *A Story and a Song*? What is the primary message of this story for you?

2. How might the meaning of *Stone Soup* apply to the beginning storyteller?

3. What offense did the gossiping clams commit? What was their punishment?

Chapter 3: How to Tell a Folktale

Name _____

Story Exercises:

1. Refer back to the previous chapter and apply "Learning the Basics of the Story" and "Making a deeper personal connection to the story" to the folktale you have chosen to tell.

2. Make a storyboard for the story.

3. Tell the story to someone else without referring to your lists or to your storyboard.

Reflection:

1. What is the most important thing you've learned in this chapter?

2. What questions do you have? Is there a topic on which you need more information or further clarification?

3. What folktales do you remember from your childhood?

4. How have folktales influenced your life?

Chapter 3: How to Tell a Folktale

Study Questions:

1. What does it mean to trust a story?

2. How do you awaken your deep understanding of the folktale pattern?

3. What are two of the ways that folktales provide delight to listeners?

4. What does it mean to say that folktales are traditional? How and why do folktales change?

5. Why would someone say that a story can be more important than food?

6. Name and briefly describe two of the features of folktales that can aid in learning and remembering the story.

7. Why is it important to use color when you make a storyboard?

8. How is a folktale like an animal in a zoo?

Chapter 3: How to Tell a Folktale

Name _____

9. List three tips for telling a story with your whole body.

10. What are the guidelines for creating a derivative version of a folktale?

11. What is the lesson for storytellers in Dovie Thomason's story about the gift of a turtle she gave to a friend?

12. What has been more important to Dovie's training than classroom instruction?

13. How do Fran Stallings and Hiroko Fujita tell stories together?

14. How did Fujita-san learn the joy of stories?

The Stories:

1. This version of the "Magic Orange Tree" begins with the opening "Cric? Crac!" This is a traditional opening designed to assess the attention and readiness of the audience so the teller can begin the tale. The story has many of the features of folktales discussed in the text. What are they? Of what other story does the story remind you?

2. "Aslaug the Deep Minded" does not rely on repetition or magic. What features or functions of the folktale does it incorporate?

3. What features and functions of the folktale does the story "Paca and Beetle" demonstrate? Does the story remind you of another you have heard? If so, what is it?

4. What features of the folktale are present in "The Tale of the Lizards' Tails"?

5. Trickster characters are common in folktales. How does Monkey trick Crocodile?

Chapter 4: How to Tell a Myth, Legend or Hero Tale

Name _____

Story Exercises:

You've told one story and you are preparing to tell the second. Reflect on your first experience:

- **Selecting the story:** How did you pick your first story? How much time did you invest in finding a story that gave you delight?

- **Relating to the story:** How did you learn your first story? Will you try different strategies to learn the second one? Was the story a good match for you?

- **Preparing to tell:** How did you prepare yourself to stand in front of the audience? Was it effective for you? Will you keep the same strategy or will you try something different as you prepare your second story?

- **The telling experience:** What was your level of comfort as you told the story? What did you learn about yourself as a storyteller by telling your first story? What did the positive feedback you received from your classmates tell you about your emerging storytelling style?

- **Considering all of the above:** What is your current understanding of yourself as a storyteller? What do you know works for you? What will you do differently next time?

Chapter 4: How to Tell a Myth, Legend or Hero Tale

When you have reviewed your first experience, then move on to the preparation of your second story:

1. Once you have selected the second story you want to tell, refer back to the "Getting Started" chapter and apply "Learning the Basics of the Story" and "Making a deeper personal connection to the story" to your myth, legend, or hero tale.

2. Review the last section of this chapter and apply the suggestions to your story:

   a. What have you learned about the culture your story is from?

   b. Are there language issues you need to consider in preparing your story?

   c. Did you find more than one version of your story, and if so was that helpful?

   d. If you chose to tell a myth, what were the important metaphors and symbols in the story? How did they contribute to your understanding of the meaning of the story? What is the meaning of the story for you?

3. Did storyboarding work for you? If so, make a storyboard for your second story.

4. Tell the story as often as you can before it is time to present it in class. The more comfortable you are with the story, the more comfortable you will be in front of your audience.

Reflection:

1. What is the most important thing you've learned in this chapter?

Chapter 4: How to Tell a Myth, Legend or Hero Tale

Name _____

2. What questions do you have? Is there a topic on which you need more information or further clarification?

3. The structure of the hero's journey is based on the important transition points in human life. By the time we reach adulthood, we have all experienced at least one of these transitions, such as puberty, graduation, childbirth, or marriage. Reflect on the transitions in your own life and apply Joseph Bruchac's four step process to your experience.

4. What experiences did you have with myths, legends, or hero tales before you took this class? Had you encountered these types of stories before?

Study Questions:

1. What is a myth and how does it relate to a mythology?

2. Why do the characters in myth and legend often seem familiar to us?

3. What is a legend and what kinds of characters are they usually about?

4. Why are myths and legends categorized as "true" stories?

5. What are the three stages of a hero myth according to Joseph Campbell?

6. What role do metaphor and symbol play in myths?

7. How is story structured like a person's life?

8. List three ways to incorporate pacing into a story.

9. List two ways of showing respect for the myth, legend, or hero-tale that you choose to tell.

10. Why does Olga Loya tell epic stories?

11. According to her, who are the ancient and modern counterparts of La Llorona?

12. According to Emil Wolfgramm, what is the difference between plumbing and water?

13. Why don't Tongans need Hollywood?

Chapter 4: How to Tell a Myth, Legend or Hero Tale

Name _____

14. What advice does Emil offer literacy-based storytellers who wish to tell stories from oral cultures?

The Stories:

1. This chapter contains several stories. Did one of the types of stories appeal to you more than the others?

2. What was your favorite story and why?

3. Once you have read the stories, pick your favorite and apply Bruchac's four-step hero pattern to it.

Chapter 5: How to Tell a Story in Public

Name _____

Reflection

1. What is the most important thing you've learned in this chapter?

2. What questions do you have? Is there a topic on which you need more information or further clarification?

3. Do you feel anxious about telling a story in public? What have you learned in this chapter that will help you?

4. Where do you plan on telling your stories?

Study Questions:

1. Why is it important to tell stories in public?

2. What are the four elements to consider before telling a story in public?

3. What must you do before, during and after the performance?

4. What three general types of places are recommended for telling stories in public?

5. What are the challenges associated with using dialects or accents? Why does the author prefer not to use them?

6. What are three of the considerations to remember when telling stories to children in an elementary school class?

7. Why is it important to assess your performance once it is completed?

8. What distinguishes storytelling from other art forms based in narrative?

9. List three the things you must assess and manage when using a microphone.

Chapter 5: How to Tell a Story in Public

Name _____

10. What is the function of the local and national storytelling organizations?

The Stories:

1. What is the message of the three Zen stories? How do they relate to storytelling and performance?

2. Reflecting on the story What Happens When You Really Listen, what do you think happened when the man dove into the ocean to fetch the ring? What is the meaning of that passage for storytellers? What is the primary message of this story for you?

3. How is "The Story of the Arrowmaker" applicable to performing as a storyteller?

Chapter 6: How to Tell Fact-based Stories

Name _____

Story Exercises:

1. Identifying a subject for your fact-based story: To identify a person that you may want to tell about, think about the people who interest you.

   - Who do you admire and respect?

   - Who do you wish to emulate?

   - Who has had an impact on your life and the way you live it.

   - Did you have a childhood hero, teacher, or mentor that you could tell about?

2. Choose one of the stories in the chapter other than "Dedication Day" and analyze its structure using the three methods described in the chapter.

3. Which structure fit the story best? Say why you think it worked better for the story you chose.

Reflection:

1. What is the most important thing you've learned in this chapter?

2. What questions do you have? Is there a topic on which you need more information or further clarification?

3. What experiences did you have with fact-based stories before you took this class? Had you encountered these types of stories before?

Study Questions:

1. What is a fact-based story?

2. Briefly describe the differences between a historical story, a biographical story, and a family story.

3. What six steps does Elizabeth Ellis recommend for the development of a story from history?

4. What kinds of questions are best for prompting stories from older relatives?

Name _____

5. What is one of the key differences between fact-based stories and traditional stories such as folktales and myths?

6. What are the "Five Ps" and what are they used for? What is the 6TH 'P?' What is the other structuring device included in the chapter by Donald Davis? Which one do you think will be more useful for you?

7. What four steps does Susan Klein recommend for getting to the heart of a story?

8. What ethical considerations must guide the creation of a fact-based story?

9. What role did Colonial Williamsburg play in Rex Ellis' life when he was young?

10. Rex Ellis says, "It's hard to hate someone whose story you know." How has he applied that at Colonial Williamsburg?

Chapter 6: How to Tell Fact-based Stories

The Stories:

1. Apply the second Donald Davis structuring device, the one that begins "There is a normal world" to Michelle Mostaghim's, "The Boy".

2. Review Elizabeth Ellis's tips on how to create a historical story. Read LynnAnn Wojciechowicz's story about Phillis Wheatley and give examples of three of Ellis's strategies that have been used in the story.

3. Who is the story "Escaping Pancho Villa" about? How do you feel about the ending of the story?

4. Apply "The Five P's" to "The Haunted Cuckoo Clock."

Chapter 7: How to Tell a Personal Story

Name _____

Developing a Personal Story

Select the memory or an anecdote that you want to craft into a story and then use the following sequence of questions and prompts to prepare it for telling:

1. Briefly describe the memory or anecdote.

2. What does the story mean to you? What changed as a result of this experience?

3. Why is it worth telling and hearing?

4. How does it fit into the overall pattern of your life and experience?

5. Think about your anecdote and complete the phrase "From that day on . . ." in relation to it. How did that help clarify the meaning of the story?

6. Describe the People, Place, Problem, Progress and Point in your story that will create a vivid set of Pictures for your listeners.
   - Who are the **People** in your story?

   - What **Place** is your story set in?

   - What is the **Problem** that your story revolves around?

- What is the **Progress** or resolution to your story?

- What is the **Point** of your story?

7. Describe the Character, Crisis, Discovery, and Lesson Learned in your story:
   - Who are the **Characters** in your story?

   - What is the **Crisis** the story is built around?

   - What **Discovery** is made that leads to the resolution of the story?

   - What **Lesson** was learned by you as a result of the incident?

8. Once you have worked through these steps, you should have the elements of a story instead of an anecdote. Now tell your new story to someone else. Note the response, and ask if your listener has any questions. How did it go?

9. Do you need more information from someone else that could help the story? Do you need permission from any of the characters in the story? If so, what do you need to know and from whom will you learn it?

10. Incorporate any new information into your story and tell it again. As with the previous stories you have told, the more you tell it, the better your story will be and the better prepared you will be to tell it.

Chapter 7: How to Tell a Personal Story

Name _____

Reflection:

1. What is the most important thing you've learned in this chapter?

2. What questions do you have? Is there a topic on which you need more information or further clarification?

3. What experiences did you have with personal stories before you took this class? Had you encountered this type of story before?

Study Questions:

1. Why are personal stories important?

2. What is the difference between an anecdote and a story?

3. What is the function of the phrase "From that day on. . ." in crafting a story?

4. How do I find a topic for a personal story?

5. What must the teller know about the characters in a personal story?

6. How does the inclusion of sensory details enhance the listeners' experience of a story?

7. What is the storyteller's primary concern when considering whether to alter the "facts" of a story?

8. What is the fourth "D" and how should I handle it?

9. Why must the emotions in a story be resolved before it is told?

10. What about the other people in my story? What is my responsibility to them?

11. Who is Michael Lacapa and what is he known for?

12. What kind of stories did Donald Davis learn from his grandmother? For what kind of stories is he best known?

The Stories:

1. Read the four personal stories. Choose one of them and then apply one of Donald Davis' story rubrics to it. What did you learn about the story by doing this?

Chapter 8: Applications of Storytelling

Name _____

Reflection:

1. What is the most important thing you've learned in this chapter?

2. What questions do you have? Is there a topic on which you need more information or further clarification?

3. How might you apply storytelling in your own life or work?

Study Questions:

1. What kinds of work do storytellers do in educational settings?

2. State which three of LynnAnn Wojciechowicz's nine reasons for infusing storytelling into the curriculum make the most sense to you and say why.

3. In which healing setting can you imagine story being beneficial in your own life?

4. How is story used in organizational settings?

5. What is the "salmon story"?

6. What are the challenges of developing stories for use in interpretive settings?

7. Who is Allison Cox and for what is she known?

8. What was Don Doyle's "minor miracle"?

9. Why should we, as storytellers, have no fear of the Internet and other new technologies?

10. With whom does the future of storytelling lie?

11. How will you integrate storytelling into your life from this point on?

Chapter 8: Applications of Storytelling

Name _____

The Stories:

1. To whom, or in what contexts, can you imagine telling the "Jataka Tale of Friendship"?

2. What feelings did you have when reading "Mike's Moment"?

3. What does the story demonstrate about the power of any story, even "The Three Billy Goats Gruff," to provide a context for change?

4. Who was changed by the transformative moment in the story and how?

5. How does "The Goblin's Glove" by Allison Cox relate to the situation in which she used it?

6. Why is it such a good match for its audience?

Appendix B

Forms

Story Summary & Analysis Worksheet

Name _____

Title of Story:

Author/Collector:

Source (Book Title or Web Address):

Publisher: Copyright Year:

Type of Story (Genre):

Ethnicity or Culture Reflected in Story:

Summary: What is the story about?

Analyze the following aspects of the story:

Audience: Who would enjoy this story?

Theme (Big ideas or lessons):

Describe concepts, skills, and/or values that this story could help teach:

What emotions, ideas, or memories does this story evoke for you?

Where and how might you use this story?

In-Class Telling Report Form

Name _____

The title of the story:

The author and source:

Cultural context:
The genre (pourquoi, folktale, myth, hero tale, family story, personal story, etc.):

Where and how you found it:

Why you chose this story:

What Feedback you got from the class:

What you liked about your performance and what you will change next time:

What you learned about the story and yourself from this telling:

Name _____

INSTRUCTION SHEET

Each student is required to tell stories in an outside-of-class setting at least three times during the semester to audience of six or more.

This may be to three different audiences or to the same audience on three separate occasions.

For each telling the student must fill out the **Preparation Form for Teller.** Most of the page should be filled out before the telling, but the last question should be answered after the telling.

Also, for each telling, the student needs to print and give a copy of the **Performance Observation Form** to an observer—the person in charge of the group or the person who has agreed to be the observer. This person should fill out the form and give it to you immediately after your performance.

When all three tellings have been completed, the student needs to write a **Summary Paper** about the whole experience.

PREPARATION FORM FOR TELLER

Preparation

What will you tell? List your story or stories, author, type, and source of story (e.g. African Folktale).
Each storytelling event needs to be approximately 15 minutes long.

Where will you tell? Describe the type of event or activity. Describe the setting (i.e. inside or outside, size of room, time of day etc.)

Who are your audience members? (Must be 6 or more) Give as many details as you can about the makeup of your audience.

Why did you choose this particular story or stories to tell? What is your goal?

Reflection

How did it go?

What kind of feedback did you get?

What did you learn?

Comments on the experience:

Name _____

PERFORMANCE OBSERVATION FORM

(To Be Filled Out by Observer)

_____

Name of Storyteller

Observer's Name and Role (teacher, supervisor, etc.)   [Please Print]

_____

Date of Telling _____

Place of Telling _____

Number of People in Audience: _____

Approximate Ages of Audience Members _____

Title of Story(ies): _____

_____

What did you like <u>best</u> about the storyteller's performance?

_____

Observer's Signature

SUMMARY PAPER

When you have completed all three outside-of-class tellings, write a short paper answering the following questions. This Summary Paper should be stapled as the first page of a packet that includes the Preparation and Observation sheets for all three tellings. Remember, you are writing a *short essay,* not just answering questions, so go into detail describing the experiences.

1. Which of the three tellings went the best? Why?

2. Which of the three tellings were you least happy with? Why?

3. What changes would you make if you were to have the opportunity to re-plan and re-do this project?

4. How would you evaluate your overall experience?

5. Can you see yourself telling stories outside of class in the future? If so, in what context, where, what types of stories, for what type of audience?

Name _____

STORYTELLING EVENT REPORT FORMAT

A. State the date, time, place, and name of the event. Also describe the culture(s), ethnicity(ies), and/or geographic region of the tellers.

B. In a well-developed paragraph – about half a page typewritten – objectively describe the event. Who performed? For how long? What stories were told? What was the venue like? How many people were there?

C. In another well-developed paragraph – about half a page typewritten – give your subjective evaluation of the event. What did you like or dislike and why? What was your favorite part of the experience?

D. Please staple proof of attendance to the back of the report. This could be a ticket stub, a program, or a note with a signature from the person in charge.

Index

Copyright Acknowledgments